Dear Dr. Chang Wuk Kang,

10/12/21 긍정 에너지 감사 드림

ANONYMOUS MINOR CHARACTERS IN THE JOHANNINE NARRATIVE

The Christological and Doxological Significance of the Characterization in John 4, 5, and 9

NATHAN HAHN

XULON PRESS

Xulon Press
2301 Lucien Way #415
Maitland, FL 32751
407.339.4217
www.xulonpress.com

Paperback ISBN-13: 978-1-6628-2602-3
Hard Cover ISBN-13: 978-1-6628-2603-0
Ebook ISBN-13: 978-1-6628-2604-7

For my wife Lisa with love

Table Of Contents

Acknowledgements

I AM THANKFUL TO GOD FOR GRANTING ME THE grace and allowing the time, health, and wisdom that enabled to accomplish this work. Give all the glory to our Lord's Name. It is also a pleasant privilege to express my gratitude to those who helped me this work to complete successfully.

First and foremost, I am deeply grateful to my supervisor, Prof. Dr. Ernest van Eck who thoroughly read every draft of each chapter and gave prompt comments/corrections along with great interest, encouragement, and kindness. Without his direction and guidance, I could not complete. His careful reading undoubtedly improved the scope of this work. However, any flaws which remain are my own responsibility.

I also owe special gratitude to Prof. Dr. Ju Hur at ACTS University who suggested and inspired me to research the minor characters in Johannine narrative. He also provided many resources for this study. I should also express special thanks to Prof. Dr. Moon Hyun Kim at Korea Christian University for the encouragement and provide his works on the Johannine characterization. Also, thanks to Late Retired Pastor Dr. Won Sang Lee and Dr. Jeong Koo Jeon who always encouraged me to finish my thesis. I also want to express my appreciation to Rev. Sydney Seiler who read each chapter to smooth my English.

I have debts to Garden Presbyterian Church members who support and allow the senior pastor to pursue this study for a long time.

Finally, my greatest special thanks and love are reserved for my dear wife, Lisa who prayed, supported, and trusted me throughout good and hard time. She has been indeed a strong pillar of my life and ministry for which I remain eternally grateful. Also thanks to my three children, Joy, Faith, and Timothy who love and support me always. I dedicate my thesis to my wife and three children.

Soli Deo Gloria!

Endorsements

Characters and characterization have received considerable attention and achievement in biblical scholarship for the last few decades. Rev. Hahn has carefully treated the Johannine narrative as literature, socio-cultural history, and theology and showed meaningful advance with special reference to the four anonymous minor characters – the Samaritan woman, the royal official, the lame man, and the man born blind delineated in chapters 4, 5, and 9. This impressive work provides a challenging and lucid account of the central issues in characterization as well as plot in John's Gospel and allows the author to present a distinctive and nuanced analysis of Johannine narrative techniques for its Christological and doxological significance. This fine piece of academic contribution encourages scholars, pastors and informed Christians to read once again John's Gospel with a fresh perspective, fixing our eyes on God's glorious purpose/will mysteriously yet progressively unfolded in encountering relationship between Jesus the Logos and "all anonymous minor characters" today. Without any doubt, readers academic and pastoral, have been enriched in various ways by this telling Ph.D. dissertation.

Ju Hur
Author of *A Dynamic Reading of the Holy Spirit in Luke-Acts*
(Sheffield Academic Press, 2001)
Professor of New Testament Studies,
ACTS University, South Korea
President of Korean Evangelical Society
of New Testament Studies

I studied the characters within John's gospel as a university professor for a long time, but this time when I read Hahn's Ph.D. thesis, I acknowledged the academic excellence of his writing. Hahn reveals the identity of Jesus through the minor characters' inter-relationships with Jesus, and through the narrative exegetical work of the 'anonymous' and 'minor' characters within the gospel of John. Furthermore, he presents the author's Christological and doxological significance through a socio-cultural-historical analysis. This thesis stands out for its excellence in completing a three-dimensional and in-depth narrative analysis versus a simple narrative character analysis. For many years, Hahn's passion as the pastor of a minority immigration church assimilates into his excellent insight as a scholar, thus this wonderful achievement has come to fruition. His exceptional insight into a narrative analysis of John's gospel stands out. Hahn is analyzing the meaning of narrative characterizations in depth through a 'narrative-social-cultural-historical' approach, and the development of the theological themes unfolded through characters. Additionally, his main theological arguments are balanced with a sense of academic prestige. Hahn, a pastor of an immigrant church for the Korean minority, goes beyond simply academically analyzing the 'anonymous' and 'minor characters' in John's Gospel, but he also shares their religious journey with us. Like today's readers, the characters in the Scriptures choose their own path, either autonomously or bounded, playing a role that the author wants. In the narrative of John 4, 5, and 9, Hahn reveals the Jesus' identity, and the glory of God through their assigned roles as the anonymous minor characters who encounter Jesus.

I pray that this outstanding thesis will be read by many more readers. It is a great pleasure to recommend this book in the name of the Lord for the publication of his wonderful work.

Moon Hyun Kim
Author of *Healing Hurts: John's Portrayals of the Persons in Healing Episodes* (Korea Christian University Press 2005) Professor of New Testament Studies, Korea Christian University, South Korea

Foreword

R EADING THE GOSPEL STORIES ABOUT JESUS AS narratives is to focus on aspects such as plot, events, time, space, characters, point of view, and ideological perspective. Through the lens of his ideological perspective, each of the gospel writers narrated their specific understanding of Jesus, thus drawing a very specific (theological) picture of Jesus.

To unravel the ideological perspective of the narrator of the gospel of John, for example, is to study the way in which the narrator plots (narrates) story time (i.e., narrated time), how space is described as focal space or general space, and especially how the characters in the story are presented. In regards to the latter, the relationship between the narrator and his characters, as well as the way in which the relationships between the different characters are described, are important keys that can be used to unravel what the narrator wants to communicate to the reader.

Two types of characters can normally be identified in narratives; simplex (flat) characters, and complex (round) characters. Flat characters normally presents one ideological perspective throughout a narrative, while round characters normally develop as the plot of a narrative unfolds. Also important when one analyze characters in a narrative is to distinguish between those characters who merely play a decorative role in the development of the plot, and those who, in their emotions, observations, insights, and thoughts, carry or embody the ideological perspective (theology) of the gospel writers.

In Hahn's estimation, several of the so-called 'minor characters' in John' gospel exactly do that. Using what he calls a 'narrative-social-cultural-historical' approach, he explores the characterization of the anonymous minor characters in John 4, 5, and 9, clearly show the author's Christological and doxological point of view.

Hahn's study of the Samaritan woman in John 4 indicates that although she initially did not clearly confess Jesus as her Savior, she progressively overcomes several barriers, eventually shows her faith in Christ, and acts as a true disciple of Jesus when she starts to share her testimony of Jesus as the Savior of the world.

In analyzing the character of the royal officer in John 4:46-54, Hahn convincingly argues that that the healing narrative of the royal official's son shaped by the narrator to demonstrate the journey from a faith that is superficially and externally based on signs and wonders to an authentic faith, and to recognize that those miracle signs characterize Jesus as the life-giver. The royal official is seen more than a type of positive faith-response to Jesus.

The third 'minor character' Hahn focuses on is the lame man at the pool of Bethesda in John 5. In the lame man's healing narrative, the narrator depicts his healing in such a way that the healing intertwine with the characterization of Jesus as the Son whom God the Father sent to do God's work. The short narrative shows that Jesus choosing to heal the lame man on the Sabbath has significant messianic implications, and that Jesus is not looking for His own glory, but for the glory of God the Father unlike the Jewish religious leaders.

Hahn finally analyzes the narrative of the man born blind in John 9. This narrative, Hahn argues, is narrated by the narrator in such a way that Jesus, as the Son of God the Father, reveals God who has the authority to perform miracles, and values the giving of life over the Jewish Sabbath tradition. Jesus also demonstrated His divine authority to forgive sin and give eternal life to those who believe in Him. In order to emphasize the point of Christology and doxology in the narrative, the narrator, in this narrative, reveals Jesus' identity, and as such indicates that the healing narrative of the man born blind has deep messianic implications.

Hahn's study of the minor characters in John's gospel not only makes a contribution to the study of characterization in John, but also to the theological message the gospel wants to convey. By 'resurrecting' the so-called anonymous or minor characters in John, Hahn has brought them to life, showing how these characters embodies what maybe can be seen as the main theological focus of John's gospel, namely that God gives life.

Prof Ernest van Eck
Author of *Galilee and Jerusalem in Mark's Story of Jesus:
A Narratological and Social Scientific Reading*
(University of Pretoria HTS Supplementum Series 7, 1995)
Department of New Testament and Related Literature
Faculty of Theology and Religion

Abstract

T HE AIM OF THIS STUDY HAS BEEN TO CLOSELY
examine anonymous minor characters found in the Johannine
narrative, especially those in John 4, 5, and 9 in order to find
out the author's Christological and doxological point of view as
reading by means of a "narratological and exegetical approach,"
considering social, cultural and historical material with serious
attention given to the text. This study starts briefly surveying the
current debate on characterization in Johannine narrative. It also
addressed the gospel's context in terms of its literary structure and
how this would be examined.

This study identifies a significant research gap: although
modern scholars have approached characterization based largely
on whether or not they see characters primarily as plot functionaries, Johannine characters are best understood by their interactive
relationship to other characters and to the structural systems of
meaning that compose a narrative. In their encounters with Jesus
and others, the author reveals Jesus' identity. It is very important
in reading the Johannine minor characters that not only a narrative text-centered approach but also a socio-cultural-historical
approach is used. It is in this way that an argument could be made
for the doxological and Christological significances of the anonymous minor characters in the narratives of the Samaritan woman
in John 4, the invalid at the pool in John 5, and the man born blind
in John 9.

After examining and applying multiple approaches in looking
at the minor characters in John's gospel, it became clear that narratives use plots and interrelationships among characters to project

an ideological or theological point of view. The narrator reveals the true identity of Jesus through conversations that these characters have with either Jesus or with other characters. Subsequently, to fully understand the text and thus recognize the ideological or theological perspective of the narrator, the reader or implied reader needs to consider the characters' social, cultural and historical contexts.

The author's theological points of view as shown in the Prologue repeatedly appear in the anonymous minor characters in John 4, 5, and 9. The Prologue prepares the reader or implied reader by setting the stage so that the Johannine narrative can be approached with knowledgeable anticipation, while the main themes regarding the deity and glory of Jesus Christ are developed in John 4, 5, and 9 and, of course, throughout the narrative. As the Johannine plot unfolds, the revelation of God evidenced in the words and works of Jesus Christ generates a diversity of responses among the characters from rejection to belief. These characters' responses to the revelation of the Father through the Son in terms of their identity, character, mission, and relationship further serve the author's goal. The criterion for the author's characterization is the characters' response to Jesus and God's revelation as revealed in Christ, His teachings, and His works. The Johannine plot, meanwhile, revolves around John unfolding the revelation of the Father through the Son, Jesus Christ, in terms of the individuals' response as well as their identity, character, mission, and relationship. Having defined this methodology, the following studies will employ this social-cultural-historical approach together with a narrative approach to identify the theological points of view of the author as John 4, 5, and 9 are analyzed and exegete. The significance of this will be evidenced in the glory of Jesus Christ who came to this world to save through faith in Him.

CHAPTER 1

Introduction

CHRISTOLOGICAL AND DOXOLOGICAL THEMES permeate the entirety of Scripture. The prominent places held by both the Christological and doxological themes in the Johannine narrative are unquestioned. The Gospel pictures Jesus not merely as a miracle performer who heals the sick, but also as the one in whom eternal life and God's glory appear personified. As is well known, the Prologue of John's gospel (Jn. 1:1-18) establishes a connection between God's act of creation through his λόγος ("Word") and His act of providing salvation through the incarnate λόγος, Jesus. The term–'λόγος'– appears in John's gospel in Christological sense in the Prologue and functions as a unique term for Jesus in the rest of the Gospel on Jesus' preexistence. It also clearly connects with the doxological theme of the Gospel as shown in John 1:14, a key verse of the Prologue that announces the incarnation of the λόγος in flesh, emphasizing its significance for the Johannine narrative as a whole. Later Jesus Himself proclaims that He only works for God's glory in John 7:18.

That said, most studies of the Christological and doxological themes in the Johannine narrative have focused on major characters in it, such as either Jesus Himself, what He is quoted by the narrator as having proclaimed, or His disciples' and what they are described as having witnessed. What is often overlooked but worth closer examination are how the Christological and doxological themes can be seen in the anonymous minor characters of

1

Johannine narrative founded in chapters 4, 5 and 9, particularly given that these minor characters contribute to the development of the plot and the Christological and doxological themes. This paper is designed to provide this closer examination.

As Culpepper points out "The Gospel of John is distinctive in its treatment of the minor characters of the gospel story. Characters which do not appear in the other gospels have etched themselves indelibly in Christian tradition because of their roles in John: Nicodemus, the Samaritan woman, the lame man, the blind man, and Lazarus."[1] In those stories the characters are a construct by the narrator/ author put together with various purposes in mind. According to Chatman, what are commonly included under the term character are personality traits.[2] This study seeks to examine primarily how these minor characters contribute to the author's theological point of view in regard to Christological and doxological themes.

Over the centuries scholars have wrestled with the interpretation of character and characterization in texts. Among the issues that have often arisen include the relationship between characters and plot.[3] Of course the importance of these characters is not tied to their particularly identity as individuals but rather how their character is a paradigm of traits. The term "character" can therefore be applied here as a "paradigm of traits." A good example of this is the characterization of the lame man and the blind man and how they are closely related to the plot of the healing story. To fully understand and portray those characters, we need to look both at the sign of healing as well as at the dialogue between

---

[1]   R. Alan Culpepper, *Anatomy of the Fourth Gospel: A Study in Literary Design*, 1983, 132.

[2]   Shlomith Rimmon-Kenan, *Narrative Fiction*, 1989, 37.

[3]   Moon Hyun Kim, *Healing Hurts: John's Portrayals of the Persons in Healing Episodes*, 2005, 14-18.

them and Jesus. In the Johannine narrative, Jesus' miracle signs are significant in that the author's distinctive theological points of view become evident in his depiction of these signs. Keener states, "Signs fulfill a specific literary function in the Fourth Gospel, summoning the reader, like witnesses in the narrative, to either faith for rejection."[4]

An examination of these anonymous minor characters is therefore crucial to understanding the full systematic and biblical theology that emerges from the Christological and doxological themes in the Johannine narrative even beyond that found in examinations of the major characters.

1.1 SURVEY OF THE CURRENT DEBATE ON CHARACTERIZATION ON JOHANNINE NARRATIVE

No one can argue the importance of Culpepper's *Anatomy of the Fourth Gospel* to contemporary Johannine research. Culpepper undertook an analysis of the literary design of the Johannine narrative helped by a deep awareness of contemporary literary theory. It was groundbreaking at that time to argue that the narrative should be read as a coherent story with emphasis on the world that the author depicts within the text.

---

4   Craig S. Keener, *The Gospel of John: A Commentary vol. 1*, 2003, 251.

Over the past decade or so, there has been a surge of interest in the characters of the Johannine narrative.[5] In 2006, Philip Esler and Ronald Piper drew on social-identity theory to examine the family of Lazarus, Mary, and Martha as important prototypes or ideal characters for the implied reader of the Johannine narrative.[6] In 2007, there was Bradford Blaine's dissertation, *Peter in the Gospel of John*.[7] Blaine employs a narrative-critical approach that takes seriously both the Fourth Gospel's source and its historical setting.

In 2009, there were three more dissertations published. Christopher Skinner's *John and Thomas: Gospels in Conflict*,[8] analyses Johannine characters with view of evaluating the thesis that the Johannine narrative contains an "anti-Thomas polemic." After looking at Thomas, Peter, Nicodemos, the Samaritan woman, Mary, Martha, Philip, Judas (not Iscariot), and the disciples as a representative group, he concluded that Johannine presentation

---

[5] Andrew T. Lincoln, 'The Lazarus Story: A Literary Perspective', in Richard Bauckham and Carl Mosser (eds.), *The Gospel of John and Christian Theology*, 2008, 211-32; Marianne Meye Thompson, 'The Rising of Lazarus in John 11: A Theological Reading', in Richard Bauckham and Carl Mosser (eds.), *The Gospel of John and Christian Theology*, 2008, 233-44; Ruben Zimmerman, 'The Narrative Hermeneutics of John 11: Learning with Lazarus How to Understand Death, Life, and Resurrection', in Craig Koester and Reimund Bieringer (eds.), *The Resurrection of Jesus in the Gospel of John*, 2008, 75-101; Steve A Hunt, 'Nicodemos, Lazarus, and the Fear of the "the Jews" in the Fourth Gospel', in Gilbert van Belle, Michael Labahn and P. Maritz (eds.), *Repetition and Variation in the Fourth Gospel: Style, Text, Interpretation*, 2009, 199-212; Cornelis Bennema, "The Character of John in the Fourth Gospel", 2009, 271-84.

[6] Philip Esler and Ronald Piper, Lazarus, Mary and Martha: *A Social-Scientific and Theological Reading of John*, 2006.

[7] Bradford B. Blaine, Jr. *Peter in the Gospel of John: The Making of an Authentic Disciple*, 2007.

[8] Christopher W. Skinner, *John and Thomas: Gospels in Conflict? Johannine Characterization and the Thoams Question*, 2009.

of Thomas is part of a wider literary pattern within the story where multiple characters misunderstanding of the mission and message of Jesus are depicted, and thus the charge of an "anti-Thomas polemic" on John's part is unfounded. Separately, in her book *Imperfect Believers*,[9] Susan Hylen examines Nicodemos, the Samaritan woman, the disciples, the Jews, Martha, Mary, Peter and the Beloved Disciple, and draws out an important element of their characterization: ambiguity. She argues that it is difficult to discern whether these characters exercise a satisfactory belief in Jesus. Many characters seem to grasp important insights about Jesus but fail to believe or understand in other key areas.[10] Lastly, Cornelis Bennema's book, *Encountering Jesus*,[11] provides more character studies than the preceding dissertations. Bennema demonstrates a concern for an overarching theory of character. He considers nearly all of John's characters using a method that categorizes characters into one of four categories: agent, type, character with personality, or individual. In addition to his classification system, his discussion of each character is accompanied by a chart that plots the character's appearances, identity, speech and actions, character classification, degree of characterization, and response to Jesus. In the process, Bennema demonstrates his concern for developing a comprehensive theory of character.

---

[9] Susan Hylen, *Imperfect Believers: Ambiguous Characters in the Gospel of John*, 2009.

[10] However, this study will argue some characters are definitely shown that they did not fail to believe Jesus as Savior.

[11] Cornelis Bennema, *Encountering Jesus: Character Studies in the Gospel of John*, 2nd ed., 2009.

1.2 CONTEXT IN TERMS OF THE LITERARY STRUCTURE OF THE JOHANNINE NARRATIVE

The structure of the Johannine narrative reflects some of the most carefully composed literature in the New Testament. The author explicitly said in his purpose statement that the aim of his Gospel was to present Jesus as the promised Messiah of the Old Testament and the unique Son of God (Jn. 20:30-31), and toward that end the author's primary means of revealing Jesus as the divine Messiah is through the use of the seven signs (σημεῖα) in the narrative and their attendant contexts of teaching in John 1-12, commonly referred to as the Book of Signs.[12]

Jesus' first two signs are purposefully placed by John in the beginning chapters of the Gospel, often called the Cana Cycle (Jn. 2-4)[13] because the signs were performed in Cana of Galilee and form a literary bracket around these three chapters.[14]

The remaining sign miracles of Jesus are also purposefully located throughout the subsequent chapters of the section frequently designated as the Festival Cycle (Jn. 5-12).[15] These chapters are so designated because the sign miracles and their attendant

---

[12]   The term "Book of Signs" as a reference to John 1-12 is now widely accepted by most Johannine scholars. It is most associated with C. H. Dodd, *The Interpretation of the Fourth Gospel*, 1953, x and Raymond E. Brown, *The Gospel according to John (I-XII)*, 1966, cxxxviii.

[13]   Gerald L. Borchert, *John 1-11*, 1996, 151-222.

[14]   These three chapters of John 2-4 form a literary unit because they are not only bounded geographically by the Cana miracles, but they also thematically presenting Jesus as the life-giving Messiah who grants eternal life to those who believe. See F. J. Moloney, "From Cana to Cana (John 2:1-4: 54) and the Fourth Evangelist's Concept of Correct Faith, in "*Studia Biblica 1978 II: Papers on the Gospels: Sixth International Congress on Biblical Studies, Oxford, 3-7 April 1978*, ed. E. A. Livingstone, 1980, 2:185-213.

[15]   See Francis J. Moloney, *Signs and Shadows: Reading John 5-12*, 1996.

narratives and discourses are set in the context of Jewish festivals.[16] This cycle begins with an "unnamed" feast (Jn. 5:1-47) and then runs through a year of festivals from Passover (Jn. 6:1-71) through Tabernacles (Jn. 7:1-10:21), Dedication or Hanukkah (Jn. 10:22-42), and then back to Passover (Jn. 12:1).[17]

1.3 CHRISTOLOGICAL AND DOXOLOGICAL SIGNIFICANCE

The doxological theme is central to all of Scripture. Such an assertion is axiomatic: God's redemptive plan and work as revealed in the λόγος are ultimately designed to glorify God and are thus doxological in their very essence. Naturally all divisions of systematic theology, particularly Christology and soteriology, have a similar doxological backdrop. The unique place John's gospel has as both a historic Gospel narrative and the one Gospel most

---

[16] R. Alan Culpepper, *The Gospel and the Letters of John, Interpreting Biblical Texts*, 1998, 148-149. Aileen Guilding interprets the whole Gospel on the basis of the feasts, proposing that John's Gospel was developed as a set of festival lectionary readings in ancient Palestine synagogues (*The Fourth Gospel and Jewish Worship: A Study of the Relation of St. John's Gospel to the Ancient Jewish Lectionary System*, 1960). Although her main thesis has found little general acceptance among Johannine scholars, her study points out the importance of the Jewish feasts to the background of the Gospel, just as Francis J. Moloney concludes in his critique of Guilding's work, "It is better to allow the context to determine the use of the feasts rather than vice-versa" (*The Gospel of John*, 1998, 165.

[17] Gerald L. Borchert, "The Passover and the Narrative Cycles in John," in *Perspectives on John: Method and Interpretation in the Fourth Gospel*, ed. Robert B. Sloan and Mikeal C. Parsons, 1993, 308-9. Some scholars include chapters 5-12 in the Festival Cycle, whereas others include only chapters 5-10. The latter say that chapters 11-12 set the stage for Jesus' sacrifice as the Passover Lamb. Brown says these chapters point to Jesus moving toward the hour of His death and glory (*Gospel according to John I-XII*, 419-98). Gary M. Burge similarly calls John 11-12 "Foreshadowing's of Jesus' Death and Resurrection" (*Interpreting the Gospel of John*, 1992, 76-77).

markedly distinguished by its rich Christology and soteriology makes a closer understanding of its doxological theme even more important, and is critical to understanding John's motivation under the inspired leading of the Holy Spirit in his writing. This is why Schnackenburg says, "The Johannine Christology is essentially ordained to soteriology. Everything that the Johannine Jesus says and does, all that he reveals and all that he accomplishes as 'signs,' takes place in view of man's attaining salvation, in view of his gaining divine life."[18]

To enable a robust and full understanding of the Christological and doxological themes in the Johannine narrative, it is important to look beyond what we see revealed through the major characters of God, Jesus, the Jews, and the disciples to aforementioned minor characters.[19] This includes the Samaritan woman and the royal officer in John 4, the lame man in John 5, and the blind man in John 9. Although each minor character alone does not fully demonstrate all of the significant aspects of both Christological and doxological themes, it would be wrong to separate these themes because they are inherently interrelated, and thus both can be inferred even if only one or the other is present.

Although Brown noted the aspects of the characters of the Johannine narrative,[20] it is interesting to note Bennema's argu-

---

[18]   Rudolf Schnackenburg, *The Gospel According to St. John*, 1990, 155.

[19]   R. Culpepper introduces four types of characters in John's gospel, Jesus and the Father, the disciples, the Jews, the Minor characters. Culpepper, *Anatomy of the Fourth Gospel: A Study in Literary Design*, 1983, 101-144.

[20]   Raymond Brown, *The Gospel According to John I-XII*, 1966, 175-176, "And if we analyze the repartee at the wall, we find quite true to life the characterization of the woman as mincing and coy, with a certain light grace. Though characters like Nicodemus, this woman, the paralytic of John 5, and the blind man of John 10 are – to a certain extent – foils used by the evangelist to permit Jesus to unfold his revelation, still each has his or her own personal characteristics and fitting lines of dialogue."

ment that many characters in the Johannine narrative are not simply types or figures deployed to make a theological point about how one can encounter Jesus; rather, the study of characters which began with the rise of literary critical approaches to the text contributes to the shaping of the narrative and the allure of the Gospel as a work of engaging narrative.[21] The interaction of these characters with Jesus can lead to significant insights into the dynamics of the Johannine narrative.

1.4 METHODOLOGY

In any research of the biblical themes in Scriptures, the exegete must exercise discipline in strictly adhering to an exegetical process wherein the text is permitted to speak for itself in the context of the passage. For this specific thesis, therefore, this study begins to examine by means of narrative, literary, social, and historical criticism the author/narrator of the text that includes anonymous characters in John 4, 5 and 9. Before doing this, an exegesis of the Prologue will be done employing a method that seeks to understand and relate the author's theological points of view that emerge in his use of characterization in John 4, 5, and 9.

Culpepper argues that most of Johannine minor characters are types that the reader can recognize easily, and he constructs in relation to the author's ideological point of view an extensive taxonomy of belief-responses in which a character can progress or regress from one response to another.[22] As Powell notes, "Characters are the actors in a story, the ones who carry out

---

[21]   Cornelis Bennema, *Encountering Jesus: Character Studies in the Gospel of John*, 2009, 40. Bennema provides a useful review of the studies of character in contemporary critical literature.

[22]   See Alan Culpepper, *Anatomy of the Fourth Gospel*, 1983, 102-4 and 14-48.

the various activities that comprise the plot,"[23] reinforcing that the author without a doubt intends to reveal theological truths through the narrative, and of course that includes the anonymous minor characters depicted in his narrative. This study will, therefore, explore the literary traits of these anonymous minor characters in terms of the following three aspects: 1) narrative point of view and focalization in narratology,[24] 2) character presentation in that the theological perspective of the narrator is put into focus, and 3) plot function whereas plot refers to a narrative flow or narrative pattern. In addition, the implications of the author's intention will be noted through these text-centered and literary theological approaches.

As Anderson noted, "Diachronic literary theories have sought to explain John's literary and theological perplexities by means of postulating several stages in the composition of the Gospel."[25] That would be the Christological and doxological significance with those anonymous minor characters in John 4, 5, and 9.

As such, the methodology employed in this study to some degree essentially combines both a "diachronic analysis," defined as a methodological approach characterized by its treatment in terms of narrative, literary, social, and historical criticism, as well as a "synchronic analysis" primarily concerned with enabling the text itself to yield the depth and richness of its meaning that in turn implies the theological significances. In commencing in this study, it is clear that there has not been much research on these minor characters, applying diachronic or synchronic analysis.

---

[23]   Mark Allen Powell, *What is Narrative Criticism?*, 1983, 51.

[24]   Andries G. Van Aarde, *Focusing on the Message: New Testament Hermeneutics, Exegesis and Methods*, 2009, 390-391.

[25]   Paul N. Anderson, *The Christology of the Fourth Gospel*, 1996, 26.

Most commentators merely compare the characters Nicodemus with the Samaritan woman.[26]

1.5   PLAN OF RESEARCH

After the introduction of Chapter 1, this study briefly surveys the past and present studies or debates on characters and characterization, and theories in the Johannine narrative by examining the relative literature in Chapter 2. It will also deal with the relationship of the author's characterization in the narrative and the plot and will identify research gaps on the topic of characteristics of minor Johannine characters. There is an integral relationship between the characters of narrative and its plot. Johannine characters are best understood by their interactive relationship to other characters and to the structural systems of meaning that compose a narrative. In their encounters with Jesus and others, the author reveals Jesus' identity. It is very important in reading the Johannine minor characters that not only a narrative text centered approach is used, but also a socio-cultural-historical approach. It is in this way that the argument would be made for the doxological and Christological significances of the anonymous minor characters in the narratives of the Samaritan woman in John 4, the invalid at the pool in John 5, and the man born blind in John 9.

In regard to the methodology of the thesis in Chapter 3 outside of that used in the exegesis of the Prologue, this study will share Resseguie, Bennema, and Kim in an attempt to examine

---

[26]   For example, Culpepper, *The Gospel and the Letters of John A Study in Literary Design*, 1998, 139.

characters by means of narrative-critical approach.[27] In doing so, however, this chapter will demonstrate the insufficiency of the narrative or literary approach alone. The social, cultural and historical approach to the text is also needed. The narrator reveals the true identity of Jesus' conversations these characters have with either Jesus or other characters. To fully understand the text and thus recognize the ideological or theological perspective of the narrator, the reader or implied reader needs to consider the characters' social, cultural and historical contexts. Thus, it will be called the narrative-social-cultural-historical approach that will be used looking at the minor characters in John 4, 5, and 9. Also examined will be the author's point of view on theological and ideological matters.

Chapters 4, 5, 6 and 7 explore each of the anonymous minor characters in terms of the narrative and literary function of each character in relation to its theological significance in the literary structure of the context. An emphasis will also be placed on how these minor characters focus on God's glory and Jesus' identification.

Chapter 4 will analyze the character of the Samaritan woman in John 4 and exegetes the text using a narrative-socio-cultural-historical approach. Although the Samaritan woman in John 4 did not clearly confess Jesus as her Savior, it is clear that through the narrative she progressively overcomes the barriers, eventually shows her faith in Christ, and acts as a true disciple as she shared her testimony. She appears to be progressive in her growing faith, increasingly perceptive and receptive to what Jesus has been saying, why he has been saying it, and who He claimed to be (Jn. 4:19-20,

---

[27] James L. Resseguie, *A Narrative-Critical Approach to the Fourth Gospel in Characters and Characterization in the Gospel of John*, 2012 and Cornelis Bennema, *Encountering Jesus: Character Studies In the Gospel of John*, 2nd ed., 2014, and Moon Hyun Kim, *People Who Encountered Jesus: Studies Johannine Characterization*, 2017.

25, 29). In the end she proves seriously open to the idea that Jesus might be the Messiah. Her subsequent testimony and confession shows that she has drank of the living water. The Samaritan woman in the narrative thus displays her honesty, open-mindedness, perceptiveness, responsiveness, and boldness to witness. Also, the narrator shows Jesus affirmation that Hs coming was first to the people of Israel, showing how Jesus asserted Jewish salvation historical primacy, while the woman asks about the place of worship (Jn. 4:22). This keeps the salvation historical pattern of the Old Testament intact, which moves from the people of Israel to the Gentiles.

The characterization of the Samaritan woman in the narrative is seen in her transformation. When she learns how much Jesus knows about her, she is attracted to Him in a new way, looking for Him to solve her sin problems that involves the relationship of God to man. The resolution that Jesus proposed was not what she expected, but she embraces it progressively. In that embrace, she is transformed to share the gospel like a disciple. The reader or implied reader is told the narrator's theological messages through the plot and characterizations of Jesus and the Samaritan woman: Jesus' mission by the Father in order to reach out the Samaritans, the meaning of the living water and true worship, the ideal type of discipleship, and Jesus' identification as the Messiah and the Savior of the world.

Her character offers a model of transformative encounter with Jesus. She moves from a position ripe with erotic overtones, exemplifying a character that might well take advantage of such a situation, to a position where she has abandoned thought of herself and serves to bring a message of salvation to her neighbors. Through her transformation and service God is glorified.

Chapter 5 will analyze the character of the royal officer in John 4:46-54 and exegete the text with a narrative-socio-cultural-historical approach. The healing narrative of the royal official's son is designed to demonstrate the journey from a faith that is superficially and externally based on signs and wonders to an authentic faith, and to recognize that those miracle signs characterize Jesus as the life-giver. It is a climax to the series of encounters people have with Jesus in the Cana Cycle of John 2-4. Both the Samaritan woman and the royal official reach an authentic and deepened faith in Jesus and testify to others so that they have become authentic believers, showing the power of the witness of the authentic faith in Jesus who is the life-giver for those who respond with faith in His words. Thus, the royal official is more than a type of positive faith-response to Jesus. The reader or implied reader can under-stand the official as a character who reveals individuality, and in the process thus learn something of his authentic faith through this character. The author may have intended that the reader or implied reader would make a connection between Jesus' life-giving word and the Word of life (cf. John 1:1).

The reader is instructed in some of the most important Johannine beliefs. What has been said in the Prologue (Jn. 1:1-18) is being proclaimed and acted out in the story of Jesus (Jn. 1:19-4:54). Above all, the reader now knows the nature of a right relationship with Jesus. The Prologue's teaching on the life-giving power that comes from believing and receiving the incarnated word (Jn. 1:12-13) happens in the story of Jesus as people accept or reject his word.

Chapter 6 will analyze the character of the lame man at the pool of Bethesda in John 5 and exegete the text with narrative-so-cio-cultural-historical approach. In the lame man's healing narra-tive, the author establishes that the lame man and the story of his healing are intertwined with the characterization of Jesus as the Son whom God the Father sent to do God's work. Jesus has the divine authority and power to heal the lame man. The reader or implied reader clearly sees that the Jewish religious leaders' charges against Jesus are false because the healing was God's act and Jesus did the healing according to God's will. The author also shows through Jesus encounters with the Jewish religious leaders that the lame man healing miracle sign has eschatological implications. The lame man's healing belongs within the horizon of eschatology.

In His discourse of defense, Jesus as the Son of God the Father reveals God who has the authority to perform miracle and values the giving of life over the Jewish Sabbath tradition. Jesus demonstrated His divine authority to forgive sin and give eternal life to those who believe in Him. Another aspect of Jesus' healing the lame man on the Sabbath is judgment. While God the Father alone is called the judge, who will exercise the eschatological judgment, this authority has been delegated to the Son, Jesus, because of the relationship between the Father and the Son. At this eschatological judgment everyone will be raised. The Son, Jesus, will judge based on belief or unbelief concerning Him: a resurrection of life or a resurrection of condemnation. Because of their delusion or blindness and looking for glory from men, the Jewish religious leaders could not see their own spiritual depravity. So they accused and tried to kill Jesus, the Son. The reader or implied reader can see that Jesus choosing to heal the lame man on the Sabbath has significant messianic implications. It presents Jesus as the promised Messiah. The author also expressed that unlike the Jewish religious leaders, Jesus is not looking for His own glory, but for the glory of God the Father. All human beings are made for His glory.

Chapter 7 will analyze the man born blind in John 9 and exegete the text with narrative-socio-cultural-historical approach. In His discourse of defense, Jesus as the Son of God the Father reveals God who has the authority to perform miracle and values the giving of life over the Jewish Sabbath tradition. Jesus demonstrated His divine authority to forgive sin and give eternal life to those who believe in Him. Another aspect of Jesus' healing the lame man on the Sabbath is judgment. While God the Father alone is called the judge who will exercise the eschatological judgment, this authority has been delegated to the Son, Jesus, because of the relationship between the Father and the Son. At this eschatological judgment everyone will be raised. The Son, Jesus, will judge based on belief or unbelief concerning Him: a resurrection of life or a resurrection of condemnation. Because of their delusion or blindness and looking for glory from men, the Jewish religious leaders could not see their own spiritual depravity. So they accused and tried to kill Jesus, the Son. The reader or implied reader can see that Jesus choosing to heal the lame man on the Sabbath has significant messianic implications. It presents Jesus as the promised Messiah. The author also expressed that unlike the Jewish religious leaders, Jesus is not looking for His own glory, but for the glory of God the Father. All human beings are made for His glory.

If people acknowledge their blindness and want to receive the light, Jesus will show and enable them to see. Those who accept the light will receive the eternal life and become God's children. But those who reject the light will continue in darkness and face His judgment.

In order to emphasize the point of Christology and doxology in the narrative, the author also reveals Jesus' identity. The reader or implied reader knows that God is associated with the giving sight to the blind in the Old Testament as a sign of messianic activity. Thus, this healing narrative of the man born blind has deep messianic implications. This miracle of restoring sight provides a type of the messianic blessings to be realized through faith.

In this healing narrative, the author intends to show the contrast between the man born blind and the Jewish religious leaders. The reader or implied reader can clearly understand the characters of the man born blind. He is obedient, courageous, open-minded, willing to give testimony, taking risks, and remains faithful to Jesus until the end. He displays a remarkable progress in his understanding of Jesus. In this way, his characteristics are very similar to that of the Samaritan woman. However, the man born blind reaches his understanding of Jesus not in a reflective encounter with Him, but in a confrontation with the hostile Jewish religious leaders. That shows his faith developed stronger than the Samaritan woman.

Chapter 8 summarizes the conclusions of the previous chapters and briefly draws out the implications of the results of this study: the significance of characterization found in John 4, 5, and 9, the narrative-socio-cultural-historical approach with other characters in Johannine narrative, and the theological significance of the Johannine characterization.

To sum up, this study of narrative-social-cultural-historical approach of anonymous minor characters in John 4, 5, and 9 will be attentive to the author's theological point of view, particularly his Christological and doxological themes. It will apply a contextual and a comparison/contrast approach in examining the author's characterization of those characters, and relational and comprehensive in encountering with Jesus within the overall plot.

CHAPTER 2

Current Studies On Characterization On The Johannine Narrative

---

2.1 INTRODUCTION

TㅎIS CㅎAPTER REVIEWS THE VARIOUS STUDIES on characterization on John's gospel over the past decade or so. After the review, the study will identify the research gaps to fill as the study explores the relations between characters and plot in John's gospel and explains the characteristics of minor Johannine characters. There are distinctive aspects of minor characters in John. In the next chapter, the method that will be used to explain the characteristics of the minor characters in John will be discussed.

2.2 CURRENT STUDIES ON CHARACTERS AND THEORIES

Over the past three decades there have been lots of interests in the characters of John's gospel.[28] Most scholars of Johannine studies has been viewed that Johannine characters have a representative aspect. In other words, the characters in John's gospel serve as examples or models of how one might respond to Jesus. Following the trail of Collins[29], in its epic study of Culpepper's book, *Anatomy of the Fourth Gospel*, he states that the characters "represent a continuum of responses to Jesus which exemplify misunderstandings the reader may share and responses one

---

[28] See the following essays: James M. Howard, 'The Significance of Minor Characters in the Gospel of John', *BibSac* 163, 2006, 63-78; Humphrey Mwangi Waweru, 'Jesus and Ordinary Women in the Gospel of John: An African Perspective', *Swedish Missiological Themes* 96, 2008, 139-159; Andrew T. Lincoln, 'The Lazarus Story: A Literary Perspective', in Richard Bauckham and Carl Mosser (eds.), *The Gospel of John and Christian Theology*, 2008, 233-244; Steven A. Hunt, 'Nicodemus, Lazarus, and the Fear of the "the Jews" in the Fourth Gospel', in Gilbert van Belle, Michael Labahn and P. Maritz (eds.), *Repetition and Variation in the Fourth Gospel: Style, Text, Interpretation*, 2009, 199-212; Cornelis Bennema, 'The Character of John in the Fourth Gospel', *JETS* 52, 2009, 271-284. Also the following magnificent books: Christopher W. Skinner, eds. *Characters and Characterization in the Gospel of John*, 2012; Steven A. Hunt, D. Francois Tolmie, and Ruben Zimmermann, eds. *Character Studies in the Fourth Gospel: Narrative Approaches to Seventy Figures in John*, 2013; Cornelis Bennema, *Encountering Jesus: Character Studies In the Gospel of John*, 2009; Christopher Skinner, Characters and Characterization in the Gospel of John, 2013.

[29] Raymond F. Collins, "The Representative Figures in the Fourth Gospel, *The Downside Review* 94, 1976, 24-46; 95, 1976, 118-132 (Reprinted in 1990) and added a second essay in "From John to the Beloved Disciples: An Essay on Johannine Characters." *Interpretation* 49, 1995, 359-69.

might make to the depiction of Jesus in the Gospel."[30] According to Culpepper, Johannine characters represent seven possible responses to Jesus[31]:

1. rejection like most of Jewish religious leaders;

2. acceptance without open commitment like Nicodemus;

3. acceptance of Jesus as a worker of signs and wonders like the lame man;

4. belief in Jesus' words as like the Samaritan woman;

5. commitment in spite of misunderstandings like the disciples

6. paradigmatic discipleship like the Beloved Disciple; and

7. defection like Judas.

It is important to recognize that Culpepper's study of Johannine characters begins with insights derived from contemporary literary criticism, like E.M. Forster's classic work on the novel.[32] Culpepper cites Forster's well-known distinction between "flat" and "round" characters. Forster distinguishes "flat" characters, which are sometimes called types from "round" characters, which are complex in temperament and motivation. He states that the test of a round character is whether it is capable of surprising in a convincing way. If it never surprises, it is a flat character. If it does not convince, it is flat pretending to be round. Culpepper observes that characters are different from people in that the transparency of characters distinguishes them from the real people, and his distinction between "life by value" and "life by time" (in the former, life is marked by

---

[30]   Alan Culpepper, *Anatomy of the Fourth Gospel: A Study in Literary Design*, Philadelphia: Fortress Press, 1983,104.

[31]   Ibid, 146-148.

[32]   E. M. Forster, *Aspect of the Novel: The Timeless Classic Novel Writing*, Orlando, FL.: Harcourt, Inc., 1962.

crucial moments; in the latter, life is controlled more by chrono-logical sequence).[33] He then argues in relation to John's ideological point of view, an extensive taxonomy of belief-response in which a character can progress or regress from one response to another.[34] He explores the entire literary anatomy of John's Gospel, of which characterization is one important aspect. In doing so, he describes almost all the relevant Johannine characters.

Stibbe's work on Johannine characters shows how narrative criticism can be applied to John's gospel.[35] Stibbe puts forth the theoretical considerations that must be taken into account with characterization, emphasizing that readers must 1) construct char-acter by inference from fragmentary information in the text such as in ancient Hebrew narratives; 2) analyze characters with refer-ence to history rather than according to the laws of fiction; and 3) consider the Gospel's ideological point of view, expressed in John 20:31.[36] Actually, he emphasizes how John portrays the various characters in his Gospel throughout his commentary.[37]

Meanwhile, Tilborg focuses his attention to certain select women in John's gospel such as Maria, Jesus' mother, Martha and Mary of Bethany, and Mary Magdalen.[38] He argues that in their loving relationship only Jesus' mother, Mary does not abandon Jesus and Jesus is the obedient son. However, in relationship with

---

[33] Alan Culpepper, 1983, 102-103.

[34] Ibid, 145-48.

[35] Mark Stibbe, *John as Storyteller: Narrative Criticism and the Fourth Gospel*, 1992 and *John's Gospel*, 1994.

[36] Mark Stibbe, *John as Storyteller: Narrative Criticism and the Fourth Gospel*, 24-25; Mark Stibbe, *John's Gospel*, 10-11.

[37] Ibid.

[38] Sjef van Tilborg, *Imaginative Love in John*, Biblical Interpretation Series 2, 1993.

other women, he finds a negative portrayal. Jesus is inviting and open to women in the beginning but there is a phase in the story where this openness disappears and Jesus retreats from this relationship to them and returns to the male group.

Beck explores the concept of anonymity in relation to discipleship, arguing that only the anonymous characters serve as models of appropriate response to Jesus.[39] He argues that anonymity facilitates readers' identification with, and imitation of, characters in John's Gospel. He concludes that the anonymous characters most closely model the paradigm of discipleship, of appropriate response to Jesus whereas named characters are inappropriate models for reader identification and imitation.

Another scholar who is interested in women characters, Fehribach, presents them as brides who function to help portray the Johannine Jesus as the messianic bridegroom in her feminist historical analysis of the women characters in John's gospel.[40] She devotes an entire monograph to investigate the type of "interactive characterization" in John. She presents how interactions between Jesus and women characters serve to bring out the important facets of other characters in the narrative. She concludes that John's Gospel does not present a community of believers in which women are equal to men. According to Bennema, her theoretical discussion of character is minimal, but she nevertheless draws on character types in Hebrew Bible, Hellenistic-Jewish literature, and Greco-Roman literature in her analysis of Johannine women.[41]

---

[39] David R. Beck, *The Discipleship Paradigm: Readers and Anonymous Characters in the Fourth Gospel*, Biblical Interpretation Series 27, Leiden: Brill, 1997.

[40] Adeline Fehribach, *The Women in the Life of the Bridgroom: A Feminist Historical-Literary Analysis of the Female Characters in the Fourth Gospel*, 1998.

[41] Cornelis Bennama, *Encountering Jesus*, 2014, 10.

Thus, it is necessary to investigate the significances or the specific aspects of each character since characters are interactively related to other characters given in the text. The author uses characters and events in order to communicate his messages with readers or implied readers through the whole plot of the narrative. The characters are not only portrayed as representative figures, but also are portrayed as living characters in their own right, communicating significant meanings in John's Gospel.

Resseguie wrote a monograph on point of view in John's gospel.[42] He surveys the characters from a material point of view and classifies them according to their dominance or social presence in society or culture rather than their faith response.[43] For example, the lame man who represents the marginalized of society, is free from the constraints of the dominant culture and even acts counter culturally by violating the Sabbath. He argues that the characters' material points of view contribute or relate to the John's Gospel overall ideology. In a later work on narrative criticism, he analyzes a few characters in John's gospel like Judas, the man born blind, and Mary Magdalene.[44] Interestingly, Van Aarde also argues that the ideological perspective of the narrator is evident in whatever the view point character does, says, thinks, and in the manner in which he or she acts and speaks.[45] Thus, the ideological perspective is reflected in the story in which the narrator employs the characters in its context of cultural historical background with psychological, temporal, and spatial data.

---

[42]   James Resseguie, *The Strange Gospel: Narrative Design and Point of View in John*. Biblical Interpretation Series 56, 2001.

[43]   Ibid., 109-68.

[44]   James Resseguie, *Narrative Criticism of the New Testament: An Introduction*, .2005, Ch. 4.

[45]   Andries G. van Aarde, *Focusing on the Message: New Testament Hermeneutics, Exegesis and Methods*, 2009, 409.

Conway's article on Johannine characterization is significant.[46] She challenges the consensus view that Johannine characters represent particular belief-responses. She criticizes the "flattening" of characters and argues that Johannine characters show varying degrees of ambiguity and do more to complicate the clear choice between belief and unbelief than to illustrate it. Instead of positioning the minor characters on a spectrum of negative to positive faith-response, she claims that the minor characters appear unstable in relation to Jesus. In doing so, the characters challenge, undercut and overthrow the dualistic world of the Gospel because they do not line up on either side of the belief/unbelief divide.[47] This study agrees with her argument that the minor characters are often presented as too simplistic like flat or round.

Koester, in his monograph on John, has a chapter on characterization, subscribing to the idea that each of John's characters represents a particular faith-response.[48] He examines the character of Jesus, and then surveys fourteen characters who meet Jesus. Koester's strength is that he interprets the Johannine characters on the basis of the text and its historical context, a reading Kim calls narrative-historical.[49] He claims a narrative-historical reading helps to analyze characters in light of John's cultural and historical context. Koester sees many parallels between John's story and ancient Greek drama or tragedy where characters are types who convey general truths by presenting a moral choice. However, Bennema argues that characters in Greek tragedy could be more

---

[46]   Colleen M. Conway, "Speaking through Ambiguity: Minor Characters in the Fourth Gospel," *Biblical Interpretation 10*, 2002, 324-41.

[47]   Ibid, 339-40.

[48]   Craig R. Koester, *Symbolism in the Fourth Gospel: Meaning, Mystery, Community*, 2nd ed., 2003, 33-77.

[49]   Moon Hyun Kim, *A Narrative Reading of John's Healing Episodes*; 2005, 24-25.

complex and round.[50] Also, he sees many Johannine characters do not fit the category of type. They are more complex, ambiguous, and round.

Howard surveys how some of minor characters contribute to the development of the plot and the purpose of John's gospel.[51] Howard, after he examines the minor characters in Johan and their responses to Jesus's miraculous signs, concludes that each of the characters represents either belief or unbelief. He sees that each character reveals the Messiah in a different way and reflects some degree of change either positively or negatively after their encountering with Jesus.

Bennema, in his study of the Johannine characters, attempts to reverse the plain view that Johannine characters are types, have little complexity, and show little or no development.[52] Following Brunett's study,[53] he argues that the differences in characterization in the Hebrew Bible, ancient Greek literature, and modern fiction are degrees of characterization rather than kind. He has sharpened his theory further.[54] He outlines a comprehensive theory of character that comprises three aspects: 1) the study of character in text and context, using information from the text and other sources; 2) the analysis and classification of characters along complexity, development and inner life and plotting the resulting character on a continuum of degree of characterization from agent to type to personality to individuality; and 3) the evaluation of characters

---

[50] Cornelis Bennema, *Encountering Jesus*, 13.

[51] James Howard, "Significance of Minor Characters," 63-78.

[52] Cornelis Bennema, *Encountering Jesus*, 2009.

[53] Fred W. Burnett, "Characterization and Reader Construction of Characters in the Gospels," *Semia* 63, 1993: 3-28.

[54] Christopher Skinner, ed., *Characters and Characterization in the Gospel of John*, 36-58.

in relation to author's point of view, purpose and dualistic worldview. He then applies his theory, showing that only eight out of twenty-three characters are "types" in John.

Hylen wrote on Johannine characters that it is hard to evaluate its characters.[55] Like Conway, she presents an alternative strategy for reading John's characters, arguing that they display various kinds of ambiguity.

Skinner edited a book including seven essays on methods or models for reading Johannine characters, followed by seven essays on specific characters such as God, John the Baptist, Nicodemus, the Samaritan woman, Martha and Mary, the Beloved Disciple, and Pilate.[56] However, Bennema argues there is no clear connection between the essays on methods or models and the essays on specific characters in the book.[57]

Hunt, Tolmie, and Zimmermann published a book same year which provides a comprehensive analysis of seventy Johannine characters. It is an important reference work for those who study Johannine characters.[58]

2.3   CHARACTERIZATION AND PLOT

To fully explore and examine characterization of the Johannine characters, one needs to look into narrative theories and methods that have been developed over time. In fact, characterization has

---

[55]   Susan E. Hylen, *Imperfect Believers: Ambiguous Characters in the Gospel of John*, 2009.

[56]   Christopher W. Skinner, ed., *Characters and Characterization in the Gospel of John*, 2013.

[57]   Cornelis Bennema, *Encountering Jesus*, 2009, 19.

[58]   Steven A. Hunt, D. Francois Tolmie, and Ruben Zimmermann, eds. *Character Studies in the Fourth Gospel: Narrative Approaches to Seventy Figures in John*, 2013.

only recently become a focus of modern literary studies. Modern approaches to characterization ultimately vary based on whether the approach sees characters primarily as plot functionaries or not. On one hand, there are those who see characters as functioning in subordination to plot, following Aristotle's famous dictum[59] that "the plot is the first principle and it was the soul of tragedy: character comes second." On the other hand, there are those who see characters as autonomous beings, not just as mere plot functions.

Chatman and Hochman argue that literary characters should be read as more "lifelike" than their subordination to plot development.[60] Again, the question that scholars of character face is whether to view characters over plot, or plot over characters. It would appear that ultimately characters and plot are not independent in narrative, but both are interdependent. Van Aarde states that the events and actions in a narration are determined by the relations of the characters.[61] He argues that their interactions contribute to the development of certain characters in the plot. There is an integral relationship between the characters of a narrative and its plot. Characters exist and interact to develop the plot. The characters can have their significance through the reading experience to the reader. As the reader encounters a text, the reader constructs the characters in accordance with the narrative sequence and the accumulated textual information given up to that point in the text.[62]

Having argued that, the characterization is a cumulative effort. Each character or characters are continuously constructed

---

[59]   Aristotle, *Poetics* 6, Loeb Classical Library, 1092, 19.

[60]   Seymour Chatman, Story and Discourse: *Narrative Structure in Fiction and Film*, 1978, 119 and Baruch Hochman, *Character in Literature*, 1985, 13-58.

[61]   Andries van Aarde, *Narrative Criticism*, 387.

[62]   John Darr, *On Character Building: The Reader and the Rhetoric of Characterization in Luke-Acts*, 1992, 46.

throughout the reader's experience of reading the text. To understand the significance of a particular character, therefore, one
needs to be sensitive to the narrative sequence and accumulation.
According to Fehribach, this is particularly important at those
places in the text where the implied author leaves gaps for a reader
to fill in and those places where the implied author utilizers read-
er-victimization.[63] Springer states that character is not given to us
by the author like a gift in the hand or like a picture on the wall, but
it does in fact accumulate.[64] This makes sense since the narrative
itself moves across time, so does the development or revelation of
the character. We must turn the page in order to find out what else
there is to know about the character, what new actions and choices
there may be to expand or modify our understanding, what deci-
sions we are to make about whether the character is fixed or in a
process of change, individual or antithetical to another character,
minor or main. Hochman argues that we must concentrate our
consciousness on the reciprocity between characters in literature
and people in life in order to understand characters adequately.[65]
The importance of a character's place within the structural orga-
nization of the narrative and within the entire set if relationships
that comprises the narrative must therefore be emphasized. Thus,
Johannine characters are also best understood by their interactive
relationship to other characters and to the structural systems of
meaning that compose a narrative.

It is in this way that an argument will be made in the coming
pages for the doxological and Christological significances of the
anonymous minor characters in the narratives of the Samaritan

---

[63]   Fehribach, *The Women in the Life of the Bridegroom: A Feminist Historical-
Literary Analysis of the Female Characters in the Fourth Gospel*, 18.

[64]   Mary Doyle Springer, *A Rhetoric of Literary Character: Some women of
Henry James*, 1978, 179.

[65]   Baruch Hochman, *Character in Literature*, 59.

woman in John 4, the invalid at the pool in John 5, and the man born blind in John 9.

2.4 CHARACTERISTICS OF MINOR JOHANNINE CHARACTERS: IDENTIFYING THE RESEARCH GAP

Analyzing minor Johannine characters can be helped by understanding the interactive relationship between those characters to other characters as well as to the structural systems of meaning of a narrative. The question then is how to view Johannine characters in a narrative plot structure.

It seems difficult to agree with many like Collins and Culpepper who argue Johannine characters are meres representative types, "flat" and one dimensional with the sole exception of Jesus, who is "round" and complex. The flat character presents only one ideological perspective in a narrative plot. On the other hand, the round character often acts in unexpected way, and at times is hesitant, uncertain and complex.

Others dismiss that flat vs. round comparison model. Hochman argues that such a dichotomy between flat and round characters cannot be established.[66] Emphasizing the role of the reader, Galef suggests that the reader's response is really the significant factor since the concept of roundness is an illusion anyway.[67] Conway also points out a glaring discrepancy in her article,[68] asserting there is little agreement among scholars on what each character typifies or represents. She argues that the Johannine characters portray varying degrees of ambiguity, causing instability and resulting in

---

[66] Ibid, 44.

[67] David Galef, *The Supporting Cast: A Study of Flat and Minor Characters*, 1993, 6.

[68] Colleen Conway, "Speaking through Ambiguity: Minor Characters in the Fourth Gospel," 2002.

responses to Jesus that resist or undermine the Gospel's binary categories of belief and unbelief.

In the end, it appears difficult to simplify Johannine characters as flat, especially when it comes to minor characters. Upon examination of the minor characters in John's gospel, it is clear that they demonstrate unpredictable roundness and fully complicated personalities, disqualifying them for any definition of being "flat." Two prime examples of this would be the case of the Samaritan woman in John 4 and the man born blind John 9.

Galef states that "minor characters in their paucity of detail invite the reader's elaboration; flat characters though lacking depth, are finished creations, possessing what one might call contextual closure. A successful minor character may invite curiosity, but well drawn flat character provokes no further probing".[69] Conway asserts that he or she may take on an aspect of autonomy, a mimetic quality along with whatever functional role a character may play.[70] That means minor Johannine characters often seem real to the reader as autonomous being. The essential role of minor characters provides a deep and visible movement to the narrative. Galef argues that the analysis of minor characters will inevitably reveal the painstaking construction of the works: how the author intends to get from alpha and omega, or what contrast he has in mind, or what thematic principles he is stressing.[71]

Thus, even when a minor character seems truly "flat" because of its insignificant role, it may not be a strict "flat." He or she may

---

[69]   David Galef, *The Supporting Cast: A Study of Flat and Minor Characters*, 3. He continues to say that though perhaps best suited as brief representational type, they may nonetheless occasionally play protagonist roles. 6.

[70]   Colleen M Conway, *Men and Women in the Fourth Gospel: Gender and Johannine Characterization*, Soceity of Biblical Literature Dissertation Series 167, 1999, 59.

[71]   David Galef, *The Supporting Cast: A Study of Flat and Minor Characters*, 22.

appear to have unfathomed depths, mainly because the light of exposition never illuminates him or her.[72] I agree with Conway saying that minor Johannine characters are mistakenly dismissed as flat and underdeveloped because biblical hermeneutics of characterization differ from the modern novel.[73]

Although Stibbe, Koester and Kim provide a literary-historical approach, the majority of scholars who have studied Johannine characterization have limited themselves to a mere literary approach. As Bennema argues that the social-historical world in which John's story occurs should be examined beside the text itself,[74] this study will adopt a narrative-historical-cultural approach. It is very important, in studying the Johannine minor characters, that not only a narrative text centered approach is used, as happened in the past. In doing so, it will become clear that the theological significances of the minor Johannine characters can be studied in a more comprehensive manner when a narrative text centered approach is complimented by a social-historical approach.

---

[72]   Ibid., 6.

[73]   Colleen Conway, *Men and Women in the Fourth Gospel: Gender and Johannine Characterization*, 59.

[74]   Cornelis Bennema, *Encountering Jesus*, 23.Cu

CHAPTER 3

The Narrative-Social-Cultural-Historical Approach

3.1 INTRODUCTION

T HIS CHAPTER POSITS A METHOD OF EMPLOYING
a narrative-social-cultural-historical approach on characterization on John's gospel, especially for minor characters in John 4, 5, and 9. Up to now it has been much more common to employ a text-centered narrative or literary approach for studying characterization in John's gospel. However, as noted in Chapter 2, using a social-cultural-historical approach to complement a narrative approach is much more conducive to understanding the ideological or theological perspective of the author or implied author as well as the point of view of the narrator.

3.2 INSUFFICIENCY OF NARRARIVE OR LITERARY APPROACH ALONE

Like Culpepper, many scholars who studied Johannine characterization are inclined to focus on narrative or literary criticism. Unfortunately, narrative or literary criticism has been criticized for disregarding the historical context in the interpretation of gospel narratives. Stibbe argues that many narrative critics have neglected the community orientation of gospel narratives, and in the process have distanced themselves from sociological criticism.[75] He continues to state that gospel narratives are composed according to Hebrew and Greco-Roman storytelling conventions. This study agrees with Rhoads' argument that the interpretation of gospel narratives should draw upon our knowledge of the history, society, and culture of the first century Mediterranean world as a means to help us understand the stories better.[76] The approach advocated here is to read texts as historical data to identify the theological viewpoints and religious practices of the first-century Christians, properly setting them in their social and cultural context. Such an approach begins by describing how the texts came into being, and then adding social, cultural, and historical knowledge to understand fully the characterization of the author.

In describing "historical criticism," Ashton, who is a strong defender, asserts it is not a mere method but an approach, or even an attitude – adopted with the conviction that the path to understanding the past lies in the attempt to place all human achievements, social, political, and religious structures, as well as writings and works of art, in their original historical context. For Ashton, therefore, the term 'historical' is all embracing.[77] Thus, he also suggests that there is no obvious reason why the two approaches of narrative criticism and historical criticism should not be combined, and it may be argued that the best practitioners of the historical

---

[75] Mark W. G. Stibbe, *John as Storyteller: Narrative Criticism and the Fourth Gospel*, Society for New Testament Studies Monograph Series 73, 1992, 67.

[76] David Rhoads, "Narrative Criticism: Practices and Prospects," in *Characterization in the Gospel: Reconceiving Narrative Criticism*, eds. David Rhoads and Kari Syredeni, 1999, 268. If we believe John's gospel is non-fictional narrative and refers to events and people in the real world of the first century Mediterranean world, it is necessary to fill gaps in our knowledge of the social, cultural, historical context, not using our imagination as through reading a fictional novel.

[77] John Ashton, *Studying John: Approaches to the Fourth Gospel*, 1994, 184.

critical method showed a keen sense of the literary qualities of John's gospel.

Another reason that characterization requires social, cultural, and historical approach is that the characterization in first century Greek literature was not simple. We cannot insist that the first century literature has no psychological interest in character, or that characters move towards personality.[78] It is difficult to read a character solely from the surface of the text. Since a character is conveyed mainly through the character's speech and actions rather than the narrator's limited statements, a reader or implied reader must reconstruct the character through inference. That is why Chatman argues that to restrain a God-given right to infer and even to speculate about characters would be an impoverishment of the aesthetic experience.[79] He continues to state that we reconstruct character by inferring traits from the information of the text.[80] The highlighting of the reader's need to infer character traits from the information dispersed in the text goes back to Iser.[81] Iser and Darr's characterization not only concentrates on the role of the author, but also on how readers participate in the building

---

[78] Bennema argues that characterization in ancient Greco-Roman literature and modern literature is not identical but has different emphases: the ancient did not give character as much individual and psychological emphasis as the moderns do in the Western world. (Christopher Skinner, ed. *Characters and Characterization in the Gospel of John*, 38-39).

[79] Seymour Chatman, *Story and Discourse: Narrative Structure in Fiction and Film*, 1978, 117.

[80] Ibid., 119-120. He also argues later that because the trait is often not named explicitly in the text but must be inferred, readers will usually rely upon their knowledge of the trait-name in the real world, so traits are culturally coded (123-125).

[81] Wolfgang Iser, "The Reading Process: A Phenomenological Approach," *New Literary History 3*, 1972, 279-299; *The Act of Reading: A Theory of Aesthetic Response*, 1978, 53-85.

of literary characters.[82] Darr presents two interpretative models: readers build characters, and critics build readers.[83] He continues to explain four critical premises for his theory: 1) texts are stable, but schematic, linguistic entities; 2) all texts function rhetorically; 3) meaning inheres in neither text nor reader alone, but is produced in and through their interaction; and 4) the writing, reading, and interpretation of texts do not occur in a vacuum, but rather are conditioned and enabled by cultural context.[84] Thus, the reader or implied reader should also consider the social, cultural, and historical context present at the time in which the narrative unfolds to understand the text, not just employ a literary or narrative approach. The "implied reader" is a concept well known to narratological critics that can come in a variety of forms. A reader may be explicitly constructed in the text, for instance, Luke's addressing of Theophilus in the prefaces to Luke's gospel (Lk. 1:3) and Acts (1:10), or John's use of "you" in asserting who is called upon to believe in John's gospel (Jn. 19:35; 20:31). The possible characteristics of that reader directly addressed by the author may indeed ultimately differ from all those who actually will take the text in hand. Alternately, the reader may be more subtly implied by the kinds of appeals and assumptions that are built into a text. As those appeals and assumptions become more tenuous and blurred, the image of the implied reader becomes more subject to the imaginative construction of the real reader who offers an interpretation of the text.

This broader lens approach explores the literary and social-cultural approaches that are supposed to help a reader or implied reader to understand the narrative's point of view. Fehribach

---

[82]   Iser, *The Act of Reading* and John Darr, *On Character Building: The Reader and the Rhetoric of Characterization in Luke-Acts*, 1992

[83]   John Darr, *On Character Building*, 1992, 16.

[84]   Ibid., 17.

identifies five aids for uncovering the literary and social conventions that would have formed the reader's horizon of expectation
regarding the female characters in John's gospel: 1) the Hebrew
Bible; 2) Hellenistic-Jewish writings; 3) popular Greco-Roman
literature; 4) the concept of 'honor and shame' as used by cultural anthropologists for the study of gender relations in the
Mediterranean area; and 5) the history of women in the Greco-
Roman world. Information about women from these five areas
will provide the twentieth or twenty-first century reader with the
"cultural literacy" necessary to understand the text as a first-century
reader might have understood it.[85] Any interpretation involves an
element of speculation, inasmuch as the interpreter or reader tries
to make sense out of the text in the absence of the author. The
reader tries to understand the meaning of the text through a process that involves a level of abstraction or aggregation that includes
acts of analysis, comparison, extrapolation, inference, and so on.
It is necessary to consider the rules of syntax and genre in relation to the wider text and knowledge of the social cultural setting of the text. The reader must aim to figure out the meaning of
the text within its original literary and social-cultural-historical
context. Van Eck states that the text is analyzed as a vehicle of
communication whose aim is shaped by the cultural and social

---

[85]   Adeline Fehribach, *The Woman in the Life of the Bridegroom: A Feminist
Historical-Literary Analysis of the Female Characters in the Fourth Gospel*,
1998, 17-18. Of course, the interpreter must be aware in reading Fehribach
that by applying such methods she fuses the modern and ancient horizons, and in merging the two horizons to bridge the vast cultural gap uses
modern terminology to understand characters in ancient literature. This
so-called "new hermeneutic," rooted in the work of philosophers Martin
Heidegger and Hans-Georg Gadamer, is developed extensively by Anthony
Thiselton in *The Two Horizons* (Exeter: Paternoster, 1980) and *New Horizons
in Hermeneutics* (San Francisco: Harper Collins, 1992).

dynamics of the social system and the specific historical setting.[86] The knowledge of the social and cultural world of first-century Mediterranean area is thus essential for understanding the personality, motive and behavior of characters in the gospels.

The Johannine characters also have historical referents and should be read within the social-historical context of first-century Judaism and not just on the basis of the text itself. The characters are real historical people. The study of the referent of Jews is therefore needed, which in turn is related to the group's identity as real people in the time of Jesus. Narrative critics, however, usually restrict themselves to the text of the gospel, effectively reading the gospel as a fictional narrative that is disconnected from reality. That is why Bennema argues that although the form of historical narrative criticism takes a text-centered approach, it also is required to examine aspects of the world outside or behind the text if the text invites us to do so.[87] Hur mentions that the readers evaluate characters in the context of each narrative in accordance with reliability of its characters.[88] Although Resseguie states that the narrative critic should be familiar with the cultural, linguistic, social, and historical assumption of the audience envisioned by the implied author, he nevertheless contends that this information must be obtained from the text itself

---

[86] Ernest Van Eck, *Galilee and Jerusalem In Mark's Story of Jesus: A Narratological and Social Scientific Reading*, Hervormde Teologiese Studies Supplementum 7, 1995, 83.

[87] Cornelis Bennema, "A Comprehensive Approach to Understanding Character in the Gospel of John," *Characters and Characterization in the Gospel of John*, Christopher W. Skinner, ed., 45.

[88] Ju Hur, "The Characterization of the Holy Spirit in Luke-Acts with Special Reference to Indirect Presentation," *Journal of the New Testament Society of Korea 22*, 2015, 412.

rather than from the outside the text.[89] Stibbe also states that characters in the gospels need to be analyzed with reference to history, and not according to the laws of fiction.[90] In reality, Boer presents a good defense for a combined historical and narrative criticism approach to John's gospel.[91]

Combining historical and narrative criticism of anonymous minor characters in John, this study will identify the manner in which a first-century reader would have understood the minor characters in John 4, 5 and 9. For instance, Martyn reads John 9 as evidence of how the author's historical situation strongly shaped his treatment of characters, pointing to the significant variety in John's wording regarding characters.[92] The characters, Martyn asserts, can be understood within a historical context in which persecution of Christians was known but not systemic, and where even Christians expelled from the Temple and Jewish society could still consider themselves Jewish, like the man born blind who is driven out by the Pharisees upon testifying of Jesus healing of his eyesight.[93] Instead of representing later Christians forcibly separated from the synagogue, the blind man may be seen as a character whose persecution confirms Jesus' identity as Israel's true leader. The Pharisees, meanwhile, seek to uphold the Sabbath but miss the activity of God manifest in Jesus. John

---

89 James L. Resseguie, *Narrative Criticism of the New Testament: An Introduction*, 2005, 32-39.

90 Mark W. G. Stibbe, *John as Storyteller: Narrative Criticism and the Fourth Gospel*, Society for New Testament Studies Monograph Series 73, 1992, 24.

91 Boer, Martinus C. de., "Narrative Criticism, Historical Criticism, and the Gospel of John", *Journal for the Study of the New Testament* 45, 1992, 35-48.

92 J. Louis Martyn, *History and Theology in the Fourth Gospel*, 1979, 39, 99.

93 Susan E. Hylen, "Three Ambiguities: Historical Context, Implied Reader, and the Nature of Faith," *Characters and Characterization in the Gospel of John*, Christopher W. Skinner, ed., 102.

thus turns the expulsion of the man born blind into evidence of the Pharisees' spiritual blindness.[94]

The vocabulary and syntax of John's gospel and cultural norms may all be situated in narrative with a likely historical context. The minor characters in John's gospel provide important clues to the author's characterization in John's literary context. As real characters they have distinctive and complex traits, even if they play only a representative role. The characters represent actual historical people, so they should be understood as evidence of the historical situation. Charlesworth demonstrates that there is a returning confidence among scholars that John's gospel contains historically accurate material as well as theological reflections about Jesus.[95] Bauckham says that the eyewitnesses' testimony offers us a theological model for understanding the Gospels in general as the entirely appropriate means of access to the historical reality of Jesus, and the eyewitnesses to Jesus life and ministry. They remain the living and active guarantors of the traditions in whose name they were transmitted.[96] And yet, characters are chosen by the process of writing and cannot easily be identified with historical people from a literary perspective. Readers have to comprehend literary characters with their knowledge of people's social, cultural, and historical setting. Thus, they often represent points of view that were typical of its readers or implied readers.

---

[94] Ibid., 103.

[95] James H. Charlesworth, "The Historical Jesus in the Fourth Gospel: A Paradigm Shift?," *Journal for the Study of Historical Jesus* 8, 2010, 3-46.

[96] Richard Bauckham, *Jesus and the Eyewitnesses: The Gospels as Eyewitness Testimony*, 2006, 5 and 290.

3.3 JOHANNINE NARRATOR'S POINT OF VIEW ON AN IDEOLOGICAL LEVEL

A narrator might be understood fully as a storyteller by whom a story is represented and evaluated in terms of narrator's point of view. Van Aarde notices that readers/interpreters of a narrative can visualize at least five levels of "point of view," namely characterization on a psychological, phraseological, temporal, spatial, and ideological level.[97] Chatman calls it "perspective" of a character in the narrative,[98] while Genette refers to it as "focalization."[99] Among these levels, this study is concentrated with the ideological or evaluative point of view which governs a work in general. It refers to the norms, values, and general worldview that the narrator or implied author establishes as operative in the narrative. Ideological point of view may be defined as the standards of judgment by which readers are led to evaluate the events, characters, and historical settings that comprise the narrative. Powell argues that readers must accept the implied author's evaluative point of view even if it means suspending

---

[97]   Andries G. van Aarde, *Focusing on the Message: New Testament Hermeneutics, Exegesis and Methods,* 2009, 392. It is Uspensky who distinguishes five different "planes" of point of view: Spatial (location of the narrator), Temporal (time of the narrator), Phraseological (speech patterns), Psychological (internal and external of the characters) and Ideological (evaluative norms). (Boris Uspensky, A Poetics of Composition: The Structure of the Artistic Test and Typology of a Compositional Form. Translated by V. Zavarin and S. Wittig, 1973, 6)

[98]   Seymour Chatman, Story and Discourse: *Narrative Structure in Fiction and Film,* 1978, 151-152

[99]   Gerard Genette, *Narrative Discourse: An Essay in Method.* Translated by Jane E. Lewin, 1980, 185. Rimmon-Kenan also calls it 'focalization' and her concept of point of view refers three facets of the text: 1) perceptual facet, 2) psychological facet, and 3) ideological facet (Shlomith Rimmon-Kenan, *Narrative Fiction: Contemporary Poetics,* 1983: 71).

their own judgments during the act of reading.[100] He continues to state that God's evaluate point of view can be determined and must be accepted as normative.[101]

The narrator tends to empathize with those characters who express God's point of view and seeks distance from those characters that do not. The gospels describe a world that includes supernatural beings and events because the gospels are God's word. The right way of thinking should be aligned with God's point of view. And God's point of view must be defined in terms of how it is described by the narrator.

The Johannine narrator usually speaks in the third person, except for the first person plural used in John 1:14, 16 and 21:24. Interestingly, Culpepper adopts Uspensky's five "planes" concepts for identifying the point of view of the Johannine narrator and proposes that 1) psychological point of view is omniscient; 2) spatial point of view is omnipresent; 3) temporal point of view is retrospective; and 4) ideological point of view is reliable and stereoscopic.[102] He explains that no narrator can be absolutely impartial: inevitably a narrator, especially an omniscient, omnipresent, omnicommunicative, and intrusive one, will prejudice the reader toward or away from certain characters, claims, or incidents and their implications.[103] As mentioned in the preceding paragraph, the most important function of the Johannine narrator is bound up in the ideological point of view. The Johannine narrator's function is to make easy communication of the author's ideological or theological point to the reader as it is manifested

---

[100] Mark Allan Powell, *What is Narrative Criticism?*, 1990, 24.

[101] Ibid., 25.

[102] R. Alan Culpepper, *Anatomy of the Fourth Gospel: A Study in Literary Design*, 1983, 21-34.

[103] Ibid., 32.

in the narrator's commentary of characters and incidents. His function is to facilitate communication of the author's ideological or theological point to the readers. The readers are thus brought into its value system or provided with some way of relating it to their own.

In order to grasp the Johannine narrator's ideological or theological point of view, readers may consider two poles of conflict in the narrative, similar to that seen in the other gospels. One is God's point of view and the other is point of view of Satan. Of course, the point of view of Satan is normative in a negative sense as it comprises what is wrong and untrue. The reader or implied reader tends to empathize with those characters that express God's point of view and seek distance from Satan's. God's point of view can be determined and be accepted as normative. The narrative is thus a powerful rhetorical device. The Johannine narrator also attempts to lead the readers to accept his ideological or theological point of view by using many rhetorical devices. Booth discusses five voices of the author: 1) direct addresses or commentary; 2) explicit judgments; 3) inside views; 4) the reliable statements of any dramatized character; and 5) all evidences of the author's meddling with the natural sequence, proportion, or duration of events.[104]

The Johannine narrator's ideological point of view takes the place of God's point of view through which he evaluates or comments on characters and incidents, certainly evident in John 4, 5, and 9. Throughout the gospel of John, the narrator presents characters as God's instruments and manifests his favoritism of some characters over others like the Pharisees or Sadducees. Therefore, like other gospel narrators the Johannine narrator holds a theocentric and Christocentric ideology. Although Culpepper states

---

[104] Wayne C. Booth, *The Rhetoric of Fiction*, 2nd ed., 1991, (originally published in 1961) 16-20.

that the reliability of the narrator must be kept distinct from both the historical accuracy of the narrator's account and the truth of his ideological point of view,[105] this study holds that the Johannine narrator is reliable and authoritative. Readers should naturally view John, his intent, and thus his and his narrative's reliability and authoritativeness on the ground that he appeals he is on God's side because he makes clear in John 20:31 the soteriological purpose of the gospel: "these are written so that you may believe that Jesus is the Christ, the Son of God, and that by believing you may have life in his name." He speaks from the ideological point of view of the Johannine community. The author's doxology and Christology are conveyed through Jesus and the narrator. Culpepper states correctly that the narrator views Jesus and his ministry from the twin perspectives of his "whence" and his "whither," and his origin as the pre-existent λόγος and his destiny as the glorified Son of God.[106]

As the anonymous characters of John 4, 5, and 6 contribute to the narrative's point of view, there are doxological and Christological significances in them where the narrator explains to the reader and shows the actions and dialogues of the narrator to be self-conscious in his understanding that Jesus is the Messiah who has come from the Father. He is going to be exalted and glorified. The narrator knows that Jesus is divine, pre-existent lo,goj and portrays Jesus as the one who continued the divine work by creating eyes of a man born blind, healing the invalid of thirty-eight years, and being himself the living water the drinking of which would leave the Samaritan woman to never thirst again. With the Samaritan woman in John 4, the invitation is framed around asking Jesus for the living water that he

---

[105]   Alan Culpepper, *Anatomy of the Fourth Gospel*, 1983, 32.

[106]   Ibid., 33.

offers her. She shows remarkable character development in the course of their dialogue. Her perspective on Jesus is progressively changed from one level to the next in the course of dialogue, and finally she says, Κύριε, θεωρῶ ὅτι προφήτης εἶ σύ ("Sir, I understand that you are a prophet") (Jn. 4:19), leaves her bucket at the well and returns to the village saying rhetorically, μήτι οὗτός ἐστιν ὁ Χριστός (Can this man be the Christ?) (Jn. 4:29). The Samaritan people in the village complete the Christological point of view in the narrative by confessing οἴδαμεν ὅτι οὗτός ἐστιν ἀληθῶς ὁ σωτὴρ τοῦ κόσμου ("we know that this is truly the Savior of the world) (Jn. 4:42).

With the healing of the invalid at the pool of Bethesda in John 5, the issues between Jesus and the Jewish authorities are exposed. Jesus healed him on the Sabbath, and Jesus identified himself with God the Father (Jn. 5:18). Thus, the issue is Jesus' identity and his violation of the Sabbath when the healing of the invalid happened. The text shows the progressiveness with a sense of inevitability to a confrontation between them. The narrative then shows a soteriological point of view. Jewish authorities try to kill Jesus for His having healed on the Sabbath, and Jesus in response declares that Father has given him authority to give life and that the tombs will be opened, and the dead will rise (Jn. 5:19-21). The man born blind in John 9 is also caught between Jesus and the Pharisees, but in contrast to the invalid at Bethesda pool in John 5, he moves step by step to an affirmation of faith in Jesus. This narrative clarifies the bases of the division among the people in response to Jesus. Seeing and believing, blindness and sin, accepting and rejecting Jesus, the disciples of Moses and of Jesus — all are developed through the blind man, the Pharisees, and the supporting cast of disciples, neighbors, and parents. The man born blind, however, acknowledges Jesus as the Messiah from God and confess that Ριστεύω, κύριε ("I believe, Lord") (Jn. 9:38) when Jesus asked, Σὺ πιστεύεις εἰς τὸν υἱὸν τοῦ ἀνθρώπου; ("Do you believe in the Son of Man?") (Jn. 9:36) and he worshiped the Lord.

3.4   THE PROLOGUE

In the prologue (Jn. 1:1-18), the author sets the tone of his gospel and writes with literary beauty while showing his theological points of view that will be seen throughout his narrative to follow. He presents Jesus as the eternal λόγος of God, and thus provides a unique point of view toward the Son of God the Father who exists from eternity past with the God the Father. Merely by studying, reflecting on, and remember the gospel's prologue, the reader or implied reader can understand and relate Christological and doxological significance of the narratives' anonymous minor characters in John 4, 5, and 9.

The author may have written this prologue to serve as the introduction of his gospel. It contains a number of themes consistent with the rest of the gospel. Important themes in the prologue that are developed later in the gospel include life (Jn. 1:4), light and darkness (Jn. 1:5, 7-9), witness (Jn. 1:7-8, 15), world (Jn. 1:10), belief and unbelief (Jn. 1:11-12), and grace and truth (Jn. 1:14, 17). These themes appear throughout the narratives of John 4, 5, and 9. Thus, the reader or implied reader is convinced that the prologue is closely linked with the rest of the narratives.

The author's subject of the prologue is ὁ λόγος ("the Word"). Most scholars propose its conceptual background of ὁ λόγος into three sources:[107]

1) Greek philosophy (Stoicism, Philo)

---

[107] Keener provides in-depth discussions of the gnostic ὁ λόγος; ὁ λόγος of Hellenistic philosophy; Philo; wisdom, word, and Torah; and John's ὁ λόγος and Torah (Craig Keener, *The Gospel of John*, 2003, 339-63).

2) The personification of wisdom

3) The Old Testament

In Stoicism current at the time in Hellenistic philosophies, ὁ λόγος was conceived as a sort of cosmic reason. It gave order and structure to the operation of the universe as an impersonal governing principle. According to the thought at the time, a bit of universal ὁ λόγος resided within people who must live in keeping with it to attain dignity and meaning. It is doubtful, however, that this definition constituted the author's primary conceptual foundation.[108] Such ὁ λόγος, Kim notes, "has no concept of a personal God, no place for historical divine acts in the incarnation, no radical view of sin, no idea of ethical renewal through the ministry of the Word and Spirit, and no hope of the resurrection and eternal fellowship with God in His kingdom."[109]

Another proposal as to the meaning of ὁ λόγος is the personification of wisdom in wisdom literature such as Proverbs 8:22-31 where wisdom is presented as a divine being. Wisdom claims preexistence and participation in God's creative activity. Late in the period of the Hebrew Scriptures and beyond that period through the first century, Jewish speculation about wisdom related it to the Torah, the written word of God. Likewise, it became identified with ὁ λόγος of God (*memra*, the Aramaic for "word"). But despite the

---

[108]   Andreas Köstenberger, *Encountering John: The Gospel in Historical, Literary, and Theological Perspective*, 1999, 52.

[109]   Stephen Kim, "The Literary and Theological Significance of the Johannine Prologue," *BibSac* vol. 166, 425. Kim quotes Geoffrey Bromiley, "Stoics," in *International Standard Bible Encyclopedia*, 1988, 621.

similarities, the use of ὁ λόγος in John 1 differs from personified wisdom in several respects.[110]

The final possibility of understanding ὁ λόγος is as depicting the Word of God in the Old Testament, viewing prologue of John's gospel within a Hebraic background rather than Hellenistic. This sees the origin of ὁ λόγος as the Old Testament and the Hebrew term rbd.. Further supporting the Hebraic background is the author's possible deliberate echoing of the Hebrew Scriptures by employing the phrase "in the beginning" to open the gospel, as well as the use of ὁ λόγος in John 1:1 that ties the verse to Genesis 1:3, which describes God's creative acts by the powerful command of His Word. This is further confirmed not only in Psalm 33:6, but also in the Old Testament prophets where repeatedly their writings begin with the words, "The word of the Lord came to" (Jer. 1:4; Ezek. 1:3; Hos. 1:1; Joel 1:1; Amos 3:1; Jon. 1:1; Mic. 1:1; Zeph. 1:1; Hag. 1:1; Zech. 1:1; Mal. 1:1). The author's adaptation of Isaiah 55:9-11 for his Christological framework has also been proposed as the background of ὁ λόγος in his gospel.[111]

Moloney suggests, "the choice of the Greek expression ὁ λόγος, whatever its background, allows the author to hint to the reader

---

[110] Köstenberger explains the differences in three points: 1) Wisdom literature presents Wisdom not as a second person of the Godhead but merely as a divine attribute already present as Creation. Jesus on the other hand is portrayed not merely as "with God" (1:1-2), but also Himself God (1:1). 2) Wisdom is not cast as a person, but merely a concept that is personified, a common literary device. But in John the exact opposite is present: Jesus, a real person, is presented in conceptual terms as ὁ λόγος. 3)The fact remains that John did not use the term σοφία ("wisdom") but the expression ὁ λόγος (Andreas Köstenberger, *Encountering John: The Gospel in Historical, Literary, and Theological Perspective*, 1999, 53).

[111] Köstenberger also argues that Isaiah 55:9-11 is God's personified Word, not Wisdom. He observes three parallels: 1) ὁ λόγος is sent by God to accomplish a particular divine purpose. 2) It unfailingly accomplishes this purpose. 3) Afterward it returns to God who sent it (Ibid. 54).

that from the intimacy between the Word and God which has been described, "the Word" will now be spoken. A word is essentially about communication. The modality of that communication has not been indicated, but if there is the Word, then it exists to say something."[112] Harris summarizes well, "Why did John choose to call Jesus the Logos in the prologue to his Gospel, and what did he mean by it? As to why the term was used, the answer probably lies with John's audience. John gave no explanation of the Logos, apparently assuming his readers would understand the idea. Greek readers would probably think he was referring to the rational principle that guided the universe and would be shocked to find that this Logos had become not only personalized but incarnate (1:1-14). Jewish readers would be more prepared for some sort of personalized preexistent Wisdom, but they too would be amazed at the idea of incarnation. John presented Jesus as the true Logos as preparation for his own presentation of Jesus as the Son of God."[113]

Thus, the thrust of the author's prologue is that ὁ λόγος for the reader or implied reader is a person. The author claims that λόγος is not a category of religious experience, nor it is speculative religious mythology. It is the person, fleshed, living, historical Son of God, Christ. Jesus Christ is the incarnation of the preexistent ὁ λόγος. That the eternal life, light, and divine origin flow from an acceptance of the story of the unseen God revealed by the incarnated λόγος. The reader or implied reader has been told who Jesus is and what He has done. The author tells how the action of God in the history takes place.

---

[112] Francis Moloney, *Belief in the Word: Reading John 1-4*, 1993, 30.

[113] W. Hall Harris, "A Theology of John's Writings," *A Biblical Theology of the New Testament*, ed. Roy Zuck, 1994, 191.

3.4.1 Literary structure of the prologue

Some scholars follow a movement in time, from preexistence (Jn. 1:1-2) into creation (Jn. 1:3-5), proceeding through the story of human condition until the incarnation (Jn. 1:6-14) and then the subsequent reception of the incarnate λόγος (Jn. 1:15-18).

If someone follows the patterns of biblical poetry like the use of parallelism, John the Baptist passages indicate that the prologue has three sections:[114]

1. The Word in God becomes the light of the world (Jn. 1:1-5)

2. The incarnation of the Word (Jn. 1:6-14)

3. The revealer: the only Son turned toward the Father (Jn. 1:15-18)

---

[114] Francis Moloney, *The Gospel of John*, 1988, 34.

Other scholars proposed that there are various forms of chiastic structure of the prologue. One proposed by Culpepper seems to be the most thorough, and thus serves a good model for discussion:[115]

A. The Word's activity in creation (Jn. 1:1-5)

B. John's witness concerning the light (Jn. 1:6-8)

C. The incarnation of the Word (Jn. 1:9-14)

B. John's witness concerning the Word's preeminence (Jn. 1:15)

A. The final revelation brought by Jesus Christ (Jn. 1:16-18)

Kysar interestingly suggests a chiastic structure focusing about the subject, ὁ λόγος as follows:[116]

Existed from the beginning (Jn. 1:1a)
Existed with God (Jn. 1:1b)

---

[115] Köstenberger agrees and adopts Culpepper' suggestion (Andreas Köstenberger, *Encountering John: The Gospel in Historical, Literary, and Theological Perspective*, 1999, 57). See Alan Culpepper, "The Pivot of John's Prologue," *New Testament Studies* 27, 1980, 1-31. He suggests a chiastic structure in which verse 12 is the center of attention. Seo outlines its chiastic structure into seven units according to Christological theme: A- The Word was God (Jn. 1:1-2) B- In the Word was life (Jn. 1:3-5) C- Through the Word all men might believe (Jn. 1:6-9) D- To those who believed in the Word (Jn. 1:10-14) C'- This was He (Jn. 1:15) B'- Grace and truth came through Jesus Christ (Jn. 1:16-17) A'- God the One and Only is at the Father's bosom (Jn. 1:18) (Young Hwan Seo, *Analysis of the New Testament Structure II*, 2007, 16; translated by Nathan Hahn). Meanwhile, although it is probable that the author designed a chiastic structure, some proposed the outline for the sake of the dividing passage according to a thematic analysis: A. The Origin and Nature of the Logos (Jn. 1:1-5) B. The Witness to the Logos (Jn. 1:6-8) C. The Manifestation of the Logos (Jn. 1:9-13) D. The Revelation of the Logos (Jn. 1:14-18) (Stephen Kim, Stephen Kim, "The Literary and Theological Significance of the Johannine Prologue," *BibSac* vol. 166, 428).

[116] Robert Kysar, *John, the Maverick Gospel* 3rd ed., 2007, 41.

Was God (Jn. 1:1c)

Was the agent of creation (Jn. 1:3)

Was life that was light to persons (Jn. 1:4)

(Was not John the Baptist) (Jn. 1:6-8)

Was in, but not recognized by the world (Jn. 1:10)

Was rejected by His own (Jn. 1:11)

Was source of power to become children of God (Jn. 1:12)

Became flesh and dwelt in the world (Jn. 1:14a)

Revealed Glory (Jn. 1:14b)

Was God's Son (Jn. 1:14c)

(John the Baptist witnessed to Him) (Jn. 1:15)

Was the means of grace and truth (Jn. 1:16)

Was superior to Moses (Jn. 1:17)

Made God known as never before (Jn. 1:18)

3.4.2 The Word's activity in creation (Jn. 1:1-5)

The first phrase of the prologue, ἐν ἀρχῇ ἦν ὁ λόγος ("In the beginning was the Word") (Jn. 1:1a) shows a parallel between the opening of the narrative and the biblical account of the beginnings of history in Genesis 1:1. Before the beginning of the history there was only God, but the author claims that even then ἦν ὁ λόγος.[117] The λόγος preexists the history and ὁ λόγος ἦν πρὸς τὸν θεόν ("the Word was with God") (Jn. 1:1b). Its existence is placed outside the limits of time and place, neither of which existed ἐν ἀρχῇ.[118] The λόγος preexists for a relationship with God. From the start the author chose the Greek ὁ λόγος to express that from the intimacy of God a word will be spoken. The λόγος exists to say God's

---

[117] Brown argues the word ἦν in John 1:1 conveys the notions of existence, relationship, and predication contrasting ἐγένετο in John 1:3, 6, 14 (Raymond Brown, *The Gospel According to John I-XII*, 1966, 4).

[118] Francis Moloney, *The Gospel of John*, 1988, 35.

revelation. The term θεὸς is familiar to the reader or implied reader of the Johannine narrative as a reference to the God revealed in the Old Testament, and the θεὸς occurs in Genesis 1:1 to refer to the Creator. The author's favorite expression for θεὸς in his narrative is πατήρ ("Father") of Jesus (Jn. 1:14, 18).[119]

The θεὸς ἦν ὁ λόγος ("the Word was God") (Jn. 1:1c) places the compliment θεὸς before the verb ἦν and does not give it an article. It means that the author avoids saying that ὁ λόγος and θεὸς were one and the same thing.[120] It indicates that ὁ λόγος and θεὸς keep their uniqueness, despite oneness due to their intimacy. Having distinguished ὁ λόγος from θεὸς, the author shows that they are God. Of course, calling ὁ λόγος God extended the boundaries of Jewish belief in Jehovah God.[121] It has been argued that John 1:1 identifies merely ὁ λόγος, Jesus as a god rather than as God because there is no definite article before θεὸς. However, this is unworthy discussion as Köstenberger explores for several reasons.[122]

The author uses a personal pronoun, οὗτος for ὁ λόγος in John 1:2, while he really repeats what has already been claimed in John 1:1. Now the reader understands more its contents of John 1:1, providing

---

[119]   Andreas Köstenberger, *John*, 2004, 28.

[120]   In terms of relationship, not only does πρὸς establish a relationship between ὁ λόγος and θεὸς, but it also distinguishes the two from each other (See Ibid., 5).

[121]   See Richard Bauckham, *God Crucified: Monotheism and Christology in the New Testament*, 1998.

[122]   After he states three reasons Köstenberger states, "Nevertheless, the force of the anarthrous θεὸς is probably not so much that of definiteness as that of quality: Jesus shared the essence of the Father, though they differed in person. Everything that can be said about God also can be said about the Word." (See Andreas Köstenberger, *John*, 2004, 28-29). Also MacLeod argues strongly against the assertion Jesus is a god, surveying many scholars' theological, literary, and grammatical reasons (See David MacLeod, "The Eternality and Deity of the Word: John 1:1-2," *BibSac*. vol. 160, 2003, 58-62).

closure as well as preparing the reader for the next verse.[123] Who might οὗτος be? The author insinuates an eventual revelation that will take place in the history by means of the story told by ὁ λόγος. The author intends that his narrative shall be read in the light of these first two verses.[124] So far, he claims that as the incarnated λόγος, Jesus alone is God come to the world. No other can stand alongside Him or take His place. Jesus shares in the infinity of God. This does not mean that people cannot know Him, but they cannot have complete knowledge of Him. He must always be in the center of the believer's approach to God, his thinking about God, and his relating to God (Jn. 14:6).

The author uses the aorist ἐγένετο in John 1:3 and the shift from the imperfect of ἦν (Jn. 1:1-2) looks back to a time in the past when πάντα δι᾽ αὐτοῦ (the Word) ἐγένετο. Moreover, οὐδὲ ἕν ("nothing") in creation took place without ὁ λόγος. The author conveyed that in the beginning the revealing act of creation took place through ὁ λόγος. Then he said, ὃ γέγονεν ("that has been made"). The perfect tense indicates that the creation took place in the past, but the significance of its plot continues into the present.[125] Calvin states, "Having declared that the Word is God and proclaimed His divine essence, he goes on to prove His divinity from His works."[126]

---

[123] Donald Carson, *The Gospel According to John*, 1991, 118.

[124] C. K. Barret, *The Gospel According to St. John*, 2nd ed., 1978, 156. He also states that "the deeds and words of Jesus are the deeds and words of God; if this be not true the book is blasphemous."

[125] The emphasis of John 1:3 is to point to creation, not incarnation. The author asserts that πάντα ("everything in creation") owes its existence to ὁ λόγος. See Donald Carson, *The Gospel According to John*, 1991, 118 and Leon Morris, *The Gospel According to John*, 1995, 71 and Herman Ridderbos, *The Gospel According to John*, 1997, 37.

[126] John Calvin, *The Gospel according to St. John, 1-10*, 1959, 9.

The λόγος speaks out of intimacy with God and makes God known, both in creation and in the presence of the λόγος itself in history. This revelation provides ἡ ζωὴ for which human beings need τὸ φῶς in John 1:4. The history of salvation is plotted from the pre-existence of the λόγος to ἡ ζωὴ and τὸ φῶς brought into the history through the presence of the incarnated λόγος, Jesus (Jn. 1:14). The author affirms that the revelation brought by the λόγος is coming into the world. According to Schnackenburg both ἡ ζωὴ and τὸ φῶς are universal religious terms,[127] but Culpepper argues that they are rooted in the Old Testament teaching.[128] At creation, τὸ φῶς was God's first creative act (Gen. 1:3-5). Later, God placed lights in the sky to separate between φῶς and σκοτίᾳ (Gen. 1:14-18). The φῶς makes it possible for ζωὴ to exist. The author asserts that ἡ ζωὴ was in Him, ὁ λόγος who is the source of ζωὴ and φῶς.

The author tells that τὸ φῶς ἐν τῇ σκοτίᾳ φαίνει ("the light shines in the darkness") in John 1:5a. He uses φαίνει, the present tense which means τὸ φῶς continues to be present despite ἡ σκοτία αὐτὸ οὐ κατέλαβεν ("the darkness has not overcome it").[129] The φῶς came when ὁ λόγος incarnated in the world and now shines.[130] Thus, the reader or implied reader may recognize τὸ φῶς keeps shining in spite of the hostile reception it received. The author speaks of how human beings respond to the revelation of God that takes place in the λόγος, Jesus Christ. The σκοτία is the world estranged from God

---

[127] Rudolf Schnackenburg, *The Gospel According to St. John, vol.1*, 1990, 242-44.

[128] See Alan Culpepper, *Anatomy of the Fourth Gospel*, 1983, 180-98.

[129] The translation "overcome" of the verb κατέλαβεν would be better than "understood," as asserted by many scholars such as Morris, Moloney, Schnackenburg, Lindars, Schlatter, and Westcott. Carson thinks the author might have both meanings in mind (Donald Carson, *The Gospel According to John*, 1991, 138). However, Calvin translates "comprehend" (John Calvin, *The Gospel According to St. John, 1-10*, 1959, 12).

[130] Herman Ridderbos, *The Gospel According to John*, 1997, 39.

in Johannine narrative, spiritually ignorant and blind dominated by Satan.[131]

It is evident that John used the opening verses of his narrative to firmly set in place the Christological planks of the framework for a worldview. As the incarnated λόγος, Jesus Christ is God, and He created all things. To reject this worldview is to choose darkness. Those who chose darkness do not want Christ as their Creator and Sovereign.

3.4.3 John's witness concerning the light (Jn. 1:6-8)

The author gives a more narrative description of the figure and role of John the Baptist in John 1:6-8. Although many scholars think it as a secondary addition to the Prologue, this section is essential to the Prologue's structure and message. As the λόγος's involvement in the events of history are found in John 1:3-5, the author continues to introduce another historical figure who ἐγένετο ("enters") the narrative (Jn. 1:6). John the Baptist was not just any man, as we can see from the narrator's point that ἀπεσταλμένος παρὰ θεοῦ ("he had been sent from God"). This phrase, ἀπεσταλμένος παρὰ θεοῦ is reminiscent of the Old Testament description of a prophet whose role was to work as a spokesperson for God. This is very unique claim since nobody else in Johannine narrative is described as having sent by God except Jesus. It is thus God's plan that μαρτυρήσῃ περὶ τοῦ φωτός, ἵνα πάντες πιστεύσωσιν δι' αὐτοῦ ("he came to testify about the light, that all might believe through him") (Jn. 1:7). Because of his testimony people might come to believe through the ζωὴ giving

---

[131] Rudolf Schnackenburg, *The Gospel According to St. John, vol.1*, 1990, 245. See Alan Culpepper, *Anatomy of the Fourth Gospel*, 1983, 180-98.

presence of the φῶς, Jesus Christ.[132] Through the λόγος, all things were created (Jn. 1:3). Now it is God's purpose that people might believe through John the Baptist's testimony.[133]

Köstenberger states well in regard to the witnesses, "This role of eyewitness is both vital and humble. It is vital because eyewitnesses are required to establish the truthfulness of certain facts. Yet it is humble because the eyewitness is not the center of attention. Rather, eyewitness must testify truthfully to what they have seen and heard – no more and no less. The Baptist fulfilled this task with distinction."[134]

John the Baptist was not the light, but ἵνα μαρτυρήσῃ περὶ τοῦ φωτός ("in order to give a witness concerning the light") (Jn. 1:8). His role was to give a witness to the light. Therefore, the reader or implied reader must not be confused. John the Baptist was a great man, but he was not the light. While he is cast in a positive light as a witness to Jesus, John the Baptist is not the light but he is a lamp (Jn. 5:35).[135] Moloney states, "The Prologue is now firmly anchored in history and, like vv. 1-5, its second section (vv. 6-14) opens with a description of the Word and a careful separation of the role of the Baptist form the role of the Word."[136]

This section of the Prologue has significance both theologically and practically. The author claims again Jesus alone is the true light

---

[132] Although it is not actual ultimate outcome, the desired result of John the Baptist's witness is that all might believe in Jesus (see C. K. Barrett, *The Gospel According to St. John*, 1978, 159 and Donald Carson, *The Gospel according to John*, 1991, 121).

[133] Raymond Brown, *The Gospel According to John I-XII*, 1966, 8-9.

[134] Andreas Köstenberger, *John*, 2004, 33.

[135] See Raymond Brown, *The Gospel According to John I-XII*, 1966, 28, Leon Morris, *The Gospel according to John*, 1995, 81, Herman Ridderbos, *The Gospel According to John*, 1997, 42, and Craig Keener, *The Gospel of John*, 2003, 393.

[136] Francis Moloney, *The Gospel of John*, 1998, 37.

of divine revelation. John the Baptist is a role model of a witness for Jesus. Dodd argues that a threefold schema in this section controls the subsequent sections of John 1 that deal with John the Baptist.[137]

3.4.4 The incarnation of the Word (Jn. 1:9-14)

The author now states the incarnation of the λόγος, the true and authentic light who φωτίζει πάντα ἄνθρωπον, ἐρχόμενον εἰς τὸν κόσμον ("enlightens everyone, coming into the world") in John 1:9.[138] The author's view of the human condition in his narrative is recapitulated in the term κόσμος. Smith explores that the author uses the term κόσμος as a virtual synonym for creation, πάντα (Jn. 1:1, 10) with no negative connotation; however, κόσμος is neutral in John 1:10 where it simply signifies the place in which the λόγος was incarnated, it is positive in John 1:2 where God created the κόσμος through the λόγος, and it is negative where the κόσμος rejects the revelation in the incarnated λόγος, Jesus Christ.[139]

As τὸ φῶς τὸ ἀληθινόν ("the true light"), Jesus is presented as the source of φῶς that enlightens people. The incarnation of the λόγος has been portrayed in the first section of the Prologue (Jn. 1:1-5) and is reiterated here in John 1:9-10. This of course does not suggest the universal salvation of all people, because the author does not speak of internal illumination in the sense of special revelation, but of external illumination in the sense of objective revelation requiring

---

[137] First, John the Baptist was not the light in (Jn. 1:19-27). Second, John came to give witness to the light (Jn. 1:29-34). Third, through John's agency all might become believers (Jn. 1:35-37). See Charles Dodd, *Historical Tradition in the Fourth Gospel*, 1965, 248-49.

[138] Carson opines that ἀληθινόν in John 1:9 delivers a sense of fundamental ultima: in Jesus God has revealed Himself in an eschatological sense (See Donald Carson, *The Gospel According to John*, 1991, 122).

[139] D. Moody Smith, *The Theology of the Gospel of John*, 1995, 80-81.

a response.[140] Not all the people accept the light, though it was available to all through Jesus' presence and His words.[141] The λόγος was in the world that has its existence through Him, (Jn. 1:10), but ὁ κόσμος αὐτὸν οὐκ ἔγνω ("the world has not known Him"). The author uses κόσμος seventy-eight times in his narrative. The term usually refers to sinful humanity (cf. Jn. 3:16). The phrase ἐρχόμενον εἰς τὸν κόσμον is used to describe Jesus as the One who enters the world from the outside and returns to His place of the presence of God the Father (cf. Jn. 13:1, 3; 14:12, 28; 16:28; 18:37).

In John 1:11, the author tells more specific identification of the place and people who have not known and have not received Him. He came to τὰ ἴδια ("His own place") and οἱ ἴδιοι αὐτὸν ("His own people"). The reader or implied reader knows and understands what is meant. Many in Israel, especially the Jewish religious leaders οὐ παρέλαβον ("did not receive") the λόγος, Jesus. They failed to recognize Jesus as the Messiah, the Savior of the world. They rejected the light including all of the signs He performed which demonstrated His deity and messiahship. Schnackenburg argues that the author's reference is not to Jesus' earthly ministry but to Israel's history prior to the incarnation of Jesus.[142] However, the reference is more likely anticipatory of the λόγος's incarnation in John 1:14.[143] Anyway, the author underscores the irony of the world — His own

---

[140]   See Raymond Brown, *The Gospel According to John I-XII*, 1966, 9 and also Andreas Köstenberger, John, 2004, 35.

[141]   Gerald Borchert, *John 1-11*, 1996, 113

[142]   Rudolf Schnackenburg, *The Gospel According to St. John*, vol.1, 1990, 256. Brown also agrees with Schnackenburg, citing the parallel of Wisdom in 1 Enoch 42:2 (See Raymond Brown, *The Gospel according to John I-XII*, 1966, 30).

[143]   See Alan Culpepper, "The Pivot of John's Prologue," *New Testament Studies* 27, 1980-81, 13-14; Donald Carson, *The Gospel According to John*, 1991, 122; Herman Ridderbos, *The Gospel According to John*, 1997, 43; and Francis Moloney, *The Gospel of John*, 1998, 37.

people —rejecting the One through whom it was made. They reject Jesus' claim of equality with God and His revelation of the God the Father through the words He spoke and the signs He committed. Brown points out, "The basic sin in John's gospel is the failure to know and believe in Jesus."[144] The entire Johannine narrative is taken up with the story of the confrontation between the Jews and Jesus as it appears in narratives of the anonymous minor characters of John 4, 5, and 9.

The message of a negative response was found for the first time in John 1:5. However, the negative response from those to whom the λόγος came (Jn. 1:11) is complemented by the positive response of others, and results of such a response (Jn. 1:12-13). The author places the verbs λαμβάνω and πιστεύσω in parallel in John 1:12, ὅσοι δὲ ἔλαβον αὐτόν ("To those who receive Him") to τοῖς πιστεύουσιν εἰς τὸ ὄνομα αὐτοῦ ("to those who believed in His name"). That is to receive the λόγος means to believe His name. Comparing the rejection of the λόγος in John 1:5, 11, the right way of λαμβάνω the λόγος is to πιστεύσω in His name. The results of belief in the name of the λόγος are narrated in the past tense, ἔδωκεν αὐτοῖς ἐξουσίαν τέκνα θεοῦ γενέσθαι ("He gave them authority to become children of God"). The authority given is not a promise but an achieved fact for those who receive and believe. The aorist verb γενέσθαι indicates that people do not have to wait for later end time to become God's children. The authority to become God's children is available now to the believers. It can be realized and confirmed.

God's children οἳ οὐκ ἐξ αἱμάτων οὐδὲ ἐκ θελήματος σαρκὸς οὐδὲ ἐκ θελήματος ἀνδρὸς ("who not born of blood, nor of the will of flesh, nor of the will of husband") but ἐγεννήθησαν ("were generated") by God (Jn. 1:13). Spiritual birth is not the result of human initiative but of a supernatural origin. The author expresses natural procreation in three different terms; αἱμάτων, σαρκὸς, and ἀνδρὸς.

---

[144] Raymond Brown, *The Gospel According to John I-XII*, 1966, 10.

First, the opposite of being born of God is born by αἱμάτων. The natural descent renders a blood relationship. The author's point is that being a child of God is not a result of blood relations like a Jew who could simply presume upon descent from Abraham. Rather, by His sovereign grace it must be sought and received from God on the basis of faith in Jesus, the Messiah. Second, the natural descent renders the θελήματος σαρκὸς. It relates to what is physical/natural as opposed to what is spiritual/supernatural. Third, the natural descent renders θελήματος ἀνδρὸς. The reference to θελήματος ἀνδρὸς ("the will of husband") implies the Old Testament concept of male headship, in the present context perhaps with reference to the initiative usually taken by the husband in sexual intercourse resulting in parental determination or will.[145]

The author gives his readers the opportunity to see the world in its rebellion, as illustrated in the Jews, εἰς τὰ ἴδια ἦλθεν, καὶ οἱ ἴδιοι αὐτὸν οὐ παρέλαβον ("He came to His own, and His own people did not receive Him") (Jn. 1:11). Having seen this rebellion, the readers of the Johannine community are challenged to received and believe Him as they admit their sin and be saved.

Now, the author announces formally the incarnation of the λόγος in John 1:14; that the λόγος was coming into the world has already been mentioned in John 1:3-4, 9. Now it is thus restated, describing Him in whose name people must believe as μονογενοῦς παρὰ πατρός ("only begotten Son of the Father"). While Jesus is the only begotten Son of God, God is Father. The πατήρ is a more personal term than θεός. The author prefers πατήρ in referring to God in his narrative. As anyone who believes in Jesus becomes God's children, Jesus taught his disciples to call God πατήρ as well (Matt. 6:9).

The preexistent λόγος who was intimately with God has now σὰρξ ἐγένετο ("became flesh"). The σὰρξ denotes "all of human

---

[145] Gerald Borchert, *John 1-11*, 1996, 118

person in creaturely existence as distinct from God."[146] The ἐγένετο does not mean "change into" in the sense that Jesus ceased to be God by becoming a human being.[147] Nor of it course does it mean He "appeared human or even took on humanity."[148] The narrator's point is that God now has chosen to be with His people in a more personal way than ever before.[149] By emphasizing that Jesus σὰρξ ἐγένετο, John communicates and reveals God in the human form, the form in which He ἐσκήνωσεν ἐν ἡμῖν ("dwells among us"). The verb σκηνόω may be linked to the Hebrew verb שָׁכַן, used of the dwelling of YHWH in Israel (Ex. 33:9; 40:34-35) and root of an important word in Judaism to speak of the resting of the כָּבֵד ("glory") of YHWH over the tabernacle. In the New Testament it is used outside of this instance only in the Book of Revelation 7:15; 12:12; 13:6; 21:3. The phrase suggests that in Jesus, God has come to take up residence among His people in a way even more intimate than when He dwelt in the tabernacle. People now may meet God and hear Him in the incarnated λόγος, Jesus, who took the place of the temple.

By speak of "His dwelling," the author points to the experience of the Johannine community that can declare to have observed, in Jesus, τὴν δόξαν αὐτοῦ ("His glory"). It reveals that John saw, together with the believing community, the δόξα of God. The δόξα is a very important concept in the Johannine narrative, introduced

---

[146] Herman Ridderbos, *The Gospel According to John*, 1997, 49. See also C. K. Barrett, *The Gospel According to St. John*, 1978, 164 and Gerald Borchert, *John 1-11*, 1996, 119.

[147] Andreas Köstenberger, John, 2004, 40. He refers to J. C. O'Neill, "The Word Did Not 'Become' Flesh," 1991, 127.

[148] Leon Morris, *The Gospel According to John*, 1995, 90-91. However, Witherington suggests that Jesus took on humanity (Ben Witherington, *John's Wisdom*, 1995, 55).

[149] Donald Carson, *The Gospel According to John*, 1991, 127.

by the author in the Prologue. In the Old Testament, the δόξα of God was said to dwell first in the tabernacle. As the author makes clear, the δόξα of God now has taken up residence among His people once again in Jesus. The author's doxological point of view in his narrative is that Jesus' supreme purpose is to bring glory to God, shown even in the anonymous characters in John 4, 5, and 9. As Jesus brings δόξα to God, δόξα also comes to Jesus. This continues what was already true of Jesus prior to His coming, for δόξα characterized both Jesus' eternal relationship with God (Jn. 17:5) and His pre-incarnate state (Jn. 12:41). While in the world, Jesus' δόξα is manifested to His disciples through His signs (cf. 2:11).[150] What is seen is σάρξ in the σάρξ of Jesus Christ. Precisely the visibility of the σάρξ is the point. Of course, the reader or implied reader sees the δόξα spiritually, but physical sight was also required. In the author's word, unlike Thomas who needed to see for himself before he would believe, the fact that Jesus speaks to those who do not see yet are still able to come to believe demonstrates that people can believe without seeing (Jn. 20:29). That said, people who must believe without seeing need the testimony of those who saw, which the reason is given by the author for having written his gospel.

The author asserted that that the λόγος and God have had an intimate relationship from the beginning of history (Jn. 1:1-2), enabling him to proclaim that observing the incarnation of the λόγος was the same as seeing God's revelation in history.

The narrator than goes on to proclaim that the glory of God seen was δόξαν ὡς μονογενοῦς παρὰ πατρός ("glory as of the only begotten Son from the Father") (Jn. 1:14). The intimate relationship of the λόγος and God is now declared as that between the only begotten Son and Father, a relationship foundational for the Johannine narrative which is about to begin. The author, however, carefully maintains a distinction between the only begotten

---

[150] Ibid., 128.

Son and the Father, as shown in John 1:1-2. Moloney opines, "The glory that the Son had with the Father before all time (cf. Jn. 17:5) is unknown and unknowable to the human situation (cf. Jn.1:18). The author states that what the human story can see of the divine has been seen in the incarnation of the Word, the only Son from the Father."[151] Believers cannot see the δόξα of the Father in the Son, but rather δόξα ὡς ("a glory as of").[152] His δόξα fully reflects the δόξα of the Father.

The author adds the description of the incarnated λόγος, πλήρης χάριτος καὶ ἀληθείας ("full of grace and truth") (Jn. 1:14b). The phrase πλήρης χάριτος καὶ ἀληθείας is a precise Greek equivalent of the phrase in the Old Testament Exodus 34:6, "The Lord, the Lord, the compassionate and gracious God, slow to anger, abounding in love and faithfulness." In this expression, both refer to God's covenant faithfulness to His people Israel. But it is also possible that the χάρις in the Prologue retains its original meaning of an undeserved favor. The reader or implied reader of the Johannine community has observed the visible manifestation of God, the incarnated λόγος, the only begotten Son from the Father, the fullness of the χάρις that is τὸ φῶς τὸ ἀληθινόν. According to the author, God's covenantal faithfulness found ultimate expression in God's sending His only begotten Son, Jesus.[153]

The δόξα is the shining of God's character, πλήρης χάριτος καὶ ἀληθείας which the Johannine community has seen in the incarnated λόγος, Jesus Christ, and in His life. It is intimately connected with His revelation. The author is directly alluding to the divine

---

[151] Francis Moloney, *The Gospel of John*, 1998, 39.

[152] Ridderbos renders ὡς as "in keeping with his nature as" (Herman Ridderbos, *The Gospel According to John*, 1997, 53). Also see Schnackenburg, *The Gospel according to St. John*, vol. 1, 1990, 270. Brown renders it as "in the quality of" (Raymond Brown, *The Gospel According to St. John, I-XII*, 1966, 13).

[153] J. C. Laney, *John*, 1992, 44.

aspect of His being and to its revelation as such. When Jesus Himself says that the hour has come for the Son of Man to be glorified (Jn. 12:23), He is pointing to His own death and to His death understood as revelatory event, Πάτερ, δόξασόν σου τὸ ὄνομα ("Father, glorify your name") (Jn. 12:28a).

The last time the author uses the word δόξα in his narrative is in Jesus' prayer in John 17, and again the reference is to Jesus' disciples seeing His δόξα (Jn. 17:24). Thus, Jesus' disciples who have seen His δόξα in His public life in the world will see Him in His manifest δόξα in heaven. It will include the Johannine community and all believers, of course.

3.4.5 John's witness concerning the Word's preeminence (Jn. 1:15)

The author then turns to the witness of John the Baptist. The first description of the λόγος (Jn. 1:1-2) comes to mind as John the Baptist proclaimed that ὁ ὀπίσω μου ἐρχόμενος ("One who is coming") follows him in terms of the time sequence of events (Jn. 1:15a), but, in terms of His place in God's providence He ἔμπροσθέν μου γέγονεν ("existed precedence over me"). John the Baptist explains how this could be happened, ὅτι πρῶτός μου ἦν ("because He was before me") (Jn. 1:15b).

John the Baptist serves as the prototype of the Old Testament prophetic witness to Jesus which makes his testimony an integral part of the salvation history unfolded and described by the author. In this regard, that Brodie states John the Baptist appears to be the embodiment of the Old Testament is far from being an illogical interpolation, but instead is altogether appropriate. It is as though, when the incarnation finally arrived, full of covenant love, the Old Testament stood up and cheered.[154]

John the Baptist was six months older than Jesus (Lk. 1:24, 26) and began his ministry before Jesus did (Lk. 3:1-20). Like most of the Eastern culture, the Old Testament supports the notion that the rank or honor is tied to one's age even six months older, it implied thus preeminence.[155] Because of John the Baptist age and earlier ministry, the author shows that Jesus was really πρῶτός him, and therefore legitimately to be honored above him.

John the Baptist may have simply intended to affirm that Jesus ἔμπροσθέν ("supersede over") him. If so, he spoke better than he knew.[156] Interestingly, John the Baptist's witness is anticipated here prior to its actual narration in John 1:19-34.[157]

3.4.6 The final revelation brought by Jesus Christ (Jn. 1:16-18)

The author leads the readers to a final revelation of people's reception and response to the gift of the incarnated λόγος, Jesus Christ. To the readers of Johannine community, the author explains ἐκ τοῦ πληρώματος αὐτοῦ ἡμεῖς πάντες ἐλάβομεν καὶ χάριν ἀντὶ χάριτος ("from His fullness we all have received then grace upon grace") (Jn. 1:16). For the Johannine narrative the believers receive His πλήρωμα within their hearts. They receive a χάρις that completes

---

[154] Thomas Brodie, *The Gospel according to John: A Literary and Theological Commentary*, 1993, 143.

[155] See R. K. Harrison, *BEB* 1:791.

[156] Colin Kruse, *The Gospel according to John*, 2003, 72

[157] Herman Ridderbos, *The Gospel according to John*, 1997, 55.

a former χάρις.[158] The πλήρωμα can be found in only the χάρις of God displayed in Jesus, whose purpose was to bring life abundantly (Jn. 10:10).

The author explains these two graces and their relationship in John 1:17. These two graces have been special gifts of God to the salvation history. At first, God ὁ νόμος διὰ Μωϊσέως ἐδόθη ("gave the law through Moses"). Secondly, God gave another gift which is already mentioned in πλήρης χάριτος καὶ ἀληθείας ("full of grace and truth") (Jn. 1:14b) and χάριν ἀντὶ χάριτος ("grace upon grace") (Jn. 1:16b) which is the truth. The two nouns, χάρις and ἀληθεία reappear in John 1:17b, ἡ χάρις καὶ ἡ ἀλήθεια διὰ Ἰησοῦ Χριστοῦ ἐγένετο ("grace and truth came through Jesus Christ") in which they are joined by καὶ. The χάρις that is truth supersedes and completes the first χάρις given through Moses, and it διὰ ἰησοῦ χριστοῦ ἐγένετο ("came through Jesus Christ"). The author portrays the incarnated λόγος, Jesus's coming, in terms of the giving of χάριν ἀντὶ χάριτος, affirming that the grace given through Moses was replaced by the grace bestowed through Jesus.[159] This does not mean to nullify the first χάρις, rather it respects it. The author claims that the first χάρις is now completed in the final χάρις of the truth that came through Jesus Christ. The incarnated λόγος, Jesus Christ, is now described as the perfection of God's gifts. The author tells the reader or implied reader πλήρης χάριτος καὶ ἀληθείας, the perfect grace is found in Jesus Christ. Jesus' ministry is superior to that of Moses. However, the Jewish religious leaders such as the Pharisees, calling themselves

---

[158]   καὶ χάριν ἀντὶ χάριτος has generally rendered the sense of "grace upon grace" by translating the proposition ἀντὶ as "upon," so its meaning of an abundance of grace. However, it has been questioned by some scholars and Moloney renders χάρις as "a gift" that allows ἀντὶ to keep its meaning of "a gift in place of a gift" in BAGD (See Francis Moloney, The Gospel of John, 1998, 46).

[159]   Harry Mowvley, "John 1:14-18 in the Light of Exodus 33:7-34:35," Expository Times, 1984, 137

disciples of Moses (Jn. 9:28), are furiously against the author's claim. Jesus counters by noting says that Moses wrote of Him (Jn. 5:46-47). Although the law is God's gracious revelation, it is not adequate as an instrument of the truth, the ultimate grace that came through Jesus Christ.

The author makes one more point before he turns to the narrative as he concludes the Prologue. Although the Johannine community may claim to have seen the revelation of God's δόξα in the incarnated λόγος Jesus Christ (Jn. 1:14), Θεὸν οὐδεὶς ἑώρακεν πώποτε ("no one ever seen God) (Jn. 1:18a) since no one can see the face of God and live, as Moses and others in the Old Testament narratives learned. That is, no one except One who has told the story of God's way ἐξηγήσατο ("made Him known") and is μονογενὴς Θεὸς ("the only begotten of God"). The incarnation of λόγος is not fatal to those who saw Jesus because God is manifested in flesh. The glory that was hidden in the cloud in the Old Testament narratives remain hidden, now veiled in flesh, but the veil is of a kind that permits a visible form of revelation.

John 1:18 constitutes an *inclusio* with John. 1:1.[160] There it was said that the λόγος was with God and the λόγος was God. Here in John 1:18 it is similarly said that the μονογενὴς Son was God and that He was εἰς τὸν κόλπον τοῦ Πατρὸς ("in the bosom of the Father") which is in the closest way possible He could be with God.[161]

The reason human beings cannot see God is that God is spirit and all the human beings are sinners, in direct contrast to God as holy and sinless. However the incarnated λόγος, Jesus, is Himself God, and He became a human being so that people could see God in Him (Jn. 1:14). Although He became a σὰρξ just as a human being,

---

[160] The Kysar's reference is in the section of the structure of the Prologue. Also, see Craig Keener, *The Gospel of John*, 2003, 335-8.

[161] Louw, "Narrator of the Father: ἐξηγεῖσθαι and the Related Terms in Johannine Christology," *Neotestamentica 2*, 1968, 38.

He was yet without sin and died for people so that their sinfulness no longer prevents them from having fellowship with God (Jn. 1:29). As the author shows later in his narrative, Jesus' claim of deity brought Him into conflicts with the Jewish religious leaders. This results in His crucifixion under the charge of blasphemy (Jn. 19:7).

Bauckham summarizes well this last section of the Prologue in which the author presents the incarnated λόγος, the Son Jesus Christ as "the eschatological fulfillment of the Sinai covenant, a revelation of glory that fulfills the Sinai covenant by qualitative surpassing it."[162]

The author conveys that the incarnated λόγος, the Son of God, will focus on the Father throughout his narrative to follow. The pre-existent relationship between λόγος, the Son Jesus Christ, and God is continually εἰς τὸν κόλπον τοῦ Πατρὸς. This relationship is presented as the very important reason why the incarnated λόγος was able to overcome the immeasurable chasm that had existed between God and man up to that point despite the law. This utmost intimacy of Jesus' relationship with the Father enabled Him to reveal the Father in an unprecedented way.[163]

Köstenberger states that the author makes the important point that the entire narrative to follow should be read as an account of Jesus telling the whole story of God the Father as he concludes the Prologue.[164]

---

[162] Richard Bauckham, *Gospel of Glory: Major Themes in Johannine Theology,* 2015, 50

[163] Raymond Brown, *The Gospel According to St. John, I-XII,* 1966, 36.

[164] Andreas Köstenberger, *John,* 2004, 50.

3.4.7 Conclusion

The author of the Johannine narrative in this opening Prologue sets for a range of theological point of views, consisting of mainly Christological themes:

1. The λόγος preexisted creation with God.

2. Creation was through the λόγος.

3. The λόγος become flesh.

4. Jesus Christ is the incarnation of God.

5. He counts equality with God, deity of Jesus Christ.

6. There is a personal distinction between the Son of God and the Father.

7. Jesus has taken on the human condition.

8. There is the ultimate intimacy in Jesus' relationship with God the Father.

9. Jesus Christ is superior to John the Baptist, the greatest prophet.

10. Jesus Christ is the one and only revelation of God in world history.

11. The ultimate gift of God takes place in the Law to Moses and through Jesus Christ.

12. The role of Jesus Christ is the only true light as the true agent of divine revelation.

13. Jesus Christ is the Savior to those who receive Him and believe in Him.

One of the purposes of the Prologue is to indicate to the readers how they should read the life story of Jesus within a context that begins with the Old Testament, as seen with the near literal repeating of the opening words of Genesis in the gospel of John. The author presents the incarnation of the λόγος Jesus Christ as the ultimate fulfillment of the Mosaic covenant, a revelation of glory that fulfills it unprecedentedly. He affirms that the Johannine community has access to the perfection of the former gift. They can see the revelation of the glory in His Son, Jesus Christ. Thus, the reader or implied reader can see the author's doxological point of view in the midst of his Christological themes.

With the Prologue the author wants to make clear that God has been made known in and through Jesus Christ. "Only the Son, Jesus Christ has ever seen God, and the story of His life will tell the story of God's loving action within the human history."[165] Culpepper comments with regard to the relationship to the rest of the narrative, "In the Prologue, the narrator speaks, introducing the reader to the protagonist (Jesus), clarifying His origin and identity, and foreshadowing the plot and the themes of the story, that is about to be told. … The result is that the narrator's credibility grows, and the reader is led to believe that Jesus is the Messiah, the Son of God."[166]

3.5   SUMMARY

Having applied multiple approaches in looking at the minor characters in John's gospel, it is clear that the narratives use plots and interrelationships among characters to project an ideological or theological point of view. The narrator reveals the true identity of Jesus' conversations these characters have with either Jesus or other characters. To fully understand the text and thus recognize the ideological or theological perspective of the narrator, the reader

---

[165]   Francis Moloney, *The Gospel of John*, 1998, 41.

[166]   Alan Culpepper, *The Gospel and Letters of John*, 1998, 116-17.

or implied reader needs to consider the characters' social, cultural and historical contexts.

The following chapters will employ this social-cultural-historical approach together with a narrative approach to identify the theological point of view of the author or implied author as John 4, 5, and 9 are analyzed and exegete. The significance of this will be evidenced in the glory of Jesus Christ who came to this world to save through faith in him.

As shown in the Prologue, the author's theological points of view reappear in the anonymous minor characters in John 4, 5, and 9. The Prologue prepares the reader or implied reader by setting the stage so that the Johannine narrative can be approached with knowledgeable anticipation. The main themes regarding the deity and glory of Jesus Christ are developed in John 4, 5, and 9 and, of course, throughout the narrative.[167] As the Johannine plot unfolds, the revelation of God evidenced in the words and works of Jesus Christ generates a diversity of responses among the characters from rejection to belief. These characters' responses to the revelation of the Father through the Son in terms of their identity, character, mission, and relationship further serve the author's goal of presenting. The criterion for the author's characterization is their response to Jesus and God's revelation as revealed in Christ, His teachings, and His works. The Johannine plot, meanwhile, revolves around John unfolding the revelation of the Father through the Son, Jesus Christ, in terms of the individuals' response as well as their identity, character, mission, and relationship.

---

[167] While he underscores the literary and theological emphasis on the Prologue, Carson summarized well in the introduction of the Prologue of his commentary, saying "The Prologue is a foyer to the rest of the Fourth Gospel, simultaneously drawing the reader in and introducing the major themes." (Donald Carson, *The Gospel according to John*, 1991, 111).

CHAPTER 4

The Samaritan Woman
(John 4:3-42)

I N TERMS OF THE LITERARY STRUCTURE OF HIS
gospel, John placed the story of the Samaritan woman just
before healing episode of the royal official's son, the point that
marks the end of the first cycle of the sign miracles (σημεῖα),
often called the Cana Cycle (Jn. 2-4)[168], because they were performed in Cana of Galilee. John 2-4 form a single literary unit
not only because they are bounded geographically by the Cana
miracles, but also because they are a unit thematically, presenting
Jesus as the life-giving Messiah who grants eternal life to those
who believe.[169]

The literary structure of John's gospel is brilliantly intertwined
with its profound theology. While the Cana Cycle reveals Jesus as
the Messiah and emphasizes the importance of believing in Him
to receive eternal life, the Festival Cycle (Jn. 5-12)[170] develops the
theme of the increasing opposition among Jewish leaders toward

---

168 Gerald Borchert, *John 1-11*, 1996, 151-222.

169 See Francis Moloney, "From Cana to Cana (John 2:1-4:54) and the Fourth
Evangelist's Concept of Correct Faith", in *Studia Biblica 1978 II*.

170 See Francis Moloney, *Signs and Shadows: Reading John 5-12*, Minneapolis:
Fortress, 1996. Some scholars include only chaps. 5-10. They say that chaps.
11-12 set the stage for Jesus' sacrifice as the Passover Lamb. Brown says
these chapters point to Jesus moving toward the hour of His death and glory,
The Gospel according to John [I-XII], 419-98.

Jesus. These chapters are so designated as a whole because the sign miracles and their attendant narratives and discourses are set in the context of Jewish festivals.[171]

In characterizing the story of the Samaritan woman and Jesus, analysis of the narrative's plot as well as the event itself gives the reader or implied reader a clear understanding of Jesus' identification. Many scholars have interpreted and assessed that the author or implied author intended, through the story of the Samaritan woman and Jesus, to summon an Old Testament betrothal type-scene by drawing attention to the patriarchs, a well, and a woman such as in Genesis 24 (Abraham's servant for Isaac and Rebekah), Genesis 29 (Jacob and Rachel), and Exodus 2 (Moses and Zipporah).[172] Without denying her symbolic role as a bride or a betrothal type, the reader does not need to interpret the whole narrative as a symbolic story. This would seem to be somewhat of an allegorical interpretation. As a historical and real person, the Samaritan woman is important in her own

---

[171]   R. Alan Culpepper, *the Gospel and the Letters of John, Interpreting Biblical Texts*, 1998, 148-149.

[172]   For example, R. Alan Culpepper, *Anatomy of the Fourth Gospel*, 136; Robert Alter, "Biblical Type-Scenes and the Uses of Convention," in the *Art of Biblical Narrative*, 1981, 47-62; E. Aitken, "At the Well of Living Water: Jacob Traditions in John 4," in Craig A. Evans, ed., *The Interpretation of Scripture in Early Judaism and Christianity*, 2000, 342-352; Sandra Schneiders, "Inclusive Discipleship (John 4:1-42)," in *Written That You May Believe: Encountering Jesus in the Fourth Gospel*, 1999, 135; Mark Stibbe, *John*, 68-69; Lee, *The Symbolic Narrative of the Fourth Gospel: The Interplay of Form and Meaning*, 1994, 67; Craig Koester, "*Symbolism in the Fourth Gospel: Meaning, Mystery, Community*, 2nd ed., 2003, 48-49; Adeline Fehribach, *The Women in the Life of Bridegroom*, 17-19 and 49-51; Craig Keener, *The Gospel of John*, 586; Mary Coloe, "The Woman of Samaria: Her Characterization, Narrative, and Theological Significance," in *Characters and Characterization in the Gospel of John*, 2013, 186-187; Moon Hyun Kim, "The Samaritan Woman in John 4:3-42, Who is She?: Centering on the Literary 'Betrothal-Type' Scene & Characterization," *Hanshin Theological Studies 62*, 2013, 31-64.

right in that she evidences true discipleship and functions as an example for the reader or implied readers.

The below narrative structure for the story of the Samaritan woman posits five "acts" that unfold in the passage. The acts consist of distinct dialogues between Jesus and many different characters that work together to construct the characterization of Jesus and the Samaritan woman in a progressive fashion.

Narrative structure (Jn. 4:3-42)

A. Act I: The setting (Jn. 4:3-6)

B. Act II: Jesus and the Samaritan woman I (Jn. 4:7-15)

　　1. Initial encounter (Jn. 4:7-9)

　　2. From ordinary water to living water (Jn. 4:10-14)

　　3. The woman's response (Jn. 4:15)

C. Act III: Jesus and the Samaritan woman II (Jn. 4:16-30)

　　1. Jesus the prophet (Jn. 4:16-19)

　　2. From the prophet to the Messiah (Jn. 4:20-26)

　　3. The woman's confession to her people (Jn. 4:27-30)

D. Act IV: Jesus and his disciples (Jn. 4:31-38)

　　1. His disciples' confusion (Jn. 4:31-33)

　　2. Father's will and work (Jn. 4:34)

　　3. His disciples' mission (Jn. 4:35-38)

E. Act V: Jesus and many Samaritans (Jn. 4:39-42)

　　1. The initial belief of many Samaritans (Jn. 4:39)

　　2. The Samaritans request Jesus staying (Jn. 4:40a)

3. Jesus' response (Jn. 4:40b)

4. Many more believed (Jn. 4:41)

5. Jesus, the savior of the world (Jn. 4:42)

Before Jesus arrives in Samaria, the author has already set the scene for this encounter by what the gospel has already claimed about Jesus' identification through John the Baptist. In the Prologue, John the Baptist is described as οὗτος ἦλθεν εἰς μαρτυρίαν, ἵνα μαρτυρήσῃ περὶ τοῦ φωτός ("He came as a witness, that he might witness concerning about the light") (Jn. 1:7). He speaks of himself as φωνὴ βοῶντος ἐν τῇ ἐρήμῳ ("a voice crying in the wilderness") (Jn. 1:23), then as ὁ φίλος τοῦ νυμφίου ("the friend of the bridegroom") (Jn. 3:29) before Jesus' journey through Samaria. The narrator has focused on Jewish characters so far, and now moves into the world of Gentile, Samaria beyond the world of Jewish.

4.1 ACT I: THE SETTING (Jn. 4:3-6)

In 4:3-6 Jesus left Judea and headed for Galilee again. Unexpectedly, however, we see Him then going through Samaria. There were two ways to go from Judea to Galilee: either a more direct route through Samaria, or via a route that circumvents Samaria along the valley of the Jordan. Even though it was a shorter route, Jews usually for socio-cultural reasons chose to bypass Samaria and opt for the longer, circuitous route which \ involved crossing the Jordan and traveling on the river's east side. Samaria had no separate political existence at that time, being under the jurisdiction of the Roman procurator.[173]

But the ἔδει (Jn. 4:4) shows a certain urgency, as Schnackenburg says. Jesus *had* to go through Samaria; this was not a simple

---

[173] Andreas Köstenberger, *John*, 2004, 146.

pragmatic decision about geography.[174] Although the exact motivation for Jesus' journey through Samaria is not clear, what is clear
is that he wanted to reach out to people beyond the Jews. Jesus'
going through Samaria was according to God's plan and will.[175]

Jesus stopped at the sixth hour (probably around noon) at
Sychar, famous as the site of Jacob's well. The small town of Sychar
was located about two miles east of Nablus, east of Mount Gerizim
and Mount Ebal. Subsequent to the conquest of Jerusalem by the
Roman general Pompey, Sychar apparently replaced Shechem as
the most important Samaritan city.[176]

'πλησίον τοῦ χωρίου ὃ ἔδωκεν Ἰακὼβ [τῷ] Ἰωσὴφ τῷ υἱῷ αὐτοῦ'
("near the field that Jacob had given to his son Joseph") reflects
the customary inference from Genesis 48:21-22 and Joshua 24:32
that Jacob gave his son Joseph the land at Shechem that he had
bought from the sons of Hamor (Gen. 33:18-19) and that later
served as Joseph's burial place (Ex. 13:19; Josh. 24:32). Jacob's well
was seemingly a convenient stop for pilgrims travelling between
Galilee and Jerusalem.

The narrator would cue in readers to the time of day inasmuch
as it helps establishes part of the story's setting. Noon time would
be hot, explaining why Jesus needed to sit down and also why He
would be thirsty and hungry while His disciples were away buying
food (Jn. 4:8). Wells probably were carved out from solid limestone
rock with a small curb remaining to guard against accidents. This

---

[174] Rudolf Schnackenburg, *Gospel According to St. John, vol. 1,* 1990, 422.

[175] Many scholars interprets it this way: see Raymond Brown, *The Gospel
According to John,* 1966, 169; C. K. Barrett, *The Gospel According to St. John,*
1978, 230, Donald Carson, *The Gospel According to John,* 1991, 215-16; Mark
Stibbe, *John,* 1993, 65; Leon Morris, *The Gospel According to John,* 1995,
226; Herman Ridderbos, *The Gospel according to John,* 1997, 153; Francis
Moloney, *The Gospel of John,* 1998, 116 & 120; George Beasley-Murray, *John,*
1999, 59; Colleen Conway, *Men and Women in the Fourth Gospel,* 1999, 105.

[176] Andreas Köstenberger, *John,* 2004, 146, referring to Martin Hengel.

is probably where Jesus sat down. The narrator presents Jesus as a human being, contrary to the claims of readers or implied readers of docetic-style interpretation.[177]

4.2 ACT II: JESUS AND THE SAMARITAN WOMAN I (Jn. 4:7-15)

An anonymous Samaritan woman suddenly appears on the scene. The woman is a social outcast because of her sinful lifestyle and low reputation in her community. That is why she came to draw water alone (Jn. 4:7) and at the hottest time of the day. According to cultural norms at the time, Jesus is not supposed to talk with her because she is a woman and because she is a Samaritan. The narrator casually informs readers that Jesus' disciples had gone into the town of Sychar to buy food. That Jesus allowed his disciples to buy food from Samaritans indicates a certain freedom from the regulations of Jews who would have been unwilling to eat food handled by Samaritans.

That Jesus talked with a woman appeared offensive given the cultural norms at the time, which is why the disciples were stunned when they returned (Jn. 4:27). There were also social and moral barriers between Jewish people and Gentiles.[178] Yet Jesus presents to her an imperative: δός μοι πεῖν ("Give me a drink") (Jn. 4:7b). Even the woman's response shows that the encounter was shocking to her, asking how a Jew could ask for a drink from a Samaritan woman (Jn. 4:9). Here, the narrator adds a point of clarification: οὐ γὰρ συγχρῶνται Ἰουδαῖοι Σαμαρίταις ("For Jews are not dealing wih Samaritans"). Generally, Jews avoided contact with Samaritans,

---

[177] Herman Ridderbos, *The Gospel according to John*, 1997, 153; Donald Carson, *The Gospel According to John* ,1991, 217; Leon Morris, *The Gospel According to John* ,1995, 228.

[178] See Craig Keener, *The Gospel of John*, 2003, 591-601.

especially Samaritan women. Samaritans were thought to be in a continual state of ritual uncleanness. Therefore, the woman is surprised when Jesus asked, δός μοι πεῖν ("Give me a drink").

In this short first moment of encounter the theme of ὕδωρ ζῶν ("living water") is introduced (Jn. 4:7, 9, 10), about which Jesus will elaborate later (Jn. 4:13, 14), emphasizing that the water of which He speaks is not the same as physical water.

When she asked Πῶς σὺ Ιουδαῖος ὢν παρ᾽ ἐμοῦ πεῖν αἰτεῖς γυναικὸς σαμαρίτιδος οὔσης; ("How is that you, a Jew, ask a drink from me, a woman of Samaria?") in John 4:9b, Jesus does not answer her question. Rather He announces that if she knew two truths, τὴν δωρεὰν τοῦ θεοῦ καὶ τίς ἐστιν ὁ λέγων σοι ("the gift of God and who is saying to you"), she would need only to ask him the ὕδωρ ζῶν ("the living water") and it will be given to her (Jn. 4:10). These two truths signify the foundational basis for the whole scene. The first truth will concentrate on the living water, τὴν δωρεὰν τοῦ θεοῦ ("the gift of God), and the second truth will be focused on τίς ἐστιν ὁ λέγων σοι ("who is saying to you"). The genitive in τὴν δωρεὰν τοῦ θεοῦ indicates that Jesus promises a gift that has its origins in God. It is life-giving revelation of God, which only Jesus makes known. It was God who was known to be the source and giver of life. It takes the place of nurturing water such as Jacob's well water. In fulfillment of the Old Testament prophetic vision (Zech. 14:8; Ezek. 47:9), Jesus inaugurated the age of God's abundance of grace.[179]

However, because the woman didn't understand Jesus' words, she asked the physical meaning of ὕδωρ ζῶν. Having known the depth of the well and the fact that Jesus does not have a bucket to draw with, she asks calling Jesus more respectively "Κύριε" (Jn.

---

[179] Leon Morris (*The Gospel According to John*, 1995, 230) and Donald Carson (*The Gospel According to John*, 1991, 218) identify it as eternal life; Rudolf Schnackenburg (*Gospel According to St. John, vol. 1*, 1990: 431) suggests that the gift is either the Holy Spirit or eternal life, or both.

4:11). She is asking more than she realizes. She is only able to explain the origins of the water in terms of the Jacob tradition, that the water in the well has its origins in the gift of Jacob. She takes it for granted that the giver of the gift was Jacob. And Jesus cannot be greater than Jacob (Jn. 4:12). The woman's claim that τοῦ πατρὸς ἡμῶν Ιακώβ, ὃς ἔδωκεν ἡμῖν τὸ φρέαρ καὶ αὐτὸς ἐξ αὐτοῦ ἔπιεν ("our father Jacob, who gave us the well and he himself drank out of it") is purely traditional. Genesis does not record Jacob digging a well, much less his drinking from it or giving it to others. There is a mention that Jacob bought and gave Shechem to Joseph (Gen. 33:19; 48:22).

Not only she is unable to reach beyond the physical understanding of ὕδωρ ζῶν, but she is also stuck with her own traditions. She cannot imagine Jesus might be the Messiah who surpassed the patriarch Jacob. Her inability to accept Jesus' words becomes more evident in His further promises of ὕδωρ ζῶν (Jn. 4:13-14). The narrator identifies Jesus as the Creator and life-giver who gives the gift of ὕδωρ ζῶν. Beginning his words with reference to physical water, Jesus points out that Πᾶς ("everyone") who drinks of the water from the well will thirst again (Jn. 4:13). He then promises that ὃς δ᾽ ἂν ("whoever may") drinks of the water that he will give will never thirst because it will become in him a spring of water welling up to ζωὴν αἰώνιον ("etenal life"). The phrase οὐ μὴ διψήσει εἰς τὸν αἰῶνα ("will never be thirsty to the age") is an emphatic negation.

The response of the woman in John 4:15 shows that she has misunderstood Jesus' words in a physical sense. She takes his words on ὕδωρ ζῶν and makes it her own. It seems Jesus' words are rejected. Yet despite her confusion, the woman continues to engage with Jesus in her quest for understanding. She is clearly interested in the ὕδωρ ζῶν that Jesus has to offer but is still at a loss as to its origin.[180] Conway comments that the woman's response in

---

[180]   Donald Carson, *The Gospel According to John* ,1991, 220.

John 4:15 does not indicate a development in her understanding of Jesus' identity yet.[181]

4.3 ACT III: JESUS AND THE SAMARITAN WOMAN II (Jn. 4:16-30)

The narrator developed the theme of τὴν δωρεὰν τοῦ θεοῦ ("the gift of God") in John 4:10a during Act II of the encounter between Jesus and the Samaritan woman. In Act III he elaborates the theme of τίς ἐστιν ὁ λέγων σοι ("who is saying to you") in John 4:10b. Moloney concludes that the literary structure of the third act parallels that of the second act.[182]

5   A relationship is established, initiated by a command from Jesus (Jn 4:7-9 // Jn 4:16-20)

6   Jesus' words transcend the apparent basis of the relationship (John 4:10 // Jn 4:21-24)

7   The woman makes an intermediate response to Jesus' words (Jn 4:11-12 // John 4:25)

8   A final intervention from Jesus takes place (Jn 4:13-14 // John 4:26)

9   The woman gives a concluding response (John 4:15 // Jn 4:28-29)

There is a contrast transition from John 4:15, with the woman's asking that she no longer διέρχωμαι ἐνθάδε, and Jesus command that she calls her husband and ἐλθὲ ἐνθάδε in John 4:16. Actually, there are three commands from Jesus in John 4:16 "ὕπαγε, φώνησον, and ἐλθὲ." The woman's marital status becomes the focus

---

[181]   Colleen Conway, *Men and Women in the Fourth Gospel*, 1999, 115-16.

[182]   Francis Moloney, *The Gospel of John*, 1998, 127.

81

of concern. Her reply, that ἄνδρα οὐκ ἔχω ("I have no husband") in John 4:17, is to be regarded as a correct reflection of her situation. She regards herself as not married to the man with whom she is currently living. Jesus credits her for telling the truth καλῶς εἶπας ("you have spoken correctly"). He then proceeds to tell her of the details of her marital history that reveals the nature of her sinful life in John 4:18, πέντε γὰρ ἄνδρας ἔσχες, καὶ νῦν ὃν ἔχεις οὐκ ἔστιν σου ἀνήρ·("For you have had five husbands and the one you have now is not your husband"). The word ἀνήρ could mean either "man" or "husband." Thus, Jesus may be telling the woman that she has had five "men" and that the one she is now living with is not her "man," that he may be ἀνήρ of another woman. In other words, she is a serious fornicator.[183]

Jesus' knowledge of these facts shocked her. The effect of Jesus' words seems to be that the woman is hurt and sobered by his knowledge of her secret but is liberated from the need to go on concealing it. Jesus removes her doubts. Not only is she surprised with ὕδωρ ζῶν in John 4:10, but also his knowledge of her secret sinful life. That's why she confesses, Κύριε, προφήτης εἶ σύ ("Sir, you are a prophet"). The Samaritans awaited the prophet like Moses (Deut. 18:15-18), who was not identified with the Messiah though. However, there is no definite article before προφήτης and the woman's use of the verb θεωρῶ makes this a limited confession. There is no evidence of any spiritual insight that would suggest she was convicted that Jesus must be the Messiah (cf. Jn. 4:25-26). That said, one may consider it a progress that she calls Him as "Ἰουδαῖος" in John 4:9, and "Κύριε" in John 4:11, 15, 19, and προφήτης in John 4:19.

At this point the narrator changes the subject of the prophecy to true worship (Jn. 4:20-26). For the woman's problems surpassed

---

[183]   Charles H. Giblin, "What Was Everything He Told Her She Did?" *New Testament Studies* 45, 1999, 148-152.

her personal life and extended also to her people's wrong way of worship service. Just as Judaism was branded as lacking in experiential knowledge of true spiritual regeneration in narrative of Nicodemos in Ch. 3, so here Samaritanism is cast as devoid of knowledge of what constitutes the true worship that God requires. The conversations regarding worship service helps her and provides her with a better understanding of Jesus. On the basis of her perception that Jesus is a προφήτης, the woman raises the question of Gerizim and Jerusalem where the worship service should take place, an age old problem debated between Samaritans and Jews.[184] The narrator shifts the interests in woman's marital status to the person of Jesus as προφήτης.

"οἱ πατέρες ἡμῶν" in John 4:20 refers back to Abraham (Gen. 12:7) and Jacob (Gen. 33:20), who built alters in this region. Mount Gerizim was the site where the Israelites were blessed by Moses (Deut. 11:29; 27:12). It is unclear precisely when the Samaritans built a temple at that location. Samaritan tradition places construction in the 5th century B.C., though Josephus claims that the temple was built in 332 B.C.[185] Schnackenburg argues that Samaritan tradition may be closer to the truth than is Josephus since the names mentioned by Josephus coincide with those of Nehemiah 13:28.[186]

The dispute between Jews and Samaritans regarding the proper place of worship service had been an issue for centuries when the Samaritan woman raised the question on the subject with Jesus. Josephus explores an argument between Egyptian Jews and Samaritans before Ptolemy Philometor in around 150 B.C. as to whether the sanctuary was to be on Mount Gerizim or Mount

---

[184] Rudolf Schnackenburg, *Gospel According to St. John, vol. 1*, 1990, 434.

[185] Andreas Köstenberger, *John*, 2004, 154 referring to *Ant.* 11.8.4.

[186] Rudolf Schnackenburg, *Gospel According to St. John, vol. 1*, 1990, 434.

Zion.[187] That Samaritan beliefs regarding the sanctuary of Mount Gerizim continued intensified is illustrated by an incident in A.D. 36 involving a Samaritan troublemaker that was put down by Pilate. During Jesus' conversation with the Samaritan woman, Mount Gerizim would have been in view. From Jacob's well, they may even have been able to see the temple's ruins, perhaps turning to look at them when the woman mentioned the place.

Jesus responded to John 4:20 to draw the woman into a deeper understanding of His person and role, "Πίστευέ μοι, γύναι." This command is followed by a promise of a future time when the debate between the Jews and the Samaritans will become irrelevant. The woman may be waiting for the revelation of a new place, but Jesus speaks of worship of God as τῷ Πατρί in John 4:21c. The questions of the place and time of worship as asked by the woman remain. Before he answers them, Jesus speaks strongly of the superiority of the Jewish tradition (Jn. 4:22).

The narrator uses the plural ὑμεῖς that Jesus treats the woman as a representative of the Samaritan people. Jewish tradition affirmed the religious supremacy of Jerusalem. Jews bear within them the authentic revelation of God, while the Samaritan traditions have no such authority. Jesus owns his origins among Jewish people by using ἡμεῖς, as he criticizes the Samaritan people and their tradition with the use of ὑμεῖς. As a Jew, Jesus is part of a long tradition in which God has revealed himself and his will for his people. And Jesus, whom the woman had earlier called "Ἰουδαῖος" in John 4:9, is the one who brings salvation. In the Jew, Jesus, salvation has come: ὅτι ἡ σωτηρία ἐκ τῶν Ἰουδαίων ἐστίν ("For the salvation is from the Jews") (Jn. 4:22b). Jesus reveals to the world both Himself and the way to the Father. Jesus thus indicates that the woman would be faced no longer with a choice between two places. The Samaritans' worship at Mount Gerizim was based on ignorance

---

[187] Andreas Köstenberger, *John*, 2004, 154 referring to *Ant.* 13.3.4 §74.

regarding Israel's role in God's plan for salvation. The narrator affirms that the Jewish people are the instrument by which God's redemption is mediated to others. This contrasts with Samaritans' religious ignorance.

At this point Jesus informs the woman of the new time: ἀλλὰ ἔρχεται ὥρα καὶ νῦν ἐστιν (But the hour is coming and is now here") (Jn. 4:23a). Jesus also announces that the new place for true worship is already present because Jesus is present. In present time, when both Gerizim and Jerusalem are surpassed as places of worship, the true worshiper worships God the Father ἐν πνεύματι καὶ ἀληθείᾳ ("in spirit and truth"), but it is the Father who ζητεῖ ("seeks") such worshipers (Jn. 4:23). The woman had spoken of the worship of οἱ πατέρες ("the fathers") in John 4 20a; Jesus responds by speaking of worship of τῷ Πατρὶ ("the Father") that is a direct object, a dative of personal interest, suggesting personal relationship. That is the new relationship created in the life of the genuine worshipper.[188] Okure says that the ζητεῖ by God the Father signifies not a passive desire on his part but his causative action in the individual without which a genuine human response is impossible.[189] Jesus teaches her the way God acts. As a spirit God is everywhere so that she can worship him in any place. The proper worship of him is a matter of spirit rather than physical location.

The author later put πνεύματι καὶ ἀληθείᾳ ("spirit and truth") together in the expression τὸ πνεῦμα τῆς ἀληθείας ("the spirit of the truth") in 14:17, 15:26, 16:13, referring to the Holy Spirit. Therefore, the narrator points the readers or implied readers ultimately to worship in the Holy Spirit. Stibbe puts it that true

---

[188] Rudolf Schnackenburg, *Gospel According to St. John, vol. 1*, 1990, 436-37.

[189] Teresa Okure, *The Johannine Approach to Mission: A Contextual Study of John 4:1-42*, 1988, 116.

worship is paternal in focus (the Father), personal in origin (the Son), and pneumatic in character (the Spirit).[190]

The hour has now come when the only acceptable δεῖ προσκυνεῖν ("it is necessary to worship") is total commitment of one's life and action toward the Father, sharing already in the gift ἐν πνεύματι ("in spirit"). Jesus' identity is still to be discovered, so she falls back on another of her traditions. She says, οἶδα ὅτι Μεσσίας ἔρχεται, ὁ λεγόμενος Cριστός· ὅταν ἔλθῃ ἐκεῖνος, ἀναγγελεῖ ἡμῖν ἄπαντα ("I know the Messiah is coming, who is called Christ. When He is coming, He will tell us all things") (Jn. 4:25). She raises the question of a Messiah and Christ without using the definite article, as she did when she accepted Jesus, a prophet (Jn. 4:19). So far, she has called Jesus by the titles – "a Jew," "Sir," "a prophet," and now she suggests that he might be "Messiah Christ." Her confession of Messiah Christ who will show us all things may come from her understanding of Jesus' knowledge of her past marriage life. However, she ignores Jesus' comment that true worship may take place now (Jn. 4:23).

Most English translators see Jesus' response in John 4:26 as an acceptance of the woman's suggestion that He might be the Christ. But Moloney disagrees saying that Jesus' response of ἐγώ εἰμι ("I AM") to the woman's suggestion answers the question of "who is it?" which is the repeating the words of John 4:10b.[191] It seems the woman still does not understand Jesus's mention of ἐγώ εἰμι ("I AM") and on true worship, especially considering her comment in John 4:29. However, the author's point is clear while his major claim for Jesus ἐγώ εἰμι ("I AM"), appearing for the first time and it is the climactic pronouncement of the dialogue upto this point. It also is congruent with the author's purpose statement, John

---

190   Mark Stibbe, *John*, 1993, 64.

191   Francis Moloney, *The Gospel of John*, 1998, 130.

20:31. The woman knew about the coming of the Messiah, and she encountered Jesus. Now she was faced with the claim that these two figures were one.[192] The narrator establishes a paradigm for sharing the gospel with those who don't know Jesus' true identity. The Messiah, Jesus the Jew, bears witness to a Samaritan woman although he is reluctant to identify himself openly to the Jews. He has no such hesitation in the case of the Samaritan woman.[193]

The disciples upon return to the scene observed that the woman's confession remains unresolved that, as they express surprise that Jesus is talking with a woman (Jn. 4:27-30). They returned just as the conversation between Jesus and the woman was almost at its conclusion. They were shocked. The author uses ἐθαύμαζον, showing their amazement because it is bad enough that a female is conversing with an unrelated male in a public place at an unusual time. The reader is also told that she considered the most significant item in this conversation Jesus' remarks on her shameless sexual behavior. Schnackenburg says, "The awe of His friends makes the mystery of the revealer stand out more strongly."[194] But none of them asked τί ζητεῖς; ἤ, τί λαλεῖς μετ᾽ αὐτῆς? ("What do you seek? Or Why are you talking with her?") The reason why they refrain from questioning Jesus here is that the woman is still there, so that an opening challenge would have created an awkward situation.[195] Also, the disciples silence may be out of respect for Jesus.

The woman ran away, leaving her water jar behind. It seems that her leaving the jar behind could be a sign that she would have to return. The narrator signals that the story of the encounter with

---

[192] Herman Ridderbos, *The Gospel according to John*, 1997, 165.

[193] Raymond Brown, *The Gospel According to John I-XII*, 1966, 173; cf. Leon Morris, *The Gospel According to John*, 1995, 241.

[194] Rudolf Schnackenburg, *Gospel According to St. John, vol. 1*, 1990, 443.

[195] Donald Carson, *The Gospel According to John*, 1991, 227.

the Samaritan woman has not come to an end, given that her water jar is still there when she returns to the village saying, δεῦτε ἴδετε ἄνθρωπον ὃς εἶπέν μοι πάντα ὅσα ἐποίησα· μήτι οὗτός ἐστιν ὁ Χριστός; ("Come, see a man who told me all that I ever did. Can this be the Christ?") (Jn. 4:29). She invites them to see "ἄνθρωπος," not the Lord or Messiah. Even so, she remains very suspicious that he might be the Messiah. She only mentioned Jesus' knowledge of her marital situation. It seems that through the initial encounter, she remained uncertain about the exact nature of Jesus' identity even though clearly showing progress.

Her response to Jesus in John 4:7-15 was to reject the word of Jesus. As the encounter progresses, she became prepared to accept that he might be a prophet (Jn. 4:19) and even Messiah (Jn. 4:25). Her understanding can progress further after Jesus directly and clearly makes himself known to her as ἐγώ εἰμι ("I AM") (Jn. 4:26). As she goes into the village and asks μήτι οὗτός ἐστιν ὁ Χριστός; ("Can this be the Christ?") the question is posed rhetorically in John 4:29b. By John 4:30 the narrator tells the Samaritans are beginning to make their way toward Jesus. So, the literary frame for Act IV closes with Jesus' discourse with the disciples.[196]

4.4   ACT IV: JESUS AND HIS DISCIPLES (Jn. 4:31-38)

His disciples urge Jesus to eat something, and then they ponder about the apparent oblivious comment Jesus makes about food and his assertion that His true sustenance comes from His mission of making God known outside Israel. For Jesus to fulfill that mission is more important than any physical food. The disciples misunderstand, just as the Samaritan woman did. Yet while the Samaritan woman's misunderstanding involves a failure to recognize what Jesus could offer her, the disciples' misunderstanding concerns

---

[196]   Dorothy A. Lee, *The Symbolic Narrative of the Fourth Gospel*, 1994, 70.

Jesus's mission and for what Jesus lives. It is here that he tells the disciples that they too should be part of the mission to the Gentiles. While this conversation is taking place, the Samaritans from the village are on their way to Jesus and the disciples (Jn. 4:30). Jesus addresses his disciples as ὑμεῖς in John 4:35-38. Jesus provides a solid foundation of mission for His life and ministry (Jn. 4:34) and invite them to accept the challenge of mission Jn. 4:35-38).

The very first phrase, Εν τῷ μεταξὺ ("In the meantime"), indicates that the encounter that follows is an intermission. It takes place in between the departure of the Samaritan woman (Jn. 4:28) and the advent of the Samaritans (Jn. 4:39-40). While they keep calling him ῥαββί (Jn. 1:38; 49; 3:2), the disciples insist with Jesus φάγε ("eat"), using the imperative. They left Jesus at the well to go buy food (Jn. 4:8), but upon their return find he does not respond to their command to eat. Rather, he speaks of βρῶσιν ("food") that he always has to eat, but about which they do not know (Jn. 4:32). Thus, their understanding for Jesus' refusal to eat is that he must have had a source of food of which they were ignorant (Jn. 4:33). Like the Samaritan woman who was not able to accept Jesus' words on the living water, they don't understand what Jesus is saying about the food. Jesus speaks of another food, while they can only think of physical food (Jn. 4:32-33). The disciples are no better in their relationship with Jesus than the Samaritan woman. Indeed, she is progressively better in understanding of Jesus (Jn. 4:16-30).

Jesus begins to elucidate the ἐμὸν βρῶμά ("my food") which nourishes Him, which the disciples could not understand (Jn. 4:34). The clarification is fundamental to the gospel presentation of Jesus' relationship with the Father, and the consequence of that relationship. Jesus explains, ἐμὸν βρῶμά ἐστιν ("my food is") 1) ἵνα ποιήσω τὸ θέλημα τοῦ πέμψαντός με ("to do the will of Him who sent me") 2) καὶ τελειώσω αὐτοῦ τὸ ἔργον ("and to finish His work") (Jn. 4:34). The nourishment of Jesus is found in His doing the will of the Father who sent Him, which will bring the completion of His mission. It is startling that the narrator tells Jesus' claiming of τελειώσω αὐτοῦ τὸ ἔργον ("finishing His work"). The future tense of τελειώσω points the reader toward some future moment when Jesus' perfect obedience to the Father will lead to the perfection of His work. He affirms his commitment to complete the redemptive work at the cross that God has given to do. The unity between Father and Son here relates primarily not to unity in essence, but to unity in purpose.[197] It is now clear why Jesus had to pass through Samaria (Jn. 4:4), which in the beginning of the story was regarded by the disciples as strange. It was the will of the Father. His food is to be present in this Gentile land, dealing with the Samaritans.

The final words of the discourse move to the mission of the disciples (Jn. 4:35-38). Although they may be following him into the mission, the harvest ahead is there to reap. Jesus' opening words on their mission remind them τετράμηνός ἐστιν καὶ ὁ θερισμὸς ἔρχεται; ("there are yet four months, and then comes the harvest") (Jn. 4:35a). They are reminded of the commonsense knowledge and the physical reality of the fields around them, that the harvest is still four months more away. According to Brown, the saying "Four more months and then comes the harvest" appears to have been a common proverb,[198] though there is no evidence for its existence except a similar expression in Jeremiah 51:33 in the context of judgment.[199] The proverb may simply indicate the need for patience, similar to the saying "Rome was not built in a day."[200]

---

[197] Rudolf Schnackenburg, *Gospel According to St. John, vol. 1*, 1990, 448.

[198] Raymond Brown, *The Gospel According to John I-XII*, 1966, 181.

[199] Rudolf Schnackenburg, *Gospel According to St. John, vol. 1*, 1990, 449.

[200] Herman Ridderbos, *The Gospel according to John*, 1997, 168.

However, Jesus contradicts this seemingly common fact, telling them to open their eyes that they might see the advent of the Samaritans (cf. Jn. 4:30) as He describes. Jesus' statement may be metaphorical rather than literal, pointing his disciples to the approaching mass of Samaritans as a "white field." Thus, he says that the crops are already white, emphasizing that the fields are ready for harvesting. The coming Samaritans who are responding to the initial belief of the Samaritan woman are already white for harvest (Jn. 4:35b). Jesus draws a distinction between the sower and the reaper in John 4:36. The disciples are to work as reapers in a harvest that has been sown by Jesus through His encounter with the Samaritan woman. Jesus as the sower who initiates the change of the heart toward true belief and the disciples who reap the harvest, the sower and the reaper rejoice together (Jn. 4:36b). Jesus has told them to open their eyes that they may become reapers of a harvest they did not sow and thus enter the joy of Jesus' union with the Father. This story shows that the proverb ὁ λόγος ἐστὶν ἀληθινὸς ("the saying is true"). Jesus sows and the disciples reap (Jn. 4:37).

Commentators interpret the identity of the sowers and reapers differently. Early church fathers like Irenaeus have taken the sower to represent the patriarchs and prophets paying the way for the apostles. Others have identified John the Baptist who prepared the way for Jesus' mission and who did in fact rejoice with Jesus (3:29).[201]

Many interpret the sower to represent Jesus, or the Father and Jesus (Mk. 4:3, 14).[202] Keener suggests Jesus and the Samaritan woman who brought the town to him are considered in the

---

[201] Leon Morris, *The Gospel According to John*, 1995, 281-282; Francis Moloney, *The Gospel of John*, 1998, 141.

[202] For example, John H. Bernard, *A Critical and Exegetical Commentary on the Gospel of John* 2, 1928, 380; J. R. Michaels, *John*, 1989, 58.

most immediate context (Jn. 4:29-30, 39).[203] Having examined many commentators' interpretations, Schnackenburg interprets the intent of the expression in terms of the missionary work, so that the narrator's perspective shifts from Jesus to the time of the church.[204] Thus, ἐγὼ ἀπέστειλα ὑμᾶς ("I sent you") refers to his disciples in anticipation of their later commissioning by Jesus in 17:18 and 20:21.

The narrator explains to Jesus' followers that others have done the hard work and His followers are the beneficiaries of the labors of others, like Jesus or John the Baptist. The reader is told that a fruitful harvest often is contingent on the labors of others.

4.5   ACT V: JESUS AND MANY SAMARITANS (Jn. 4:39-42)

As the disciples disappear from the scene the Samaritan woman and Samaritans come to Jesus. The narrator shows that Samaritans believe in and proclaim Jesus as a Savior in this brief and climatic episode. Historically, Jesus' mission in reaching out to the Samaritans may have been preparatory for the early church's effort. Theologically, the author may seek to show that the Samaritan mission of the early church was based on precedent in Jesus' own ministry. His pattern of ministry in John's narrative coincides with the ministry of the early church as in Acts 1:8. In John's gospel Jesus' first ministry was in Judea (Jn. 3), and then in Samaria (Jn. 4), and then Gentiles (Jn. 12:20-32).

Many of the Samaritans from the village believed in Jesus on the basis of the Samaritan woman's testimony, εἶπέν μοι πάντα ἃ ἐποίησα ("He told me all things that I ever did") (Jn. 4:39), repeating

---

[203]   Craig Keener, *The Gospel of John*, 2003, 626.

[204]   Rudolf Schneckenburg, *Gospel According to St. John, vol. 1*, 1990, 454.

the words in John 4:29. They join the Samaritan woman's faith, πολλοὶ ἐπίστευσαν εἰς αὐτὸν τῶν Σαμαριτῶν διὰ τὸν λόγον τῆς γυναικὸς μαρτυρούσης ("many of the Samaritans believed in Him because of the word of the woman's testimony") in John 4:39. As such, they appear to progress beyond the woman's understanding of Jesus. The woman's testimony provided the initial momentum for them to come to Jesus, but now they have heard for themselves and have drawn their own conclusion.[205] The secondary testimony is no substitute for a direct personal encounter with Jesus.[206]

They ask Jesus, ἔμεινεν ἐκεῖ δύο ἡμέρας ("to stay there two more days") in John 4:40b, and he did. It is still exceptional that he stayed with them even a short two days since they were Samaritans. Jew's hesitations regarding ritual purity, which cause them to refrain from association with Samaritans, was not a concern for Jesus (cf. Jn. 4:9). His stay was not to be drawn out, however: He had to move on after two days, being directed by the Father.

During that time the harvest extended beyond those who had come out to see him and πολλῷ πλείους ἐπίστευσαν διὰ τὸν λόγον αὐτοῦ ("many more believed because of His word") (Jn. 4:41). The contrast between how people believed in Him in John 4:39 compared to John 4:41 should be noted. The initial crowd's faith is due to the Samaritan woman's testimony, and later the faith of many more is due to Jesus' words. They are more convinced that Jesus is the Savior as they have made a major step toward authentic faith. That's why they said to the Samaritan woman who had left her jar at the wall (Jn. 4:28) that Οὐκέτι διὰ τὴν σὴν λαλιὰν πιστεύομεν: αὐτοὶ γὰρ ἀκηκόαμεν ("It is no longer because of what you said we believe, for we ourselves heard"). It is interesting that the narrator changed λόγος in John 4:39 to λαλιὰ in John 4:42. It seems

---

[205]   C. K. Barrett, *The Gospel According to St. John*, 2nd ed., 1978, 243-44.

[206]   Leon Morris, *The Gospel According to John*, 1995, 250-51.

he intends to emphasize that there is only one λόγος (cf. Jn 1:1, 14). The many Samaritans believed in Jesus because of his λόγος, which reveals that Jesus is really the Savior of the world (Jn. 4:42). On the basis of hearing λόγος they came to know (οἴδαμεν) that Jesus is the Savior. Interestingly, the Old Testament never calls the Messiah 'Savior', and the expression was not a messianic title in 1st century Judaism. The Samaritan likewise did not view the Taheb as a redeemer. The LXX uses σωτὴρ ("Savior") both for God (eg., Isa. 45:15, 21) and for human deliverer such as Othniel and Ehud (Judg. 3:9, 15). By recognizing Jesus as ὁ σωτὴρ τοῦ κόσμου ("the Savior of the world"), the Samaritans accept that salvation may be from the Jews but it is for all people. This fits well with the author's consistent emphasis on the salvation for whole world offered thorough faith in Jesus (cf. Jn. 3:16-21; 12:46-47). Therefore, Jesus' mission for harvest among the Samaritans signals the return of the atheistic world to God as a sign of his universal scope of mission.

4.6   THE SIGNIFICANCE

Sukmin Cho argues that the Samaritan woman didn't confess Jesus as the Savior of the world even if she told the people in the village "Could this be the Christ?" (Jn. 4:29). Cho thus doubted the woman's faith in the Son of God or Messiah due to her silence in direct response to Jesus as recorded in the narrative.[207] That said, although the Samaritan woman did not clearly confess Jesus as her Savior, it is clear that through the narrative she progressively overcomes the barriers, eventually shows her faith in Christ, and acts as a true disciple as she shared her testimony. At first, she hesitates to converse with Him in this unusual and culturally unacceptable situation (Jn. 4:7-9). Then, she misunderstands Jesus' statement

---

[207]   Sukmin Cho, *A New Perspective on John's Gospel*, Solomon: Seoul, 2008, 204-205

in 4:10 and challenges Him (Jn. 4:11-12), but Jesus is still able to capture her attention and interest. Although she still does not understand (Jn. 4:13-15), she seems honest and open minded. Jesus speaks of himself as 'living water' that can quench people's thirst forever. She would receive eternal life if she believes in Him.

Thus, she appears to be progressive in her growing faith such that she may perceive why He has been saying what He was saying and claimed to be who He is (Jn. 4:19-20, 25, 29). In the end she proves seriously open to the idea that Jesus might be the Messiah. That's why she gives her testimony to the people and their confession shows that she has drunk of the living water. Bennema also thinks she is included among the people who confess Jesus as the Savior of the world (Jn. 4:42).[208]

The Samaritan woman in the narrative thus displays her honesty, open-mindedness, perceptiveness, responsiveness, and boldness to witness. Bennema also says this woman turns out to be a keen theological thinker and a successful missionary.[209] Also, the narrator shows Jesus affirmation that Hs coming was first to the people of Israel, showing how Jesus asserted Jewish salvation historical primacy, while the woman asks about the place of worship (Jn 4:22). This keeps the salvation historical pattern of the Old Testament intact, which moves from the people of Israel to the Gentiles. While Isaiah prophesied to the people of Israel, "I will also make you a light for the Gentiles, that you may bring my salvation to the ends of the earth" (Isa. 49:6b), Jesus' ministry opens up beyond Israel as He encounters the Samaritan woman. This leads to a theological tension and sends a message to the people of Israel that while the Messiah came first to them, others too would be the beneficiaries of his ministry. This would be the case only

---

[208] Cornelis Bennema, *Encountering Jesus Character Studies in the Gospel of John*, 2nd ed., 2014, 169.

[209] Ibid., 170.

subsequent to the crucifixion, resulting from their rejection of the Messiah. Yet Jesus had to pass through Samaria as He was willing to overcome the socio-cultural barrier, and still continues to focus His mission primarily on Israel.

Ahn observes in this narrative context, "The recurrent keyword μαρτυρία ("witness") and its cognate words weave together chapter 2 through 4. In those pericopae, the testimonies offered by the minor characters lead to the explicit manifestation of Jesus' Christological identity, i.e., Mary's disclosing Jesus' divine power, … and the Samaritan woman's witness resulting in the Samaritans' confession of Jesus as the redeemer. In the present periscope, Jesus' discourse with the Samaritan woman leads her and others to escalating faith in Christ."[210]

The climactic moment in the narrative, however, is Jesus' discussion of true worship in spirit and truth (Jn. 4:21-24). It is after this that Jesus reveals himself as the Messiah to the Samaritan woman in 4:26. During conversations with her Jesus points out that worship is not a matter of location, but is a spiritual matter just as God is spirit and thus she must worship spiritually. That might have comforted her, in that neither the worship offered by the people of Israel or that of Samaritans was satisfactory. Both must give way to true and spiritual worship of God in and through Jesus. This narrative builds up to Jesus' declaration to the Samaritan woman that he is the Messiah. Jesus is shown to be the new temple on which worship is to center. This will be followed by another Cana sign performed in relation to a Gentile (Jn. 4:46-54).

That is why Köstenberger argues the narrator has managed to illumine several important theological points:[211]

---

[210] Sanghee Ahn, *The Christological Witness Function of the Old Testament Characters in the Gospel of John*, 2014, 78.

[211] Andreas J. Köstenberger, *A Theology of John's Gospel and Letters*, Zondervan: Grand Rapids, Michigan, 2009, 204-205.

1. The reason for the antagonism toward Jesus on the part of the Jewish leadership in their lack of spiritual regeneration.

2. True, God-pleasing worship must center not on the earthly sanctuary, but on Jesus as the new temple; Jesus is the authentic manifestation of God's presence.

3. At the center of Jesus' messianic mission is His cross and the resurrection; the signs are profoundly gospel-centered.

4. People are steeped in their tradition, be it Jews (Nicodemus), Samaritans (the Samaritan woman) or Gentiles; Jesus' revelation of God has major obstacles to overcome in the form of people's preconceived notions of how (and where) God is to be worshiped.

4.7 CONCLUSION

The characterization of the Samaritan woman in the narrative is seen in her transformation. When she learns how much Jesus knows about her, she is attracted to Him in a new way, looking for Him to solve her sin problems that involves the relationship of God to man. The resolution that Jesus proposed was not what she expected, but she embraces it progressively. In that embrace, she is transformed to share the gospel like a disciple. The reader or implied reader is told the narrator's theological messages through the plot and characterizations of Jesus and the Samaritan woman: Jesus' mission by the Father in order to reach out the Samaritans, the meaning of the living water and true worship, the ideal type of discipleship, and Jesus' identification as the Messiah and the Savior of the world.

The Samaritan woman is a minor character who learns from her encounter with Jesus the Messiah a new meaning for her own life. As curiosity changes to wonder, the focus of her life shifts to mission and she engaged in a successful outreach to her people in Samaria. Her character offers a model of transformative encounter with Jesus. Attridge states this progression well: "She moves from a position ripe with erotic overtones, exemplifying a character that might well take advantage of such a situation, to a position where she has abandoned thought of herself and serves to bring a message of salvation to her neighbors."[212] Through her transformation and service God is glorified.

---

[212] Harrold Attridge, "The Samaritan Woman: A Woman Transformed" in *Character Studies in the Fourth Gospel, WUNT 314,* 2013, 280-81.

CHAPTER 5

The Royal Official (John 4:43-54)

──────

Towards the end of John 4 the author provides the story of the royal official's son. As for the literary structure of the healing narrative of the royal official's son, the author has placed it just after the Samaritan woman's encounter with Jesus, marking the end of the first cycle of the sign miracles (σημεῖα), often called the Cana Cycle (Jn. 2-4)[213] because they were performed in Cana of Galilee. The healing miracle story of the royal official' son is designated by the narrator as the δεύτερον σημεῖον ("the second sign") of the seven miracle signs (σημεῖα) performed by Jesus in John's gospel (Jn. 4:54). Kim interestingly points out that not like in the Synoptics the author never uses the usual word δύναμις for miracles Jesus performed in John's gospel, and instead he uses the word σημεῖα in all his references to miracles (Jn. 2:11, 23; 3:2; 4:48, 54; 6:2, 14, 26; 7:31; 9:16; 10:41; 12:18, 37; and 20:30).[214] Ashton argues that σημεῖα are marvelous happening with a special theological significance, and that σημεῖα also demonstrate Jesus' relationship with the God the Father.[215]

The entire Cana Cycle presents a variety of responses to Jesus of the characters who emerge. This is evident beginning with the miracle of Jesus turning the water to wine in John 2:1-11, and ends

---

[213] Gerrald Borchert, *John 1-11*, 1996, 151-222.

[214] Moon Hyun Kim, *Healing Hurts*, 2005, 26.

[215] John Ashton, *Understanding the Fourth Gospel*, 1991, 521.

with the healing of the royal official's son in John 4:46-54. A chiastic structure is evident with the forming of an *inclusio* as follows;[216]

(A) John 2:1-12   Jesus' first miraculous sign at Cana of Galilee

(B) John 2:13-25   Jesus cleaning up the temple

    (C) John 3:1-21   Jesus and Nicodemus

      (D) John 3:22-36   Jesus and John the Baptist

(C[1]) John 4:1-42   Jesus and Samaritan woman

(B[1]) John 4:43-45   Jesus rejected by His own people

(A[1]) John 4:46-54   Jesus' second miraculous sign at Cana of Galilee

Van Belle and Hunt also explore the forms of inclusion seen in both the wine miracle and the healing of royal official's son: "Both narratives describe a person who comes to believe fully: the mother of Jesus (with his disciples) and the royal official (with members of his household). Between the two narratives the evangelist considers pairs of groups and/or individuals who show disbelief (the Jews in 2:12-22 and the Samaritan woman in Jn. 4:1-15), partial faith (Nicodemus in 3:1-21 and the Samaritan woman in Jn. 4:16-29), and complete faith (John the Baptist in 3:22-26 and the Samaritans of Sychar in Jn. 4:27-30, 39-42). These responses (disbelief, partial faith, complete faith) take place in both a Jewish milieu (Jn. 2:12-Jn. 3:26) and a non-Jewish milieu (Jn. 4:1-42). Indeed, the two Cana narratives themselves occur in Jewish (Jn. 2:1-11) and non-Jewish milieu (Jn. 4:43-54). Moreover, "the evangelist's own commentary is placed symmetrically: John 2:23-25

---

[216] Suk Min Cho, *A New Perspective on John's Gospel*, 2008, 183. Translated by Nathan Hahn.

appears *after* the first example of disbelief (the Jews) and John
4:43-45 appears *before* the last example of faith in the section (the
Royal Official)."[217] Moloney also thinks that this final episode in
the Cana Cycle completes a literary pattern common throughout
this section of the Gospel where the literary shapes of successive
narratives are very similar.[218]

Culpepper remarks that the character of the anonymous royal
official is one of the overlooked characters of the gospel, but then
Culpepper himself devotes merely a short paragraph to him.[219]
The narrator indicates in the setting of the scene (Jn. 4:43-45)
that Jesus moves from Samaria to Galilee, and he also comments
the reception Jesus received from the Galileans. This narrative of
the royal official reveals Jesus who restores life as the life-giving
Messiah. Brodie argues that this healing episode of the royal official's son constitutes a carefully crafted progression from the previous Samaritan woman narrative while the episode has its own
newness and integrity.[220] Schnackenburg also states that "there are
intrinsic links which connect John 4:43-54 with the preceding narrative. Jesus reached the goal for which He set out in John 4:1 ff.
and the attention is concentrated on the reception given to Jesus

---

[217] Gilbert Van Belle and Steven Hunt, "The Son of the Royal Official." 2013,
316-17.

[218] Francis Moloney, *The Gospel of John*, 1998, 151. Moloney's explanation is
slightly different from that of Van Belle and Hunt, "The first Cana story
(2:1-12) is matched by the purification of the Temple (2:13-25), and the
encounter with Nicodemus (3:1-21) is structurally parallel with the Baptist's
final witness (3:22-36). The two moments of Jesus' encounter with the
Samaritan woman are shaped in the same way (4:1-15 and 4:16-30). The
literary shape of the account of Jesus' stay with the Samaritan villagers
(4:39-42) returns as Jesus comes back to Cana in Galilee (4:43-54)."

[219] Alan Culpepper, *Anatomy of the Fourth Gospel*, 1983, 137.

[220] Thomas Brodie, *The Gospel According to John*, 1993, 226.

by His countrymen in Galilee (cf. v. 44)."[221] The author's theological point of view in this narrative is not hard to see: Faith in Jesus
and in His words is the way of life. Jesus, the Son of God, can give
life by His word.

The structure of the healing narrative of the royal official's son
is divided into four acts, while the main plot of John 4:46-53 can
be divided into two. Many scholars divide it into just two.[222] The
four acts look as follows:

Narrative structure (Jn. 4:43-54)

F. Act I: The setting (Jn. 4:43-45)

G. Act II: Jesus and the royal official, and the Galileans
(Jn. 4:46-50)

H. Act III: The royal official and his servants, and his household (Jn. 4:51-53)

I. Act IV: The epilogue

5.1   ACT I: THE SETTING (Jn. 4:43-45)

The narrator introduces two characters, Jesus (Jn. 4:43) and the
Galileans (Jn. 4:45). Jesus departed the Samaritan village (where
He stayed as the Samaritans had asked him to in Jn. 4:40) μετὰ τὰς
δύο ἡμέρας ("after two days") and came to Galilee (Jn. 4:43). The
setting of the healing narrative of the royal official's son (Jn. 4:43-
45) is well-connected with John 4:46, ἦλθεν οὖν πάλιν εἰς τὴν κανὰ
τῆς γαλιλαίας ("So He came again to Cana in Galilee"). The μετὰ

---

[221]   Rudolf Schnackenburg, *The Gospel According to St. John* vol 1, 1990, 461.

[222]   See Moon Hyun Kim, *Healing Hurts*, 2005, 27-49. Francis Moloney, *The
Gospel of John*, 1998, 150-56. However, unlike many other scholars both
Kim and Moloney include v. 46 in the introduction because vv. 43-46 serve
the present shape of the narrative as an introduction to vv. 47-54, although
v. 46 probably introduced an originally independent story.

τὰς δύο ἡμέρας ("after two days") implies that Jesus arrived at Cana on the third day after leaving the Samaritan village.[223] However, the reader or implied reader is not told exactly how long it took Jesus to get there from Sychar in Samaria. From Sychar to Cana was about 40 miles, so a trip could take two or three days.[224]

Having been rejected by the Jewish religious leaders in Jerusalem, Jesus went to back Cana in Galilee.[225] While Jesus was in Jerusalem at the Passover Feast, the Jewish religious leaders had confronted Him about His cleansing of the temple (Jn. 2:14-17). Their question about this set the stage for the narrative of the royal official. In this way the Jewish religious leaders became a thwart for the royal official and his faith when they asked Jesus, Τί σημεῖον δεικνύεις ἡμῖν, ὅτι ταῦτα ποιεῖς; ("What sign do you show us for doing these things?") in John 2:18b. Displeased by Jesus' action in the cleansing of the temple, the religious leaders challenged Him by asking for a sign. When He answered them by stating the sign would be His death and resurrection, they did not believe Him, while at the same time John notes that that after Jesus' recollection, this exchange with the Jewish religious leaders contributed to their faith (Jn. 2:19-22).

The narrator tells the reason Jesus came to Cana in John 4:44, αὐτὸς γὰρ ἰησοῦς ἐμαρτύρησεν ὅτι προφήτης ἐν τῇ ἰδίᾳ πατρίδι τιμὴν οὐκ ἔχει ("For Jesus Himself had testified that a prophet has no honor in his own hometown"). The reader or implied reader may conclude from this that Jesus' motive for his trip from Judea to Cana in Galilee was tied to the fact that "a prophet has no honor in his hometown." However, elsewhere in scripture Jesus is said

---

[223] Francis Moloney, *The Gospel of John*, 1998, 159.

[224] Andreas Köstenberger, *John*, 2004, 167.

[225] James Howard, "The Significance of Minor Characters in the Gospel of John," 1969, 69. He refers to Andreas G. van Aarde, "Narrative Criticism Applied to John 4:43-54," 1991, 124.

to be "of Nazareth" (cf. Matt. 2:23) and a Galilean (cf. Mk. 14:70). The author elsewhere notes Jesus was from Galilee when Philip told Nathanael that they had found the fulfillment of Israel's hope, Ἰησοῦν υἱὸν τοῦ Ἰωσὴφ τὸν ἀπὸ Ναζαρέτ ("Jesus of Nazareth, the son of Joseph") (Jn. 1:45c). Also, the reader or implied reader may think that the presence of Jesus' mother at Cana in John 2:1 indicates His Galilean origin. Finally, the author does not even tell us that Jesus was born in Judea, not like the infancy narratives of Matthew and Luke.[226]

How, then, can the mention of Jesus' m trip to Galilee be tied to Jesus' pronouncement of prophets having no honor in their home town? In John 4:45, the author describes Jesus's "welcome" reception from the Galileans, establishing that that the author's intent is not to claim Galilee to be Jesus' hometown.[227] In the opening of the Johannine narrative, Judea is the location for the first three days of Jesus' ministry (Jn. 1:19-42). After that, Jesus spent the next day in Galilee (Jn. 1:43-51), where he performed the first miracle sign of the revelation of δόξα (Jn. 2:1-12). Jesus returned to Jerusalem immediately after that (Jn. 2:13), remaining in Judea until He began his trip to Galilee through Samaria (Jn. 4:3-4). The narrator now reveals that Jesus leaves Samaria heading for Galilee because His own hometown is not honoring Him (Jn. 4:43-44). In Judea Jesus faced rejection from the Jews (Jn. 2:23-25). Jesus moved away from Judea due to the danger of hostility from the Pharisees (Jn. 4:1). Thus, for the author, Jesus' hometown is Judea.[228]

---

[226] Raymond Brown, *The Gospel According to John I-XII*, 1966, 187.

[227] Pryor opines that this welcome afforded Jesus on arrival in Galilee may be taken to invalidate Jesus' own prophetic statement in 4:44 (J. W. Pryor, "John 4:44 and the *Patris* of Jesus," 1987, 254-58).

[228] See C. K. Barrett, *The Gospel According to St. John*, 1978, 246; Barnabas Lindars, *The Gospel of John*, 1972, 200-01; Francis Moloney, *The Gospel of John*, 1998, 152; Mark Matson, *John*, 2002, 34.

That said, the reader or implied reader should recall John 1:1, ἐν ἀρχῇ ἦν ὁ λόγος, καὶ ὁ λόγος ἦν πρὸς τὸν θεόν, καὶ θεὸς ἦν ὁ λόγος ("In the beginning was the Word, and the Word was with God, and the Word was God") and John 1:14, καὶ ὁ λόγος σὰρξ ἐγένετο καὶ ἐσκήνωσεν ἐν ἡμῖν, καὶ ἐθεασάμεθα τὴν δόξαν αὐτοῦ, δόξαν ὡς μονογενοῦς παρὰ πατρός, πλήρης χάριτος καὶ ἀληθείας ("And the Word became flesh and dwell among us, and we have seen his glory, glory as the only Son from the Father, full of grace and truth"). Thus, the "hometown" or origins of Jesus in John 4:44 may imply a spiritual dimension. The narrator in John 1:11 told that Jesus comes to τὰ ἴδια ("his own") and οἱ ἴδιοι αὐτὸν ("his own people") did not receive Him.[229] So the transitional introduction setting of the healing narrative of the royal official's son declares a sense of Jesus' spiritual observation, ironically, that His Judaic compatriots showed him no honor, but the Galileans welcomed Him.[230]

At the same time, there is a significant difference evident between "welcoming" and "accepting" Jesus, according to John's narrative. For example Jesus negatively comments on Galileans' superficial faith in John 4:48, even though acknowledging that they welcomes Him (Jn. 4:45).[231] The reader or implied reader also may recall the welcoming response of those in Jerusalem in the

---

[229]   Leon Morris, *The Gospel according to John*, 1995, 254. He notes that John 4:44, where τιμὴ replaces the customary δόξα, illustrates the opening reference to Jesus' rejection even by "His own." See also Pryor, "Jesus and Israel in the Fourth Gospel," 1990, 216-17.

[230]   Moon Hyun Kim, *Healing Hurts*, 2008, 30; Thomas Brodie, *The Gospel According to John*, 1993, 229

[231]   Morris and Carson argue that the Galileans "welcome or receive" is another instance of Johannine irony. It was in fact a rejection because they were only interested in Jesus' miracles (Jn. 4:45). See Leon Morris, *The Gospel according to John*, 1995, 254 and Donald Carson, *The Gospel according to John*, 1991, 236.

Passover feast who ἐπίστευσαν εἰς τὸ ὄνομα αὐτοῦ, θεωροῦντες αὐτοῦ τὰ σημεῖα ἃ ἐποίει ("believed in His name when they saw the signs that He was doing") in John 2:23. The narrator tells that the Galileans had been in Jerusalem and had seen the first miracle sign Jesus performed. So the reader or implied reader may conclude that they understand Jesus as a miracle performer and welcome him with the superficial faith. Again, this reinforces that welcoming Jesus is not necessarily the same as accepting Him, in keeping with the author's point of view on authentic faith.[232]

5.2 ACT II: JESUS AND THE ROYAL OFFICIAL, AND THE GALILEANS (Jn. 4:46-50)

After the setting of the story the narrator reminds the reader or implied reader of the miracle Jesus performed the last time He was at Cana of Galilee (Jn. 4:46a), introducing a new character, the royal official whose son was very sick (Jn. 4:46b). As another anonymous minor character from the Johannine narrative, the royal official came from Capernaum, a city on the northwest shore of the Sea of Galilee. For the reader or implied reader, the author's intention in maintaining the anonymity of the character may be to allow the read to identify with the character and thus be urged to respond with his/her own faith.[233] Such use of anonymity in characters may help enhance the representative qualities of a character. Collin argues that throughout John's gospel, Johannine characters represent a type of faith response or lack of faith response to Jesus, the Son of God.[234]

---

[232] Rudolf Schnackenburg, *The Gospel According to St. John* vol 1, 1990, 464.

[233] See D. R. Beck, "The Narrative Function of Anonymity in the Fourth Gospel Characterization," 1993, 143-58.

[234] R. F. Collin, "The Representative Figures in the Fourth Gospel," 1976, 26-46.

The identity of βασιλικὸς ("royal official") is unclear. The term βασιλικὸς could be either someone in the service of the king or a relative of the king.[235] The king here is probably Herod Antipas, given that he was the tetrarch of Galilee and Perea at the time of Jesus' public ministry from 4 B.C. to AD 39.[236] Köstenberger points out, "This was the ruler whom Jesus later called 'that fox' after hearing that he was out to kill Him (Lk. 13:31-32). Still later, when summoned before Herod at the occasion of His Jerusalem trial, Jesus refused to answer any of his questions (Lk. 23:8-12). Presumably, one of the reasons for this frosty relationship was Herod's beheading of John the Baptist. But the present event takes place at an earlier stage of Jesus' ministry and Jesus in any case would not have held the royal official's employment with Herod Antipas against him personally."[237]

Looking into the context of the present Johannine narrative, Moloney thinks that the individual depicted is a Gentile officer, noting "All the other characters in 4:1-54 are Samaritans, people from the world outside Judaism. It is most likely that this particular βασιλικὸς is understood and presented to the reader by the author

---

[235] Scholars are divided for his identity: a Jewish official in service of Herod Antipas (Rudolf Bultmann, *The Gospel of John*, 1971, 206; Donald Carson, *The Gospel according to John*, 1991, 234); a Gentile officer in service of Herod Antipas (Andreas Köstenberger, *John*, 2004, 166, 169; A. H. Mead, "*basilikos*," 1985, 69-72); an officer in the army of Herod Agrippa (George Beasley-Murrey, *John*, 1991, 69); a Galilean aristocrat (Craig Keener, *the Gospel of John*, 2003, 630-31).

[236] Cornelis Bennema, Encountering Jesus, 2014, 176. See also Harold Hoehner, *Herod Antipas*, 1972. Most scholars refer to Josephus' use of the word to designate the retainers (both military and civilian) of Herod Antipas, the ruler of Galilee in the time of Jesus, whom the New Testament regularly refers to as βασιλεύς.

[237] Andreas Köstenberger, *John*, 2002, 169.

as a final example of the reception of the word of Jesus from the non-Jewish world."[238]

Whatever his identity, he appears to be a prominent individual with authority over people and who had servants (Jn. 4:51). Nevertheless, the narrator's main point is that Jesus does not turn away from the official's plea.

The royal official ἀκούσας ὅτι Ἰησοῦς ἥκει ἐκ τῆς Ἰουδαίας εἰς τὴν Γαλιλαίαν ("heard that Jesus had come from Judea to Galilee," John 4:47a), similar to how Samaritans heard of Jesus' coming from the woman (Jn. 4:39). Similar to how the Samaritans came to Jesus because they themselves heard Jesus' word (Jn. 4:39-42), in this narrative the royal official approaches Jesus after hearing about Him. The term ἀκούσας ("having heard") is an aorist temporal participle and denotes preceding action. The narrator tells that the royal official from Capernaum came to Cana in Galilee quickly as he heard Jesus was coming down from Judea and ἠρώτα ἵνα καταβῇ καὶ ἰάσηται αὐτοῦ τὸν υἱόν ("he was asking Him to come down and heal his son") (Jn. 4:47). His primary concern is not with Jesus' identity but with his son's healing.[239] The motive of his coming to Jesus is that he heard from the Galileans of the miracle sign that Jesus had performed in Jerusalem (Jn. 4:45). He believed Jesus had the ability to heal his son ἤμελλεν ἀποθνῄσκειν ("was about to die"). The narrator does not tell what kind of his sickness was involved, but indicates that it involved some kind of fever (Jn.

---

[238] Francis Moloney, *The Gospel of John*, 1998, 153. Beirne also argues that the mother of Jesus and the royal official provide a frame of corresponding exemplars of authentic faith in John 2:1-4:54 with Jesus' mother representing a Jewish model, the royal official a Gentile model (Margaret Beirne, *Women and Men in the Fourth Gospel*, 2003, 48-49).

[239] Donald Carson, *The Gospel according to John*, 1991, 238; Herman Ridderbos, *The Gospel according to John*, 1997, 176.

4:52) and that the son was at the point of death (Jn. 4:47, 49).[240] Like the Samaritans who asked Jesus to stay with them because the Samaritan woman shared the testimony and they believed in Him, the royal official was motivated by his having heard confirmation by witnesses in Galilee who had seen all the miracle wonders by Jesus. The narrator emphasizes and connects closely the faith, testimony, and hearings in John 4:39, 45 and 47. Kim states that the royal official asks Jesus to καταβῇ to Capernaum and ἰάσηται imply that Jesus should be present there in order for Him to heal his son miraculously. Those two aorist subjunctive verbs show his humble and desperate attitude, and the imperfect active verb, ἠρώτα indicates that his plea is not just one time incident but consistent begging.[241] The reader or implied reader can see the royal official's character of consistent and determined commitment to pursue Jesus as the narrator uses καταβῇ several times in John 4:47, 49 and 51. Resseguie suggests the reasons that the narrator uses it several times is because Cana is geographically located in the Galilean hills from which Jesus should go downward to Capernaum about

---

[240] The narrator describes the sickness of the royal official's son progressively. First, the narrator tells that the son of a royal official is sick in John 4:46b, τις βασιλικὸς οὗ ὁ υἱὸς ἠσθένει ("a royal official whose son was sick"). Second, the readers are informed that the son was at the point of death at the royal official's first request in John 4:47b, ἤμελλεν γὰρ ἀποθνήσκειν ("for he was about to die"). Third, the threat to the son's life is repeated for emphasis in the second request in John 4:49b, Κύριε, κατάβηθι πρὶν ἀποθανεῖν τὸ παιδίον μου ("Lord, come down before my child dies"). The aorist form in πρὶν ἀποθανεῖν contrast sharply with the present infinitive ἀποθνήσκειν in John 4:47. Fourth, the readers learn that the son's sickness caused the fever in John 4:52b, ἀφῆκεν αὐτὸν ὁ πυρετός ("the fever left him"). See Gilbert van Belle and Steven Hunt, "The Son of the Royal Official: Incarnating the Life Giving Power of Jesus' Word," 2013, 322.

[241] Moon Hyun Kim, *Healing Hurts*, 2008, 34. It points to the royal official's determination (Herman Ridderbos, *The Gospel according to John*, 1997, 176; Leon Morris, *The Gospel according to John*, 1995, 256).

fourteen miles, and Jesus doesn't intend to descend figuratively.[242] Rensberger argues that Jesus' upward or downward move has figurative or symbolic significance in the Johannine narrative.[243]

However, the narrator shocks and surprises the reader or implied reader as he tells Jesus' negative response to the royal official's begging in John 4:48b, ἐὰν μὴ σημεῖα καὶ τέρατα ἴδητε, οὐ μὴ πιστεύσητε ("Unless you see signs and wonders you will not believe"). It is not a typical response of Jesus found in the miracle episodes.[244] In this urgent situation of life and death of the royal official's son, Jesus seems to rebuke the official, although He uses the second person plural verb ἴδητε. Jesus addresses His words to the crowd, the Galileans, which included the royal official. Jesus warns them that authentic faith cannot be based on just signs and wonders. Those Galileans who are dependent on just signs and wonders do not have authentic faith. With this statement of Jesus, the author presents the reader of his theological theme that authentic faith in Jesus, as the reader familiar with Jesus is well aware, is not seen in those who have only a superficial faith based on only signs and wonders (cf. Jn. 2:23-24). Ridderbos argues that Jesus' harsh words are designed to challenge the desperate, concerned royal official to go beyond self-interest and to recognize Jesus as more than a miracle performer, thus summoning his Galilean audience to acknowledge Jesus' true identity.[245]

As for the narrator's shocking and disrupting inclusion of the statement made by Jesus, Staley argues that the narrator uses such

---

[242] James Resseguie, *The Strange Gospel*, 2001, 131.

[243] David Rensberger, "Spirituality and Christology in Johannine Sectarianism," 2002, 173-88. Also see Tat-siong Liew, "Ambiguous Admittance: Consent and Decent in John's Community of 'Upward' Mobility," 2002, 193-224.

[244] Francis Moloney, *The Gospel of John*, 1998, 153.

[245] Herman Ridderbos, *The Gospel According to John*, 1997, 176. See also Rudolf Schnackenburg, *The Gospel According to John* vol. 1, 1990, 468.

tools and devices to control the reading experience as inscribed in the text. As part of the narrator's rhetoric, Johannine language and symbolic significance are not always revealed at the textual surface. Narrative disruption or inconsistency is employed to lead the reader to see an alternative meaning from a different point of view.[246] In this manner, a narrative disruption such as this can have its own developed meaning within the narrative plot. Culpepper posits that misunderstanding between secondary characters is one of the distinctive features of the Johannine narrative. Minor characters' misunderstandings of Jesus' words may be characterized in general terms by the following elements:[247]

1. Jesus makes a statement which is ambiguous, metaphorical, or contains a double-entendre.

2. His dialogue partner responds either in terms of the literal meaning of Jesus' statement or by a question or protest which shows that he or she has missed the higher meaning of Jesus' words.

3. In most instances an explanation is then offered by Jesus or (less frequently) the narrator.

Jesus' harsh response is ignored by the royal official, who continues begging in John 4:49, saying to Jesus Κύριε, κατάβηθι πρὶν

---

[246] Jeffrey Staley, *The Print's First Kiss: A Rhetorical Investigation of the Implied Reader in the Fourth Gospel*, 1998, 21-22. He takes it from Chatman's model of narrative communication (Seymour Chatman, *Story and Discourse: Narrative Structure in Fiction and Film*, 1978).

[247] Alan Culpepper, *Anatomy of the Fourth Gospel*, 1983, 152. Therefore, misunderstandings provide either an implicit or an explicit opportunity to explain the meaning of Jesus' words and further develop the author's significant themes. Brodie also argues this narrative interruption may introduce the significant Johannine theme of faith and signs (Thomas Brodie, *The Gospel According to John*, 1993, 229).

ἀποθανεῖν τὸ παιδίον μου ("Lord, come down before my child dies"). The royal official doesn't care about Jesus' negative response. Despite Jesus' rebuke, he insists Him to go down to Capernaum before his son dies.[248] While most of scholars agree that Jesus' ambiguous negative response of John 4:48 is toward the Galileans to include the royal officer, the officer himself may have thought that Jesus is not talking to him but to other Galileans, based on his disregard of Jesus' rebuke and his continued begging. Conversely, Howard asserts that Jesus was not speaking to the royal official when He made his negative comment, but rather the crowd of Galileans.[249]

The royal official then goes on to implore Jesus to help him, only using the more respective address of "Κύριε" (Jn. 4:49). The reader or implied reader may think that the official is more desperate this time as he introduces his son as παιδίον ("child"), compared to his use of υἱόν ("son") in John 4:47, indicating the affectionate intimacy that exists between a concerned father and his child. The royal official's intimate relationship with his son is acknowledged by Jesus as He said πορεύου· ὁ υἱός σου ζῇ ("Go, your son will live") in John 4:50.[250] All of this may contribute to the reader seeing the healing of the official's son as the work of God given the parallel between the official's intimate relationship with his son and the Father's relationship with His Son Jesus. It is

---

[248] Herzog argues that the royal official's insistence reflects his most vital concern that any human preserves and prevails (Frederick Herzog, *Liberation Theology: Liberation in the Light of the Fourth Gospel*, 1972, 78).

[249] James Howard, "The Significance of Minor Characters in the Gospel of John," 1969, 70.

[250] The phrase ὁ υἱός σου ζῇ ("your son will live") may be an allusion to Elijah and the woman of Zarephath in 1 Kings 17:23. If so, Jesus' messianic activity is placed here within the compass of the miraculous healing ministry of Elijah in the Old Testament (Rudolf Schnackenburg, *The Gospel According to John* vol. 1, 1990, 467).

in this manner that Jesus answers the royal official's plea on His own terms, a long-distance miracle.[251]

Another parallel may be seen by the reader or implied reader between Jesus' rebuke of the royal official's initial plea to and Jesus' initial rejection of His mother' request in the first miracle sign that He performed at Cana (Jn. 2:4). In both cases, Jesus initial response to the request is responded to negatively, yet in both cases the persistence of the requester is responded to with the miraculous action by Jesus. As Jesus, the Son of God knows τί ἦν ἐν τῷ ἀνθρώπῳ ("what was in a man" Jn. 2:25b), He shows mercy to the royal official's desperate begging and heals his son. Beirne states that since an ambiguously negative remark is followed by a positive action (Jn. 2:7-8; 4:50), one may read Jn. 2:4 and 4:48 as tests of faith.[252] Both signs in Cana reflect the magnitude of and the subsequent fulfillment of human needs. The reader or implied reader must see the persistence of both the mother of Jesus and the royal official as their character. In the face of his son's life and death, the royal official naturally should beg Jesus repeatedly even in spite of His initial negative statement, just as the mother of Jesus had done.

Although Jesus wants to show mercy to the royal official and heal his son, He does not accede to καταβῇ ("come down") to Capernaum. He heals τὸ παιδίον ("the child") by the authority of His word and the royal official is told to go home because his son is living (Jn. 4:50). Unlike that of the Galileans, the response of the royal official is impressive. The narrator says ἐπίστευσεν ὁ ἄνθρωπος τῷ λόγῳ ὃν εἶπεν αὐτῷ ὁ Ἰησοῦς καὶ ἐπορεύετο ("The man believed the word that Jesus spoke to him and went his way") in John 4:50b. The royal official may learn and have faith in Jesus word when He rebuked the Galileans' superficial faith

---

[251]   A similar long distance miracle incident of healing is the centurion's servant in Capernaum, narrated in Matthew 8:5-13.

[252]   Margaret Beirne, *Women and Men in the Fourth Gospel*, 2003, 59.

in Jesus' signs and wonders. The narrator emphasizes ἐπίστευσεν ("believed"), as seen his use of the verb to open the sentence. The royal official believed τῷ λόγῳ ὃν εἶπεν αὐτῷ ὁ Ἰησοῦς ("the word that Jesus spoke to him"), after which the royal official without any hesitation as he went off fully accepting Jesus' command. The royal official trusts in Jesus' word even without seeing a miracle or validating sign that his son would be healed, thus demonstrating a remarkable progression from one who only seeks out Jesus on the basis of His reputation of a miracle performer. Ridderbos states that the royal official previously had merely believed in Jesus' ability to heal his son, and now he takes Jesus' word or promise that He actually has done so.[253] Culpepper says the royal official exemplifies those who respond because of the signs they see, but who are still ready to believe apart from the signs.[254] He became a model of what it means to believe apart from just signs and wonders, but also believing in Jesus' word.

The reader or implied reader can perceive the truly Johannine character of the story and the major theme of the narrative, that of authentic faith. Judge states, "As with the first Cana sign, there is an initial request to Jesus, who replies with a testing objection that is overcome in some way by the quester. Jesus then complies with the request but in His own way that makes clear that the reader can move with the evangelist or narrator to a new level of significance."[255]

---

[253] Herman Ridderbos, *The Gospel According to John*, 1997, 177.

[254] Culpepper, *Anatomy of the Fourth Gospel*, 183, 137.

[255] Peter Judge, "The Royal Official: Not So Officious," 2013, 312.

5.3 ACT III: THE ROYAL OFFICIAL AND HIS SERVANTS, AND HIS HOUSEHOLD (Jn. 4:51-53)

The second scene of the healing royal official's son shows the miracle happening as the royal official is going back from Cana to his hometown; of Capernaum, and the meeting there with his servants. The background of this scene is of course the word of Jesus, πορεύου· ὁ υἱός σου ζῇ (Jn. 4:50a).

The royal official is ἤδη καταβαίνοντος ("already going down") in John 4:51a. His going down was in obedience to Jesus' command in John 4:50a. While going down, the royal official meets his servants who tell the official ὁ παῖς αὐτοῦ ζῇ ("his son lives") (Jn. 4:51b). Although the author could have ended his recounting of this episode here, the author wants to make a theological point. When the Samaritan people encountered Jesus in the previous narrative, they believed in Jesus' word and had knowledge of who Jesus is (Jn. 4:41-42). Likewise, in this royal official's narrative, the official believes in Jesus' word as seen in his acting on it, and will come to know the authority of the word of Jesus over sickness, even at the point of death.

When the royal official hears the good news from the servants, he asks them τὴν ὥραν ἐν ᾗ κομψότερον ἔσχεν ("the hour when he got better") in John 4:52a. Köstenberger notes that the term ἐπύθετο ("inquire") used "elsewhere in this Gospel only in 13:24, often connotes an element of curiosity or intrigue, coupled with a strong desire to know some piece of information of which the questioner is ignorant."[256] Why did he inquire the time his son got better? Does he want more evidence concerning his son's healing? The reader or implied reader is already told that he believed in

---

[256] Andreas Köstenberger, *John*, 2002, 171. Other New Testament instances of this word include Matt. 2:4; Luke 15:26; 18:36; Acts 4:7; 10:18, 29; 21:33; 23:19, 20, 34.

Jesus' word in John 4:50a. Is it not a statement of faith or an incomplete faith? Is there a doubt in his mind or just checking whether Jesus' word has really the authority or not? The narrator's comment of ἐπίστευσεν αὐτὸς καὶ ἡ οἰκία αὐτοῦ ὅλη ("He himself believed and his whole household") in John 4:53b needs interpretation. Howard-Brook states that his doubts are now revealed to be perhaps the basis for Jesus' rebuke in John 4:48.[257] The royal official may have wondered if his son recovered naturally on his own. He thus needs a confirmation of Jesus' power and authority over the deadly sickness.

His servants reply, ἐχθὲς ὥραν ἑβδόμην ἀφῆκεν αὐτὸν ὁ πυρετός ("Yesterday at the seventh hour the fever left him") in John 4:52b. That was the very time at which the royal official spoke to Jesus, who said to him ὁ υἱός σου ζῇ ("your son will live").[258] If he had any doubts on Jesus, they disappeared immediately. After the official finds out the time of his son's healing, the royal official was assured as he confirmed that Jesus has the power and the authority to heal. He thus can finally have authentic faith in Jesus. Schnackenburg opines that the peculiar tension in John 4:50b and 4:53b can be resolved by speaking of John 4:50b as representing a kind of developing stage in the royal official's faith.[259] That's why the narrator confirms and completes his initial faith in John 4:50b. Moloney argues the narrator closes this story in a way that parallels John 2:11, saying "In the first Cana story others came to belief as a result of the miracle (cf. 2:11). The narrator has reminded the reader of the first Cana story in v. 46. In 2:1-12 not only does the

---

[257] Wes Howard-Brook, *Becoming Children of God: John's Gospel and Radical Discipleship*, 2001, 118

[258] Donald Carson, *The Gospel According to John*, 1991, 239; Francis Moloney, *The Gospel of John*, 1998, 162; George Beasley-Murray, *John*, 1999, 69; Gary Burge, *The Gospel of John*, 2000, 152.

[259] Rudolf Schnackenburg, *The Gospel According to John* vol. 1, 1990, 468.

mother of Jesus place all her trust in the word of Jesus and thus act as the catalyst that produces the miracle. Her initial act of faith (2:5) leads to the faith of others, the disciples (2:11). In the second Cana story an initial act of faith (4:50b) has enabled a miracle that leads to the faith of others, the official's household."[260] His servants' report brings a complete faith to his initial act of believing (Jn., 4:50). Lindars interprets that the royal official's servants have confirmed his faith, but in doing so they themselves discovered faith in Jesus.[261] Kim explores, "The distinction between 4:50b and 4:53b is suggested by the Greek syntax. In 4:50b, ἐπίστευσεν ὁ ἄνθρωπος τῷ λόγῳ ('he believed the word'), the verb ἐπίστευσεν takes a dative object τῷ λόγῳ, which reflects a faith that is not obviously firm, whereas 4:53b, ἐπίστευσεν αὐτὸς ('he himself believed'), with the verb ἐπίστευσεν being followed by an emphatic pronoun αὐτὸς, and thus reflecting of his later faith as becoming stronger."[262] The narrator emphasizes and confirms the official's authentic faith

---

[260] Francis Moloney, *The Gospel of John*, 1998, 155.

[261] Barnabas Lindars, *The Gospel of John*, 1972, 205.

[262] Moon Hyun Kim, *Healing Hurts: John's Portrayals of the Persons in Healing Episodes*, 2005, 43. He refers to Raymond Brown's commentary of the Gospel according to John.

in John 4:53b.²⁶³ His initial belief is justified and has now become true knowledge of Him. Bennema points out that the royal official expressed further belief on his knowledge basis, in which both belief and knowledge stimulate and inform each other for the Johannine dialectic.²⁶⁴ Koester correctly states that the royal official's faith was confirmed by a sign, not based upon a sign.²⁶⁵

In the meantime the narrator mentions ζῇ the third time in John 4:53, ἔγνω οὖν ὁ πατὴρ ὅτι [ἐν] ἐκείνῃ τῇ ὥρᾳ ἐν ᾗ εἶπεν αὐτῷ ὁ Ἰησοῦς, ὁ υἱός σου ζῇ ("The father knew that was the hour when Jesus said to him, your son will live."). Thus, the narrator emphasizes Jesus' authority over ἤμελλεν ἀποθνῄσκειν (Jn. 4:47b) and ἀποθανεῖν (Jn. 49b) because He is life-giver. Like the Samaritan people, the royal official believed not only in Jesus' word but also

---

263   Some Johannine scholars agree that while the royal official's belief in John 4:50 may simply have been to trust or to take Jesus at His word, his belief in John 4:53 most likely denotes a saving faith. See Rudolf Bultmann, *The Gospel of John*, 1971, 208-9; Rudolf Schnackenburg, *The Gospel According to John* vol. 1, 1990, 467-68; C. K. Barrett, *The Gospel According to St. John*, 1978, 248. However, Francis Moloney and Margaret Beirne argue that the royal official already reached authentic Johannine belief in John 4:50. His faith becomes more full and complete in John 4:53 (Francis Moloney, *The Gospel of John*, 1998, 154-55; Margaret Beirne, *Women and Men in the Fourth Gospel: A Genuine Discipleship of Equals*, 60-61). In the meantime, David Beck correctly states that if there is a difference in belief in John 4:50 and 4:53, it is not inherent in the two occurrences of πιστεύειν but must be inferred from the context (David Beck, *Discipleship Paradigm: Readers and Anonymous Characters in the Fourth Gospel*, 1997, 81). There is no intrinsic difference in meaning in πιστεύειν followed by the dative in John 4:50 and the absolute use of πιστεύειν in John 4:53. Thus, the argument for Moloney and Beirne is stronger.

264   Cornelis Bennema, "Christ, the Spirit and the Knowledge of God: A Study in Johannine Epistemology," 2007, 122-24.

265   Craig Koester, *Symbolism in the Fourth Gospel: Meaning, Mystery, Community*, 2ⁿᵈ ed., 52.

knows now its authority as God's.[266] He believes that Jesus' word is true in John 4:50b and believes in the person of Jesus based on the knowledge of Him in John 5:43b.[267] All this builds anticipation for Jesus' eschatological statement in John 5:24, ὁ τὸν λόγον μου ἀκούων καὶ πιστεύων τῷ πέμψαντί με ἔχει ζωὴν αἰώνιον καὶ εἰς κρίσιν οὐκ ἔρχεται ἀλλὰ μεταβέβηκεν ἐκ τοῦ θανάτου εἰς τὴν ζωήν ("the one who hears my word and believes in whom One sent Me has eternal life and does not come under judgment, but has passed from the death to life"). Thus, Resseguie states the narrator uses the double reference of the royal official's belief in John 4:50 and 4:53 that reflects the official's conversion from an appearance point of view to correct judgment from death to life.[268] His initial belief in Jesus' word leads progressively to an authentic faith that believes in Jesus Himself, the Messiah.

One more observation is needed for the reader or implied reader in regard to the narrator changing the royal official's description. At first the narrator introduces him as βασιλικὸς ("a royal official") in John 4:46 and 4:49. The reader thinks him as a king's official who has power and authority. But after he listened and obeyed Jesus' word, he is referred to as ὁ ἄνθρωπος ("a man")

---

[266]   The narrator uses ὥρᾳ ("hour") three times in John 4:52-53. He points out the authority of Jesus' word that has power to heal the dying son of the royal official. See also James Resseguie, *The Strange Gospel*, 2001, 133.

[267]   Some scholars make the distinction of the royal official's faith between John 4:50 and 4:53 in terms of the different objects of faith (Ernst Haenchen, *John*, 1984, 235 and Marianne Thompson, *The Humanity of Jesus in the Fourth Gospel*, 1988, 72-75).

[268]   James Resseguie, *The Strange Gospel*, 2001, 133.

in John 4:50b and then ὁ πατὴρ ("a father").[269] As a human being, he has personal relationships; as a father, he has a more intimate and passionate relationship with his son. Stibbe correctly states that "it is probable that the word παιδίον is to be taken as a catalyst for Jesus' change of attitude."[270] In particular, the man's son is very sick to the point of death. He therefore lays aside his apparent power and authority, and acts out of his love toward dying son. Once can conclude that this signifies a progressive movement of the royal official toward being more human.[271] Moloney argues that the narrator emphasizes the official's role as father intentionally.[272] As the author's theme of the John's gospel, this portrayal of the intimate father and son relationship may lead the reader or implied reader to imagine God's love for His only begotten Son.[273]

---

[269] As the father is characterized with three different substantives of "the royal official, the man, and the father," so does his son. 1) He is presented four times as ὁ υἱὸς ("the son") of the royal official in John 4:46, 47, 50, and 53. 2) The son is called τὸ παιδίον μου ("my child") in father's second request in John 4:49. 3) The son is called a ὁ παῖς ("the child") by the narrator in John 4:51. The substantive παῖς means "one's own immediate offspring, child as a son or daughter (Frederick Danker, BDAG, 750). Thus, it also develops the internal theme of the status of the royal official emerging since his use of παιδίον in John 4:49, and the narrator's description of him as ὁ ἄνθρωπος ("the man") in John 4:50b and the πατὴρ ("father") in John 4:53. See Gilbert van Belle and Steven Hunt, "The Son of the Royal Official: Incarnating the Life Giving Power of Jesus' Word," 2013, 321.

[270] Mark Stibbe, John, 1993, 72.

[271] Robert Lightfoot, St. John's Gospel, 1956, 129.

[272] Francis Moloney, *The Gospel of John*, 1998, 155. He states that a certain official (v. 46) who trusted unconditionally in the word of Jesus became the man (v. 50) and is finally described as the father (v. 53) whose faith and knowledge generate faith in others.

[273] Moon Hyun Kim, *Healing Hurts: John's Portrayals of the Persons in Healing Episodes*, 2005, 46.

It is likely that the entire household of the royal official heard from him that the time that his son was healed with consistent with the time Jesus had told him ὁ υἱός σου ζῇ ("your son will live"). As such, the entire household, having witnessed the power and the authority of Jesus' word, all believed in Jesus.[274] Conversions of entire households are presented in Acts in the case of Cornelius in Acts 11:14, Lydia in Acts 16:15, the Philippian jailer in Acts 16:31, and Crispus in Acts 18:18.[275] Also influencing the household's faith is the authentic faith now demonstrated by the royal official, of course. It is evident that he becomes a true disciple of Jesus, just as seen in the examples of anonymous minor characters in the Johannine narrative such as the Samaritan woman in the preceding narrative and the man born blind in chap. 9. That's why the reader or implied reader can think of the royal official as a representative model. Brown opines that the royal official is looked upon as representing the Galileans.[276] For Brown, Galileans may mean those who have only superficial faith, and so it could apply all human beings in this world. Thus, the royal official may represent those who may hold the belief in the author's purpose of his gospel in John 20:31. The author challenges the Johannine community to have an authentic faith and become true disciples of Jesus.

5.4 ACT IV: THE EPILOGUE

The narrative of the healing royal official's son closes with a summarizing statement from the narrator. The nature of the royal official's faith must be shown to be authentic from the narrator's

---

[274] Thomas Brodie, *The Gospel According to John*, 1993, 233. He states that the royal official is now ready to listen, and he comes to believe more strongly at each narrative stage as does his whole household.

[275] Donald Carson, *The Gospel According to John*, 1991, 239.

[276] Raymond Brown, *The Gospel According to John I-XII*, 1966, 191.

perspective, and this narrative forms another parallel with the opening miracle at Cana where those who see the sign come to full faith in Him. The attention of the reader or implied reader is thus drawn to the fact that this healing of the royal official's son is the second sign that Jesus performed in Galilee. The phrase of πάλιν δεύτερον σημεῖον ("again the second sign") in John 4:54 recalls ἀρχὴν τῶν σημείων ("the beginning of the signs") in John 2:11. The author composes a frame around these narratives of two miracle signs that extends from John 2:1 to 4:54, the Cana Cycle. The belief of the mother of Jesus in the word of her son precipitates a miracle that reveals His glory and leads others to the faith in Him in John 2:1-12. After the first miracle sign and through the narratives of Jesus' encountering characters such as Nicodemus and Samaritans, the author tells the royal official's faith in Jesus' word and His authority that leads to others.

However, many scholars raise a question of the narrator's remark of πάλιν δεύτερον σημεῖον ("again the second sign") because it does not take any account of the author's mentioning further signs in John 2:23, ὡς δὲ ἦν ἐν τοῖς Ἱεροσολύμοις ἐν τῷ πάσχα ἐν τῇ ἑορτῇ, πολλοὶ ἐπίστευσαν εἰς τὸ ὄνομα αὐτοῦ, θεωροῦντες αὐτοῦ τὰ σημεῖα ἃ ἐποίει ("Now when He was in Jerusalem at the Passover Feast, many believed in His name when they saw the signs that He was doing"). Ashton states, "It certainly looks on the face of it that two independent narratives have been stitched together at this point; and the most of recent proponents of the source theory adopt this solution, arguing that when inserting the second sign recorded in his source the evangelist did not attempt to harmonize the story by removing the word, 'second'. This does not, of course, mean that all that questions are solved."[277] It is possible that the author may have taken the story in substance from a source that also contained the first Cana miracle sign, and inserted it into his

---

[277] John Ashton, *Understanding the Fourth Gospel*, 1991, 95.

narrative with some adapted additions. The author did not wish to omit the verification of the healing as given by the source, since in his concept of the miracle sign the historical reality of the event is as important as its Christological significance. Thus, many scholars refer to the hypothetical document as a σημεῖα source used by the author.[278] Schnackenburg points out the assumption that the author is using a miracle story from a σημεῖα source:[279]

1. Like the story of the marriage feast at Cana, that of healing of the son of the royal official contains hardly any characteristics of Johannine style.

2. The journey noted in John 2:12, which now serves merely to link the miracle of the wine at Cana with the cleansing of the temple at Jerusalem, could have been originally (in the source) the introduction to the second miracle. The new story (Jn. 4:46) linked up with the goal of the journey of John 2:12, since the royal official's son lay sick in Capernaum. He may have been thought of as meeting Jesus on the road, at some distance from Capernaum. If this is correct, it was the author who decided to situate the conversation at the scene of the first miracle, a procedure understandable on several grounds: not so much to enhance the miracle by lengthening the distance, as to make the connection between the two stories clearer. They had come one after the other in the source but had now been separated by the journey to and from Jerusalem.

3. The question arises as to whether the σημεῖα source did not contain further miracles, on which the author has also

---

[278]   Rudolf Schnackenburg, *The Gospel According to John* vol. 1, 1990, 469-71; John Ashton, *Understanding the Fourth Gospel*, 1991, 90-113; J. Louis Martyn, *History and Theology in the Fourth Gospel.* 2nd ed. 1979, 164-68; See also Robert Fortna, *The Fourth Gospel and its Predecessor: From Narrative Source to Present* Gospel,1988

[279]   Rudolf Schnackenburg, *The Gospel According to John* vol. 1, 1990, 470.

drawn. In view of John 6:2 (signs wrought on the sick), it could be assumed that further healing miracles followed the two Galilean miracle stories.

In the meantime, Brodie argues that the term σημεῖα can be understood in a positive way, which is not the basis of genuine faith, but which plays as a confirmation after faith is recognized.[280] Like the first miracle sign at Cana plays the role of a confirming sign for Jesus' disciples who already believed (Jn. 2:1-4, 11), the second miracle sign is not the initial basis for the royal official's faith. Rather it completes or strengthens his faith, and in a way that fits the author's theme, ταῦτα(σημεῖα) δὲ γέγραπται ἵνα πιστεύ[ς]ητε ὅτι ἰησοῦς ἐστιν ὁ Χριστὸς ὁ υἱὸς τοῦ θεοῦ ("but these [signs] are written that you may believe that Jesus is the Christ, the Son of God") (Jn. 20:31a). The signs are not to initiate, but to strengthen belief.[281]

However, the term σημεῖα could also be used negatively when it becomes the basis of a superficial faith as it is used to characterize those in Jerusalem (Jn. 2:23-24). The reader or implied reader can take into consideration the significance of σημεῖα and πίστις, the narrator does not specifically mention the Galileans' reaction to what Jesus has done in Jerusalem (Jn. 4:45). Thus Brodie states, "The effect of Jesus' action on them was not superficial faith, but a welcoming attitude, in other words, not faith, but a predisposition to faith. And it is that same predisposition that is dramatically manifested in the royal official who had heard of Jesus."[282]

---

[280] Thomas Brodie, *The Gospel According to John*, 1993, 231.

[281] Rudolf Schnackenburg, *The Gospel According to John* vol. 1, 1990, 338.

[282] Thomas Brodie, *The Gospel According to John*, 1993, 232. Therefore, he mentions that its ultimate effects is not that of similar but contrasting reactions although Jesus' warning to the Galileans in John 4:48 recalls the reaction of those in Jerusalem in John 2:23.

5.5 THE SIGNIFICANCE

The author has presented the Samaritans as representatives of the world in the preceding narrative as they confess Jesus ὁ σωτὴρ τοῦ κόσμου in John 4:42b. The author is concerned with the problem of authentic and genuine faith against superficial faith in Galilee. He puts people of Jesus' hometown on the same pages as the people of Jerusalem (Jn. 4:45). That said, the author clearly demonstrates that they too could have an authentic and genuine faith if they brought good intention to bear as had the royal officer. They also should leave behind a superficial faith that sees only the miracle signs (Jn. 4:45), and come like the royal official and his household to faith in Jesus' word (Jn. 4:50) and to the authentic and full faith in the Son of God (Jn. 4:53).

The reader and implied reader also can see that power and authority of Jesus to give or restore life as revealed in by the author in the healing narrative of the man born blind in John 9. It is precisely in the flesh of His earthly incarnation that ὁ λόγος reveals the underlying divinity of Christ. His powerful works become crucial witnesses to which belief cannot be refused and at the same time σημεῖα which manifest His δόξα. But if σημεῖα are not grasped in faith, they are nothing but outward phenomena. That's why the narrator expresses σημεῖα καὶ τέρατα in John 4:48.

The reader or implied reader may think the healing narrative of the royal official's son is very similar to the healing miracle of the lame man in John 5 in terms of healing at a distance demonstrating Jesus' power of the restoration of life. Jesus as a life-giver is developed by the author in the revelation discourse found in John 5:19-47. In the light of its discourse Thompson points out, "There are thematic links between the story of the healing of the official' son, with its emphasis on the very hour when Jesus gave life to the little boy (4:50-53), and the discourse about the Son's life-giving authority in 5:19-47 (5:21, 25-26)."²⁸³ Both narratives emphasize Jesus' life-giving word as well as hearing and believing in that word. Thus, the discourse in John 5:19-47 stresses not only the healing of the lame man who had been sick for 38 years, but also on the healing of the royal official son. Hunt quotes from Van Belle, "Both narratives illustrate that Jesus has power over life and death, and that He, who is prophet (4:19, 44), has been sent by the Father (5:23-24; compare 5:36-37), as He is the Son of man (5:27) and the Son of God (5:25; compare υἱὸς in 5:19b, 20, 21, 22, 23b, 26)."²⁸⁴ The contrast between the two miracle signs in John 4 and 5 relates primarily to the response of those most immediately impacted by them. Therefore, the royal official ἐπίστευσεν αὐτὸς καὶ ἡ οἰκία αὐτοῦ ὅλη ("believed himself and his whole household") in John 4:53b, while the healed lame man simply reports Jesus to the Jewish religious leaders who started persecuting Jesus in John 5:15-16. The author wants to show that the miracle signs do not always lead to an authentic faith.

However, Schnackenburg argues and summarizes well that there are reasons which forbid the readers to link the second miracle of Cana with the healing of the lame man in Jerusalem:²⁸⁵

---

²⁸³ Marrianne Thompson, *The Humanity of Jesus in the Fourth Gospel*, 1998, 143.

²⁸⁴ Gilbert van Belle and Steven Hunt, "The Son of the Royal Official: Incarnating the Life Giving Power of Jesus' Word," 2013, 325. See also Marrianne Thompson, *The Humanity of Jesus in the Fourth Gospel*, 1998, 83. She says, "The signs do not merely symbolize the revelation of God's glory; they embody it in visible manifestations. Thus Jesus is revealed to be the Son who gives life (4:46-54; 5:19-29) in perfect harmony with the will of God (5:19-36)."

²⁸⁵ Rudolf Schnackenburg, *The Gospel According to John* vol. 1, 1990, 476-77. He refers to Dodd, *Interpretation* and Feuillet, "La signification theologique." And also to Van den Bussche, "La structure de Jean I-XII."

1. In the narrative sequence the story is connected with the preceding (cf. Jn. 4:43-46), and John 4:54 points back to John 2:11.

2. The miracle in Jerusalem is called a "work", not a "sign" (cf. Jn. 5:17, 19; 7:21), and though this hardly constitutes an objective distinction, it argues against their being associated as parallels in the mind of the evangelist.

3. Further healings in Galilee are mentioned in John. 6:2, and in general it seems that John 6 should follow John 4 (on which see later).

4. The notion of restoring to life gives a connection not merely with John 5, but with all that Jesus says and does. It is a viewpoint which dominates the whole Gospel. Jesus already spoke of His gift of life under the image of water in John 4:11-14.

5. In contrast to John 5, the notions of forgiveness of sin (cf. Jn. 5:14) and of judgment (Jn. 5:22f., 27-30) are missing.

O'Day also says, "In this narrative of the healing of the royal official's son, the fullness of God is also available. The physical healing provides a glimpse of the character of God in Jesus."[286] Jesus' miracle signs are clearly sightings of God that must be seen in the context of Θεὸν οὐδεὶς ἑώρακεν πώποτε ("no one ever seen God') in John 1:18a.

Therefore, the healing narrative of the royal official's son should be considered as the conclusion of the first part of Jesus' ministry, the Cana Cycle, in which the author begins to portray Jesus as the Messiah, the Son of God who gives the eternal life and shows His glory.

---

[286] Gail O'Day, "The Gospel of John: Introduction, Commentary, and Reflection," 1995, 576.

5.6 CONCLUSION

In order for the reader or implied reader to comprehend his theological point of view, the author characterizes the royal official with multiple traits. Bennema explains them well as follows:[287]

1. His willingness to come to Jesus in person and submit to his authority illustrates humility.

2. He is persistent, not deterred by Jesus' rebuke in John 4:48.

3. His inquiry and his deduction about the efficacy of Jesus' word show that he is meticulous and analytical.

4. He is a persuasive witness to his household.

The author portrays the royal official as the object of Jesus' word and action for giving or restoring life. He was the beneficiary of Jesus' second miracle sign. Although he is an anonymous minor character in the Johannine narrative, the reader or implied reader can identify his thoughts and the development of his faith to follow. His development of faith reflects the significance of one's faith response in Jesus, the Messiah, the Son of God. He either knew about Jesus' power and authority to perform miracles because he had heard it from the Galileans who had been there in Jerusalem, or he may have been there for the Passover Feast in John 2:23. So it was with an initial faith that the ruling official approached Jesus to ask and beg to heal his dying son. Then Jesus challenged him to go beyond a belief that is merely based on miraculous signs. He responded to Jesus' challenge by believing in Jesus' word. Finally, his belief was confirmed and deepened to a true knowledge of Jesus. Therefore, the royal

---

[287] Cornelis Bennema, *Encountering Jesus; Character Studies in the Gospel of John*, 2nd ed., 2009, 180.

official represents those who initially believe in Jesus on the basis of His signs and wonders but are able to progress toward more on Jesus' words and knowledge of who He is for an authentic faith. Howard thus states that the healing narrative of the royal official's son is designed to demonstrate the journey of a faith from being superficially and externally based on signs and wonders to authentic faith, and to recognize that those miracle signs characterize Jesus as the life-giver.[288] It is a climax to the series of encountering people with Jesus in the Cana Cycle of John 2-4. Both the Samaritan woman and the royal official reach an authentic and deepened faith in Jesus and testify to others so that they have become the authentic believers. It shows the power of the witness of the authentic faith in Jesus who is the life-giver for those who respond with faith in His words. Thus, the royal official is more than a type of positive faith-response to Jesus. The reader or implied reader can understand the official as a character who reveals some individuality, and in the process learn something of his authentic faith through this character.[289] The author may desire the reader or implied reader would make a connection between Jesus' life giving word and the Word of life (cf. John 1:1).

Moloney concludes that "The reader is now instructed in some of the most important Johannine beliefs. What has been said in the Prologue (Jn. 1:1-18) is being proclaimed and acted out in the story of Jesus (Jn. 1:19-4:54). Above all, the reader now knows the nature of a right relationship with Jesus. The Prologue's teaching on the life-giving power that comes from believing and receiving the incarnated word (Jn. 1:12-13) happens in the story of Jesus as people accept or reject his word. However, much still

---

[288] J. Keir Howard, *Disease and Healing in the New Testament: An Analysis and Interpretation*, 2001, 179.

[289] Peter Judge, "The Royal Official: Not So Officious," 2013, 313

remains to be revealed before the disciples will remember everything that Jesus has said and done and believe in His word and
in the Scriptures (cf. Jn. 2:22)."[290]

---

[290] Francis Moloney, *The Gospel of John*, 1998, 158.

CHAPTER 6

The Lame Man At The Pool Of Bethesda (John 5:1-47)

A FTER THE STORY OF THE SAMARITAN WOMAN and the healing episode of the royal official's son, the author placed Jesus' third miracle sign of the lame man at the pool of Bethesda. This is the first miracle within the section designated as the Festival Cycle in John 5 to John 12. This designation derives from the fact that the sign miracles and their narratives and discourses found in these chapters are set in the context of Jewish festivals.[291] This cycle begins with an unnamed feast (Jn. 5), and then a year of festivals from Passover (Jn. 6) through Tabernacles (Jn. 7-10). While the author reveals Jesus as the Messiah and emphasizes the importance of believing in Him to receive the eternal life in the Cana Cycle (Jn. 2-4), the Festival Cycle develops the theme of increasing opposition by the Jewish religious leaders against Jesus.

The characterization of the lame man at the pool of Bethesda is closely related to the plot of Jesus' healing, dialogues, and discourse in John 5:1-47. Subsequently in order to analyze the characterization of the lame man, Jewish religious leaders, and Jesus on the scene, it is necessary to look into the healing sign, the dialogues, and the long discourse of Jesus toward Jewish religious leaders that resulted from the healing. The characterization of Jewish religious leaders together with the exegesis of Jesus' discourse gives

---

[291] Alan Culpepper, *The Gospel and the Letter of John*, 148-49.

a clue to the characterization of the lame man and Jesus. Jesus' polemic discourse that follows the dialogue with Jewish religious leaders clarifies to the reader or implied reader His identification as Schnackenburg notices that a great sign in John's gospel is followed by a fundamental discourse in which Jesus reveals Himself.[292]

The narrator connects Jesus' healing of the lame man at the pool of Bethesda to His broader witness to Himself as the Son of God the Father, inasmuch as His ability to heal proves the Son has the divine authority and power to give life. As a result of this witness, only the Son should be glorified. Moreover, the Son has the authority to judge at the end of the world. The judgement and Christ's authority to execute it is thus connected with Jesus' witness to God.

The narrative structure of John 5:1-47 looks as follows:

Act I: The Setting (Jn. 5:1-3)

Act II: Jesus and the Lame Man I (Jn. 5:5-9)

Act III: The Lame Man and Jewish Religious Leaders I (Jn. 5:10-13)

Act IV: Jesus and the Lame Man II (Jn. 5:14)

Act V: The Lame Man and Jewish Religious Leaders II (Jn. 5:15)

Act VI: Jesus and Jewish Religious Leaders (Jn. 5:16-18)

Act VII: Jesus' Discourse (Jn. 5:19-47)

Jesus' Response to Charges (Jn. 5:19-30)

Jesus' Calls for Witnesses (Jn. 5:31-47)

---

[292] Rudolf Schnackenburg, *Gospel According to St. John, vol. 2*, 91.

The majority of scholars until now[293] have viewed the lame man as a negative character within the narrative, suggesting the lame man was dull, passive, and did not respond to Jesus with belief, unlike the Samaritan woman in John 4 or the man born blind in John 9. There are, however, some scholars[294] who view the lame man as a positive character, arguing that the lame man was daring in his open opposition to Jewish religious leaders as he defended Jesus and His work in healing him. The positive reading has not won much support or been considered competently. This study will show why the lame man's character is not simple or flat, but rather a little bit ambiguous, even if somewhat negative when compared with the Samaritan woman in John 4 or the man born blind in John 9.

6.1   ACT I: THE SETTING (Jn. 5:1-3)

The story takes a new turn as the narrator introduces a healing episode after the events in Cana in Galilee. In doing so, the author

---

[293]   For example, Alan Culpepper, *Anatomy of the Fourth Gospel*, 1983, 137-38; R. F. Collins, "Representative Figures," 1990, 21-23; R. F. Collins, " From John to the Beloved Disciples," 1995, 364-65; Dorothy Lee, *Symbolic Narratives of the Fourth Gospel*, 1994, 102, 109-110; Herman Ridderbos, *The Gospel according to John*, 1997, 186-90; Craig Koester, *Symbolism in the Fourth Gospel*, 2003, 52-54; Craig Keener, The Gospel of John, 2003, 643-44; Steven Bryan, "Power in the Pool," 2003, 7-22, Andreas Köstenberger, *John*, 2004, 180-83; James Howard, "Significance of Minor Characters," 2006, 71-73; Ramsey Michaels, "The Invalid at the Pool: The Man Who Merely Got Well" in Steven Hunt, *Character Studies in the Fourth Gospel*, 2013, 337-46; Cornelis Bennema, *Encountering Jesus*, 2014, 185-99; Moon Hyun Kim, *Healing Hurts*, 2005, 71-77.

[294]   Jeffrey Staley, "Stumbling in the Dark," 1991, 55-80; John Thomas, "'Stop Sinning Lest Something Worse Come Upon You': The Man at the Pool in John 5," 1995, 3-20; Sjeh van Tilborg, *Imaginative Love in John*, 1993, 218-19; Gail O'Day, *The Gospel of John*, 1995, 578-80; James Resseguie, *Strange Gospel*, 2001, 134-38; David Beck, *Discipleship Paradigm*, 1997, 89-90.

leads the reader or implied reader to the sign that Jesus will perform by Μετὰ ταῦτα ("After these things") as He went up to Jerusalem (Jn. 5:1a). The motivation for the journey was ἑορτὴ τῶν Ἰουδαίων ("a feast of the Jews"). No precise ἑορτὴ is mentioned. It may be one of three major feasts of Passover, Pentecost, or Tabernacle since Jews must go to Jerusalem for those feasts.[295] Borchert thinks that the author intentionally mentioned the feast without its name in order to keep the focus on the miracle and its attendant context of generating a Sabbath controversy, while the unnamed feast itself was not thematically related to the miracle.[296] Carson also states, "If other feasts are named, it is because the context in each case finds Jesus doing or saying something that picks up a theme related to that feast. By implication, if the feast in John 5 is not named, it is probably because the material in John 5 is not intended to be thematically related to it. Then mention of a feast of the Jews in that case becomes little more than an historical marker to explain Jesus' presence in Jerusalem."[297]

The author introduces the theme of a feast of τῶν Ἰουδαίων that will happen in the narrative. It indicates that a change of direction occurs in the narrative. The theme stated in verse 1 extends across the Festival Cycle (Jn. 5-10) that sets the theological agenda. The issue of belief has been the theme of Cana Cycle (Jn. 2-4) and now the narrative turns to the feasts of τῶν Ἰουδαίων as Jesus goes up to Jerusalem. At this point the narrator focuses on the lame man healing as a miracle that took place on the Sabbath (Jn. 5:9). The Sabbath was designed by God for a time of physical and spiritual rest or refreshment. It also serves for Israel as a way to remember their covenantal relationship to God. By Jesus' time in the 1st

---

[295]   Raymond Brown, *The Gospel According to John*, 1966, 206.

[296]   Gerald Borchert, *John 1-11*, 1996, 228.

[297]   Donald Carson, *The Gospel According to John*, 1991, 241.

Century, however, the Sabbath had been perverted. Excessive restrictive rules created by the rabbis governing the observance of the Sabbath caused keep the Sabbath holy to become an overwhelming burden.[298] This is very likely the reason why Jesus chose to heal the lame man on the Sabbath, and also why the author wanted to point out that Jesus the Messiah is Lord over even the Sabbath. Regardless, there had been growing hostility between Jesus and the Jews (Jn. 2:13-22) by the time of the Cana healing. A negative tone is already struck as the narrator mentions a feast celebrated by the Jews in verse 1. Moloney points out that the association of the feast with the Jews reflects the *Sitz im Leben* of the Johannine community, celebrating the saving presence of God in a way that differed from that of the Jews.[299] The debates between Jesus and the Jewish religious leaders in the Festival Cycle (Jn. 5-10) will intensify.

The narrator suspends Jesus' action in verses 2 through 3 to provide background. The precise location of the lame man's healing is given. The spatial setting is specified as ἐπὶ τῇ προβατικῇ κολυμβήθρα ("by the Sheep Gate a pool") in Jerusalem, called βηθζαθά in the language of the Jews, the place with πέντε στοὰς ("five colonnades"). At that time τῇ προβατικῇ was a small opening in the north wall of the temple as the sheep were washed in the pool before being taken to the sanctuary. The pool of βηθζαθά was also the place where invalids lay in hopes of being healed. Βηθζαθά may mean "house of mercy"[300] which would be adequate, given the invalids lying there in hope of miraculous healing. Thus, a large

---

[298]   A major section of the Mishnah is devoted to rules for the Sabbath (*The Mishnah*, trans. Jacob Neusner [New Haven, CT: Yale University Press, 1988]).

[299]   Francis Moloney, *The Gospel of John*, 1998, 167.

[300]   J. C. Laney, *John*, 1992, 106.

number of invalids used to κατέκειτο[301] at the pool of Bethesda. The reader or implied reader may assume that all the characters involved in the lame man healing were part of the Jewish community.[302] Also, the narrator reflects its image of a suffering sheep of Jewish community as the invalids among πέντε στοὰς are described as τυφλῶν ("blind"), χωλῶν ("lame"), and ξηρῶν ("paralyzed"). However, since the alleged healing powers of the pool were characteristics of pagan cults, the Jewish religious leaders almost certainly did not approve of such superstition.[303]

6.2   ACT II: JESUS AND THE LAME MAN I (Jn. 5:5-9)

Köstenberger comments, "Healers were much sought after in the ancient world, both in Judaism and in Greco-Roman society. Rabbinic literature speaks of one Hanina ben Dosa, who was recognized for his efficacious prayers on behalf of the sick."[304] With a socio-cultural context of Jewish feast and a traditional healing site Jesus sees a man who has been sick for thirty-eight years. Although his sickness is not specified, it seems that he is paralyzed or lame as John 5:8-9 indicates. The length of the lame man's plight indicates the hopelessness of his situation. Since his sickness has kept him from participating in the socio-cultural life, the lame man has been alienated and lonely.

---

[301]   Donald Carson, *The Gospel According to John*, 1991, 242; the imperfect tense indicates that this was customary.

[302]   D. M. Smith, *John* 2nd ed., 1999, 39. Brodie also mentions the background of the lame man healing episode is predominantly Judean because of terms like Jerusalem, Hebrew, and Sabbath (Brodie, *The Gospel according to John*, 1993, 236.

[303]   Andreas Köstenberger, *John*, 2004, 179.

[304]   Ibid. refers to notes on Hanina ben Dosa under commentary at 4:49-50.

However, since thirty-eight years is the length of the time Israel spent in the desert at Kadesh (cf. Deut. 1:45-46; 2:14), Schnackenberg sees the lame man as a symbol of the unbelieving Jewish people.[305] That the people at the pool are physically invalid people implies that they are spiritually dead. But it may not need to be read the character of lame man as a symbol that the narrator makes a theological point of encountering him with Jesus. Malina and Rohrbaugh have read the lame man as a representative of the socioeconomically deprived, not spiritually dead.[306] Stibbe also argues for a representative character by pointing to τὸν κράβαττόν ("the mat"), which is the type of bedding used by the poor.[307] But, the narrator simply tells the truth to emphasize the man's predicament with his inability to respond to Jesus with faith. Collins argues that the lame man's representative role can be understood only when he is compared with his counterpart, the man born blind in John 9.[308]

The narrator tells us that Jesus γνοὺς ὅτι πολὺν ἤδη χρόνον ἔχει ("knew that he had been already there a long time") in John 5:6 just like the encounters with the Samaritan woman (Jn. 4:18). Despite His divine knowledge of the lame man's condition Jesus asks him, θέλεις ὑγιὴς γενέσθαι; ("Do you want to be well?") The reader or implied reader should notice the significance of the term θέλεις. Θέλω connotes the attitude of a "strong and determined will," not just a wish or desire. Thus, it implies that Jesus' request demands his determined will. Meantime, Jesus' offer seems unnecessary in light of his obvious need. But Jesus may clarify what the

---

[305] Rudolf Schnackenburg, *The Gospel According to St. John vol.2*, 1980, 95.

[306] Bruce Malina and Richard Rohrbaugh, *Social-Science Commentary on the Gospel of John*, 1998, 111.

[307] Marj Stibbe, *John Reading*, 1993, 75.

[308] R. F. Collins, "Representative Figures in the Fourth Gospel," 1976, 42.

lame man really wants. Thomas suggests that ὑγιὴς is an example of double entendre, evoking misunderstanding – the lame man understands it as a question whether he wants to be healed by the pool, whereas Jesus intends to know whether the man wants to be ὑγιὴς.[309] The lame man's response, Κύριε, ἄνθρωπον οὐκ ἔχω ἵνα ὅταν ταραχθῇ τὸ ὕδωρ βάλῃ με εἰς τὴν κολυμβήθραν ("Sir, I have no one to put me into the pool when the water has been stirred up") in John 5:7 shows that he is unaware of who Jesus is. He does not understand how Jesus could help him ὑγιὴς. He is seeking just another ἄνθρωπον to carry and put him in the pool so that he might be made well. The lame man's perspective on the obstacle to his cure is that there is no one who carries him to the pool when the water was stirred. The stirring of the water could have been created by random springs. Superstition attributed the stirring of the water to an angel of the Lord who could come down from time to time (cf. the gloss in Jn. 5:3b-4 found in some later MSS).[310] Thus, Bryan points out that the lame man's understanding of God as one who periodically infuses the pool with impersonal power, which is accessed in a purely arbitrary way.[311] His complaint that there is no one who can help him to get into the pond when it is stirred up is ironic since the reader or implied reader knows that the real healing water can be found in Jesus Himself based on His encounter with the Samaritan woman in John 4.[312]

Ignoring the pool and its superstitious healing power, Jesus commands him, ἔγειρε ἆρον τὸν κράβαττόν σου καὶ περιπάτει

---

[309]   John Thomas, "Stop Sinning Lest Something Worse Come Upon You,"1995, 10.

[310]   The absence of verses 3b-4 from the earliest and best witnesses has led many scholars to omit them as not original. See Bruce Metzger, *A Textual Commentary of the Greek New Testament*, 2nd ed., 1994, 179.

[311]   Steven Bryan, "Power in the Pool," 2003, 11 & 14.

[312]   Alan Culpepper, *The Gospel and the Letters of John*, 138.

("Arise, take up your mat, and walk") in John 5:8. Jesus grants his wish unreservedly with no requirement or any mention of "faith" or "believing."[313] The reader or implied reader could be sure that the response of the lame man is an immediate obedience to Jesus' command, but this is only possible because the narrator indicates that εὐθέως ἐγένετο ὑγιὴς ὁ ἄνθρωπος ("immediately the man became well") in John 5:9 between the command and the response. It seems that the lame man is progressing from his initial response to Jesus in John 5:7, but no mention of faith on the part of the lame man and a warning from the author comes in ἦν δὲ σάββατον ἐν ἐκείνῃ τῇ ἡμέρᾳ ("now it was on that day") John 5:9b. Interestingly the narrator does not mention any response of the lame man to Jesus. The healed lame man just walked away (Jn. 5:9a). The imperative verves, ἔγειρε, ἆρον and περιπάτει suggest that the lame man needs to experience God's healing power and he did. Moloney suggests, "There are some preliminary indications in this man's story that he may be on journey to true faith. Although he began without understanding who Jesus was and what He could offer, he has responded unquestioningly to the word of Jesus."[314] But, he may or could not be on the journey to true faith, while having afraid to ex-communicate with Jewish people like before the healing happens. Interestingly, Staley views Jesus' command to the lame man to work on the Sabbath negatively, while the lame man proves to be a daring and risk-taking individual as he accepted Jesus' Sabbath

---

313 Michaels notices this in contrast to the story of the paralytic (Mk. 2:5) in which Jesus saw the "faith" of those who brought him through the roof, and the story of the royal official's son in Capernaum, where the father first believed the word Jesus said to him (Jn. 4:50), and later "believed, he and his whole family" (Jn. 4:53). See Ramsey Michaels, "The Invalid at the Pool: The Man Who Merely Got Well," 2013, 339.

314 Francis Moloney, *Signs and Shadows: Reading John 5-12*, 1996, 5.

rule breaking command.³¹⁵ However, it is unnecessary to read Jesus' command negatively when the reader or implied reader realizes that Jesus intentionally works on the Sabbath to show that He is equal with God the Father in the light of the entire text.³¹⁶ It was Jesus who made the initial approach to the lame man. Jesus offered him healing and commanded him to do certain actions. The lame man is able to act in response to these commands because Jesus has performed a miracle without the stirring water. The healing miracle performed on the lame man and his subsequent obedience come from the initiative of the sovereign Lord, Jesus. Jesus acts with the divine knowledge and power of the Creator, God. Like the creation of the world Jesus commanded three words to restore him (cf. Jn. 1:1-2).

6.3 ACT III: THE LAME MAN AND JEWISH RELIGIOUS LEADERS I (Jn. 5:10-13)

The Jewish religious leaders appear on the scene and accuse the lame man of breaking a Sabbath law as he carries his mat. The lame man does not accept responsibility for this unlawful work on Sabbath. He excuses himself saying that he only did what the healer, ὁ ποιήσας με ὑγιῆ ἐκεῖνός μοι εἶπεν, ἆρον τὸν κράβαττόν σου καὶ περιπάτει ("The man who made me well, he said to me, 'Take up your mat and walk'") (Jn. 5:11). It is not an exact quotation of Jesus' command in John 5:8, ἔγειρε ἆρον τὸν κράβαττόν σου καὶ περιπάτει ("Arise, take your mat and walk"). He missed ἔγειρε. Howard-Brook points out that while ἆρον and περιπάτει

---

³¹⁵ Jeffrey Staley, "Stumbling in the Dark," 1991, 60.

³¹⁶ Cornelis Bennema, *Encountering Jesus: Character Studies in the Gospel of John*, 2014, 189.

imply Sabbath violation, the ἔγειρε insinuate rebirth or resurrec-tion.[317] Given the resurrection connotation of the term ἔγειρε, the reader or implied reader may find the significance of the lame man's omission of this word in this narrative and reconsider the characterization of the healed lame man.[318]

Despite having healed his 38-years-old sickness all at once, this man has not moved beyond his initial understanding of Jesus in John 5:7. The Jewish religious leaders want to know τίς ἐστιν ὁ ἄνθρωπος ("Who is the man that said to you") (Jn. 5:12) but the narrator comments that ὁ δὲ ἰαθεὶς οὐκ ᾔδει τίς ἐστιν ("Now the man who had been healed did not know who it is") in John 5:13. They are willing to accept the man's excuse of breaking the Sabbath law, evidently in the hope that it will lead them to the real target of their investigation. They seem to have someone in mind whom they are looking for, possibly for other reasons. Their anger at the Sabbath healing was not the first time the religious leaders found themselves directly opposed to Jesus' actions, having encoun-tered Him once before when they challenged His act of driving the money changers from the temple (Jn. 2:18-20).

It is worth to notice that the narrator describes the lame man as ὁ δὲ ἰαθεὶς ("now the man who had been healed"). Moreover, since Jesus ἐξένευσεν ὄχλου ὄντος ἐν τῷ τόπῳ ("moved away as there was a crowd in the place"), the Jewish religious leaders cannot pursue Jesus any further (Jn. 5:13). The identity of ὄχλου and into whom Jesus disappeared is not clear, but it seems that Jesus has disappeared from the Jewish religious leaders. In summation, it is obvious this healed man's response is quite different from the man born blind healed in John 9. Basically, he blames Jesus, ὁ ποιήσας με ὑγιῆ ("who made me well").

---

[317] Wes Howard-Brook, *Becoming Children of God*, 2001, 125.

[318] Ibid.

The emergent controversy between Jesus and Jewish religious leaders centered on proper Sabbath observance. Their
leaders' objection is not against the healing itself, but rather that
the law forbade the man from carrying his mat on the Sabbath.[319]
Köstenberger in turn argues that the lame man did not actually
break any biblical Sabbath regulations, although Jewish religious
leaders may have thought of passages such as Exodus 31:12-17,
Jeremiah 17:21-27, and Nehemiah 13:15-19.[320]

In the current context of the narrative, this controversy leads
to Jesus' polemic discourse in John 5:19-47 regarding His unique
relationship with God the Father. Malina and Rohrbaugh explore
the comparison and contrast the lame man's healing with the man
born blind's healing in John 9, which also takes place on a Sabbath.[321]

Staley argues that the lame man was indeed standing up to the
Jewish religious leaders, comparing their authority with the healer,
and he then would say that ὁ ποιήσας με ὑγιῆ who also has the
power to abrogate Sabbath law.[322] Thomas also regards the lame
man's response positively, where he appears to set the authority
of ὁ ποιήσας με ὑγιῆ and therefore the healer has power over the
Sabbath law.[323] That said, it seems that Staley and Thomas are too
charitable in their characterization of the lame man's character

---

[319] Raymond Brown, *The Gospel According to John*, 1966, 208.

[320] Andreas Köstenberger, *John*, 2004, 181. The Mishnah mentions for instance
that "the generative categories of acts of labor prohibited on the Sabbath are
forty less one: he who transports an object from one domain to another" (*m.
Shabbat* 7:2). However, there was an exception to carry a bed with a person
lying on it (*m. Shabbat* 10:5).

[321] Bruce Malina and Richard Rohrbaugh, *Social-Science Commentary on the
Gospel of John*, 1998, 109.

[322] Jeffrey Staley, "Stumbling in the Dark," 1991, 61-62.

[323] John Thomas, "Stop Sinning Lest Something Worse Come Upon You," 1995,
13.

in contrast to the context of the narrative. What's important to consider here is that the lame man is ignorant of Jesus' identity because Jesus ἐξένευσεν ὄχλου ὄντος ἐν τῷ τόπῳ (Jn. 5:13). This could be read as suggesting the lame man had an opportunity to ask Jesus' identification if perhaps, He were still there. An alternative reading is to see the healed man as so happy to be healthy finally that he fails to identify the healer.[324] For him being healthy is probably more important than knowing the healer. In any case, the lame man's response is not a positive confession, leaving him failing as a witness unlike the Samaritan woman in John 4 and the man born blind in John 9. Kim states that the lame man's characterization remains ambiguous at this point of the narrative because the lame man speaks of Jesus in two ways after the healing: first, as a healer, and second, as the one who initiates the command that causes him to break the Sabbath law.[325]

6.4 ACTS IV: JESUS AND THE LAME MAN II (Jn. 5:14)

The narrator opens the new scene starting with μετὰ ταῦτα in John 5:14, separating the encounter between the lame man and the Jewish religious leaders. It is also the scene that does not mention the Sabbath. Again, Jesus takes the initiative and finds the healed lame man ἐν τῷ ἱερῷ ("in the temple"). The exact narrative space in the temple is not specified, nor is the amount of time that has passed. The institution of the Sabbath is set aside for a moment and replaced by the institution of the temple.

Jesus recalls the healing miracle, Ἴδε ὑγιὴς γέγονας ("Behold, you have become well") (Jn. 5:14b). Its perfect verb tense indicates the healed lame man's continual state of well-being, perhaps

---

[324] Moon Hyun Kim, *Healing Hurts*, 2005, 67.

[325] Ibid., 64.

comparing his healing to other healings at the pool of Bethesda that proved less than permanent.[326] Jesus commands the healed lame man, μηκέτι ἁμάρτανε ("sin no more"). Sin will lead to the healed man being worse off than he was in his earlier thirty-eight years sickness condition. The reader or implied reader may expect that "ἴδε ὑγιὴς γέγονας" is equivalent to "Behold, your sins are forgiven."[327] Thus, Jesus moves the conversation to a spiritual level by introducing the concept of sin. The syntax of Jesus' command emphasizes urgency and implies that the healed man should abstain from a pattern of sin.[328] Although Jesus did not attribute every instance of physical suffering to sin, He acknowledged that sin may well lead to all kinds of sufferings. It may be this case that the author implies the correlation between sin and judgment by mentioning χεῖρόν σοί τι γένηται ("worse may happen to you").[329]

The narrator demonstrates that Jesus transcends the theological and legal demands of the Sabbath law. The rabbis associated sin with God's punishment through suffering and death, but in the name of God Jesus speaks in the temple, breaking the Sabbath law link between the physical suffering and God's punishment. The lame man's physical problems have been overcome, but Jesus' warning indicates that more sufferings will be encountered unless the problem of sin is resolved. Sin will lead to a situation that is more damaging than physical sickness, most probably of course a reference not to a worse physical condition but rather to eternal

---

[326] Leon Morris, *The Gospel According to John*, 1995, 272.

[327] Ramsey Michaels, "The Invalid at the Pool: The Man Who Merely Got Well," 2013, 342.

[328] See Donald Carson, *The Gospel According to John*, 1991, 246; Leon Morris, *The Gospel According to John*, 1995, 272; Herman Ridderbos, *The Gospel according to John*, 1997; 189. They are against a simplistic generalization of negated present imperative although the author intends it to stop doing sin.

[329] Gerald Borchert, *John 1-11*, 1996, 235.

punishment for sin as considering the context of the narrative (cf. 5:22-30).[330] Interestingly, Michaels explores that the notion of forgiveness of sin is remarkably rare throughout most of John's gospel, saying "The Samaritan woman, with her five husbands and a partner not her husband (Jn. 4:18), is arguably a sinner, yet Jesus never explicitly identifies her as such, or condemns her, or for that matter, forgives her. The Pharisees charge the man born blind with being born altogether in sins (Jn. 9:34), but according to Jesus, neither this man sinned or his parents."[331] In Johannine narrative, sin is defined narrowly as unbelief or rejection of the Son whom God the Father sent. That's why Jesus warns μηκέτι ἁμάρτανε ("sin no more") as the author identifies him as a sinner.

Bennema also interprets sin as unbelief since the author views sin primarily as unbelief (Jn. 16:9; cf. 8:24).[332] Jesus is thus warning the healed lame man that he faces the more urgent issue of sin and judgment. There will be condemnation at the last judgment of Jesus.

From this scene of the lame man's second encounter with Jesus, the reader or implied reader becomes aware that the healed lame

---

[330] Howard-Brook argues that Jesus' warning can be related to the warning in John 3:36, "ὁ δὲ ἀπειθῶν τῷ υἱῷ οὐκ ὄψεται ζωήν, ἀλλ᾽ ἡ ὀργὴ τοῦ θεοῦ μένει ἐπ᾽ αὐτόν." (Wes Howard-Brook, *Becoming Children of God*, 2001, 126).

[331] Ramsey Michaels, "The Invalid at the Pool: The Man Who Merely Got Well," 2013, 342.

[332] Cornelis Bennema, *Encountering Jesus: Character Studies in the Gospel of John*, 2014, 192-93. Bennema argues against the positive reading of the lame man such as that offered by Thomas or Staley whose interpretation of v. 14 is not satisfying because they assume the lame man's sin is forgiven when he was healed. Interestingly, Schnackenburg also assumes that the lame man's healing incudes forgiveness of his sin (Schnackenburg, *The Gospel according to St. John*, vol. 2, 97). But the context of entire narrative tells that he has not been shown faith in Jesus at all, and how he can be forgiven without it. Culpepper points out that Jesus' warning emphasizes that the lame man is still a sinner (Culpepper, *Anatomy of the Fourth Gospel*, 1993, 204).

man is not spiritually alive. He does not have faith in Jesus, the Son of God who gives the eternal life, although he has yet another encounter with Jesus after the healing. In stark contrast to the man born blind in John 9, the lame man takes no effort to even find out the name of the healer, does not defend Jesus but instead blames Him for breaking the Sabbath law, and eventually even turns Him in to the Jewish religious leaders.[333]

The characters in the narrative will continue to debate questions regarding the proper observances of the Sabbath, but such issues should be exceeded by Jesus' words to the healed lame man in the temple.

6.5   ACTS V: THE LAME MAN AND JEWISH RELIGIOUS LEADERS II (Jn. 5:15)

As ἀπῆλθεν ὁ ἄνθρωπος ("the man went away") to answer the question asked by the Jewish religious leaders in John 5:12, the healed lame man and Jesus were separated. There is no sign of faith or of following in ἀπῆλθεν ὁ ἄνθρωπος. Rather he went to report the name of the healer, Jesus to the Jewish leaders (Jn. 5:15b). There is no reason why he had to do this. The lame man was in the clear so far as the charge of Sabbath breaking was concerned. Lincoln points out that "at no stage of the story has the narrator been interested in the man's motivations in relation to Jesus, and that does not change here. The main purpose of the narrator's statement is to strengthen the connection between the miracle story and a direct confrontation between Jesus and the Jews."[334]

The reader is told that the healed lame man's only response to Jesus' warning (Jn. 5:14b) was to report Him to them. His most

---

[333]   Sandra Schneiders, *Written That You May Believe*, 2003, 153.

[334]   Andrew Lincoln, *The Gospel According to John*, 2005, 196.

recent encounter with Jesus in the temple, where He revealed Himself who transcends the Sabbath law (Jn. 5:14), has made no impact on him. This man Jesus has just healed the lame man from a disease that left him paralyzed for 38 years. Yet there is no expression of gratitude from the healed man toward Jesus in the entire narrative, a stark contrast with the healed man born blind in John 9 who defends Jesus and pay the price by being excommunicated from the synagogue.[335] That is why so many scholars say that the lame man is a representative of unbelief.[336]

Still other scholars, however, suggest that the healed lame man is characterized as a positive witness for Jesus since he acknowledges Jesus' identity to the Jewish religious leaders. According to Staley, the lame man who has been characterized negatively in the first part of the narrative in John 5:1-8 becomes a positive character in the second part in John 5:9-15 because he took the brave, risk-taking actions of carrying his mat in contravention of the Sabbath law and then going to tell the Jewish religious leaders in person.[337] For Staley, the lame man's report to the Jewish religious leaders shows a character who serves in his own way as a

---

[335]   Herman Ridderbos, *The Gospel according to John*, 1997, 190.

[336]   Against Beck who argues that anonymity necessarily equals ideal function and positive characterization (David Beck, "The Narrative Functions of Anonymity in the Fourth Gospel Characterization, 1997, 86-90), Moloney argues that anonymous characters in the Fourth Gospel draw the reader into identification with the character. However, the reader of the Fourth Gospel hardly identifies with a man who is in league with 'the Jews' in John 5:15 (Francis Moloney, *The Gospel of John*, 1998, 173).

[337]   Jeffrey Staley, "Stumbling in the Dark," 1991, 60.

147

faithful witness to a sign performed.[338] But, the interpretations of Staley's or positive readers of the lame man are not convincing. They read the lame man's character too generously by making too many favorable assumptions about the narrator's story about him. That is why so many scholars read the lame man's character negatively, describing him as "dull and passive,"[339] "dimwitted and ungrateful,"[340] or even "a super ingrate and crassly malicious."[341] His action to go to the Jewish leaders reporting is seen as a kind of betrayal of his healer. The lame man should have known from his previous conversation with the Jewish leaders in John 5:10-12 that they want to charge Jesus with breaking the Sabbath law and that his report would cause trouble for the healer. Perhaps he had a selfish motivation of wanting to join the Jewish community since he is healthy now. Kim states that John's syntax and vocabulary underscores the lame man's active movement or involvement to commit an act of betrayal like Judas.[342] As a result, the Jewish religious leaders start to persecute Jesus for ταῦτα ἐποίει ἐν σαββάτῳ ("He was doing these things on the Sabbath") (Jn. 5:16). Thus, it is very clear that the lame man's character is negative.

---

[338] Ibid., 63. Resseguile also argues that the lame man's carrying the mat as a demonstration of health and activity, and he emphasizes the significance of the verb ἀνήγγειλεν used since the term means positive connotation in John 4:25; 16:13, 14, and 15 (James Resseguie, *The Strange Gospel*, 2001, 134-38). However, he and other positive readers make too much of the term ἀνήγγειλεν. The term may simply denote "to announce or inform or report," and the context of the entire narrative determines whether the term has positive or negative connotation.

[339] Donald Carson, *The Gospel According to John*, 1991, 246.

[340] Robert Kysar, *John's Story of Jesus*, 1984, 34.

[341] Ernst Haenchen, *John*, 1984, 247.

[342] Moon Hyun Kim, *Healing Hurts*, 2005, 74.

6.6 ACTS VI: JESUS AND THE JEWISH RELIGIOUS LEADERS (Jn. 5:16-18)

The narrator tells that the healed lame man's evidence against Jesus' being the one who broke the Sabbath law is the reason for the Jewish religious leaders indicting a legal process and persecuting Him (ἐδίωκον οἱ ἰουδαῖοι τὸν ἰησοῦν). The verb δίωκω means both "to persecute" and "to bring a charge against or prosecute"[343] The imperfect form ἐδίωκον indicates that their persecution of Jesus has been constant. From this narrative point onward there is a trial in process. Jesus defends Himself by revealing the truth. Their Sabbatical observance lies behind the prosecuting process.

Like a defense lawyer's initial appeal summary before the jury in a court, Jesus speaks to them, ὁ πατήρ μου ἕως ἄρτι ἐργάζεται, κἀγὼ ἐργάζομαι ("My Father is working until now, and I am working") (Jn. 5:17b). The Jewish religious leaders think that God could not rest on the Sabbath. Although Genesis said, "On the seventh day God finished his work that he had done, and he rested on the seventh day from all his work that he had done. So God blessed the seventh day and made it holy, because on it God rested from all his work that he had done in creation" (Gen. 2:2-3), God could not cease to work even on the Sabbath. If He did the history of the world come to an end. Thus, Jesus' claiming to be working on the Sabbath is blasphemy to them. But for the reader or implied reader who believes that Jesus is ὁ λόγος ἦν πρὸς τὸν θεόν, καὶ θεὸς ἦν ὁ λόγος ("the Word was with God, and the Word was God") (Jn. 1:1b) and ὁ λόγος σὰρξ ἐγένετο ("the Word became flesh") (Jn. 1:14a), it is the logical consequence.

Jesus claims that His Father works on the Sabbath ἕως ἄρτι ("until now"), and that He is also still working ἕως ἄρτι (Jn. 5:17). The big issue is one of relationship. His claim depends upon His

---

[343] Liddell, Scott, and Jones, A Greek-English Lexicon, 440.

relationship with God, whom He calls πατήρ μου. Morris points out that it would have been highly unusual for a Jew of that day to address God as "my Father" without some qualifying phrase such as "in heaven" in order to avoid excessive familiarity.[344] Additionally, the designation of "my Father" for Jehovah God was extremely rare in the Old Testament, only in Jeremiah 3:4, 19 and Psalms 89:26. But, Jesus called God πατήρ μου ("My Father"), claiming equality with God. That's why the Jewish leaders bring charges against Jesus trying to sentence Him to death in John 5:18. The Jewish religious leaders read Jesus' claim correctly and the charges are:

1. He has broken the Sabbath law

2. He called God His Father, making Himself equal to God by claiming that He works on the Sabbath

The Jewish religious leaders expressed a true understanding of Jesus and His claims that He cannot be controlled by Sabbath law and that God is His Father, giving Him equality with God. However, they are not able to see beyond more immediate issue surrounding Sabbath keeping traditions.

Once the charges are made, Jesus does not deny them. Instead, He boldly defends Himself and His action. A trial has been set in motion in which the prosecutors and the defendant have different answers to the same question. The defendant, Jesus, sees the Sabbath keeping traditions on the basis of His relationship with the God of Israel, His Father; the prosecutors, the Jewish religious leaders, judge that Jesus has broken the Sabbath law and deserves to die. Schnackenburg describes these developments as Jesus acting with the authority of God coming into conflict with

---

[344]   Leon Morris, *The Lord from Heaven*, 1974, 31-35.

the human keepers and advocates of God's law.[345] In the meantime, the author and his readers are aware that Jesus is ὁ λόγος ἦν πρὸς τὸν θεόν, καὶ θεὸς ἦν ὁ λόγος ("the Word was with God and the Word was God") (Jn. 1:1b) and ὁ λόγος σὰρξ ἐγένετο καὶ ἐσκήνωσεν ἐν ἡμῖν, καὶ ἐθεασάμεθα τὴν δόξαν αὐτοῦ, δόξαν ὡς μονογενοῦς παρὰ πατρός ("the Word became flesh and dwelt among us, and we have seen His glory, glory as of the only Son from the Father") (Jn. 1:14), and thus He is the source and Lord of the Sabbath (cf. Matt. 12:8). Therefore, the relationship of Jesus to God the Father and its implied Christology and doxology are crucial to John's narrative and conclusive of the following discourse as Jesus defends His case in John 5:19-30 and calls His witnesses in John 5:31-47. While the prosecutors, Jewish religious leaders, are present, Jesus speaks alone.

6.7   ACTS VII: JESUS DISCOURSE (Jn. 5:19-47)

The narrator tells only Jesus' words throughout the discourse of John 5:19-47. Jesus speaks in his own defense through a discourse with two parts:[346]

1.   Response to Jewish religious leaders' charges (Jn. 5:19-30)

2.   Jesus' calls for witnesses (Jn. 5:31-47)

---

[345]   Rudolf Schnackenburg, *The Gospel According to St. John*, vol. 2, 97.

[346]   Neyrey interestingly suggests that Jesus responds to the charges against Him in the order that He responds first to the blasphemer charge in John 5:19-29, and then to the charge of breaking the Sabbath law in John 5:30-47 (Jerome Neyrey, *An Ideology of Revolt*, 1988, 18). He doesn't include 5:30 for the blasphemy charge because he argues that although Jesus' defense in 5:30 simply denies the charge with no explanation, that is not the case of 5:19-29. But most scholars do not agree with this. Molony sees that the themes of Jesus' first defense are life and judgment and thus 5:30 should be included in the first defense (Moloney, *The Gospel of John*, 1998, 177).

The foundation of Jesus' polemic discourse is the eschatological judgment activities by God on the Sabbath that Jesus describes in the passage. Throughout, Jesus makes clear that the work He does as God the Father has entrusted Him is based on Jesus' relationship with God the Father. The reader or implied reader can see throughout Jesus' discourse both Jesus' total dependence on God the Father as well as the unity of the Father and Son depicted in John 5:19-30.[347] The introduction of Jesus' witnesses in John 5:31, ἐὰν ἐγὼ μαρτυρῶ περὶ ἐμαυτοῦ ("If I bear witness Myself") establishes a further rhetorical question that Jesus will pursue up to John 5:47.

6.7.1 Jesus' response to charges (Jn. 5:19-30)

The narrator explains Jesus' relationship with God the Father with the themes of life and the eschatological judgment by the Son's authority. As Moloney asserts, "The Sabbath question continues to be central, even though the literary form shifts from a narrative built on action and dialogue (vv. 5-18) to a monologue (vv. 19-30)."[348]

In John 5:19 Jesus opens his defense with a serious double ἀμὴν, responding directly to the charge by the Jewish religious leaders for Jesus' Sabbath law breaking (Jn. 5:18) as Jesus identifies Himself as the Son to God the Father.[349] Jesus tells how God's revelation

---

[347] What is said in v. 19 οὐ δύναται ὁ υἱὸς ποιεῖν ἀφ᾽ ἑαυτοῦ οὐδὲν is restated in v. 30 οὐ δύναμαι ἐγὼ ποιεῖν ἀπ᾽ ἐμαυτοῦ οὐδέν. The third person in v. 19 is restated in the first person in v. 30.

[348] Francis Moloney, *The Gospel of John*, 1998, 177.

[349] Carson states that breaking the Sabbath was a serious offense, but making oneself equal to God was challenging the fundamental distinction between holy, infinite God and finite, fallen human beings (Donald Carson, *The Gospel According to John*, 1991, 249).

functions in the life of the Son and for the benefit of others (Jn. 5:20). Everything the Son does flows from God the Father. The Son is totally depending on the Father in all that He does so that the Son might have the privilege of ultimate intimacy with the Father. The Son is at once with God the Father eternally as well as subordinate to Him. The negative structure of the sentence, οὐ δύναται ὁ υἱὸς ποιεῖν ἀφ᾽ ἑαυτοῦ οὐδὲν ("the Son can do nothing by Himself") (Jn. 5:19a) stresses οὐ … οὐδὲν like that double negative means the positive. The Son sees all that God the Father does, and thus He can do exactly what the Father has done. That is why Jesus claims κἀγὼ ἐργάζομαι ("I am working") as ὁ πατήρ μου ἕως ἄρτι ἐργάζεται ("My Father is working until now") in John 5:17b. Jesus also points out that something new is happening: ἃ γὰρ ἂν ἐκεῖνος ποιῇ, ταῦτα καὶ ὁ υἱὸς ὁμοίως ποιεῖ ("for whatever the Father does, and that the Son does likewise") in John 5:19b. Jesus implies that it is the Father who led the Son to the lame man and told Him to heal.[350]

Since the relationship of God the Father and the Son is love, there is no secret between them (Jn. 5:20a). The Father's love for the Son expresses itself in His free self-disclosure, and the Son's love for the Father expresses itself in His submission to the Father's will (cf. Jn. 5:30), including death on the cross.[351] The affirmation of the Father πάντα δείκνυσιν αὐτῷ ἃ αὐτὸς ποιεῖ ("shows Him all things He Himself does") turns to promise as Jesus tells the Jewish religious leaders that greater works will be shown to the Son ἵνα ὑμεῖς θαυμάζητε ("so that you may marvel") (Jn. 5:20b). The reader or implied reader can be drawn into the unique relationship between the Son and the Father, and moreover can also marvel at the Son' greater works that might be part of a revelation

---

[350] Rudolf Schnackenburg, *The Gospel According to St. John*, vol. 2, 103.

[351] Donald Carson, *The Gospel According to John*, 1991, 251.

of God the Father which reach beyond their Sabbath law. The μείζονα τούτων δείξει αὐτῷ ἔργα ("greater works than these He will show Him") in context refers to giving life and judging.[352] Jesus tells them what these greater works are in the rest of Jesus defense through John 5:21-30.

Only God of Israel can raise the dead and give life (cf. Deut. 32:39; 1 Sam. 2:6; 2 Kg. 5:7; Isa. 25:8). This lies behind Jesus' statement of ὁ πατὴρ ἐγείρει τοὺς νεκροὺς καὶ ζῳοποιεῖ ("the Father raises the dead and gives life") (Jn. 5:21a), but οὕτως καὶ ὁ υἱὸς οὓς θέλει ζῳοποιεῖ ("thus the Son also gives life to whom He will") (Jn. 5:21b). The reader or implied reader can link Jesus' statement to the lame man's healing miracle as Jesus commanded him, "ἔγειρε" in John 5:8. Only God of the Sabbath is the master of life and death, so this power of ἔγειρε from death has been given to the Son because of the existing relationship between God the Father and the Son. Jesus the Son exercises the given authority in ζῳοποιεῖ.

Also, only the God of Israel judges the world (cf. Ps. 94:2; 105:7; Isa. 26:9; 33:2; Mic. 4:3). But God the Father judges no one, rather τὴν κρίσιν πᾶσαν δέδωκεν τῷ υἱῷ ("all the judgment has given to the Son") (Jn. 5:22). At this point of narrative, the exact nature of the Son's judging activity is not described, but for now the reader can know the basis of the Son's judging authority. The reason God the Father has given it to the Son is because πάντες, including the Jewish religious leaders, should honor the Son if they wish to honor God the Father (Jn. 5:23a). As a result, anyone who does not honor the Son also fails to honor God the Father who sent Him. In fact, Jesus directly tells them that although Israel is obligated to honor God on the Sabbath, they are persecuting and plotting to kill the Son (Jn. 5:16-18). According to the author, Jesus' role as

---

[352] See Francis Moloney, *The Gospel of John*, 1998, 178; Morris, *The Gospel According to John*, 1995, 278; Rudolf Schnackenburg, *The Gospel According to St. John*, vol. 2, 105.

the Son underscores both Jesus' equality with God the Father in purpose, and Jesus' subordination to the Father in carrying out the mission. This is precisely what Jesus did: He came to earth, finished all the missions entrusted to Him even the death on the cross, and returned to God the Father.[353]

The narrator resumes Jesus' discourse opening with two uses of the double ἀμὴν in John 5:24-25, emphasizing Himself as the life-giver and the judge. The reader now knows who Jesus is, and that the reader must honor both God the Father and the Son. Jesus states with the first person singular focusing on the believer, ὁ τὸν λόγον μου ἀκούων καὶ πιστεύων τῷ πέμψαντί με ("the one who hears My word and believe the One who sent Me") (Jn. 5:24a), even though He is dealing with the Jewish religious leaders, the prosecutors. The results of His life-giving and judging presence are indicated. The one who ἀκούων Jesus' word and πιστεύων the Father who sent His Son, Jesus, ἔχει (present tense) ζωὴν αἰώνιον, καὶ εἰς κρίσιν οὐκ ἔρχεται (future tense) ἀλλὰ μεταβέβηκεν (perfect tense) ἐκ τοῦ θανάτου εἰς τὴν ζωήν ("has eternal life and will not come into judgement, but has passed from death to life"). The eternal life should be given now through faith in the revelation of God through the Son, Jesus. It is not a future promise, but now (ἔρχεται ὥρα καὶ νῦν ἐστιν in Jn. 25a). It is in conflict with contemporary Judaism, which considered the receiving of eternal life to be a future event. It thus represents a strong affirmation of inaugurated eschatology in John's gospel.[354] Jesus points to Himself as the source of life and judgment on a Sabbath festival (cf. Jn. 5:1, 9),

---

[353] Andreas Köstenberger, *John*, 2004, 188.

[354] See George Beasley-Murray, *John*, 1999, 76; Donald Carson, *The Gospel According to John*, 1991, 256; Andreas Köstenberger, *John*, 2004, 188; Francis Moloney, *The Gospel of John*, 1998, 183; Leon Morris, *The Gospel According to John*, 1995, 280; Herman Ridderbos, *The Gospel According to John*, 1997, 197.

while doing what the God of Israel has done so far. He does not eliminate the celebration of the Sabbath.

Jesus continues His argument for the authority God the Father of Israel has given. Starting with ὥσπερ γὰρ ὁ πατὴρ ἔχει ζωὴν ἐν ἑαυτῷ ("For as the Father has life in Himself") as a principle of their theological tradition, it is logical conclusion (οὕτως καὶ) that the Father τῷ υἱῷ ἔδωκεν ζωὴν ἔχειν ἐν ἑαυτῷ ("gave life to the Son to have in Himself") in John 5:26 (cf. Jn. 5:22). Jesus has already claimed that He ζῳοποιεῖ (Jn. 5:21b) and now explains how this is true. From this affirmation Jesus goes on to address that the Son judges because He is υἱὸς ἀνθρώπου ("Son of Man"). Köstenberger argues that the phrase rendered "He is υἱὸς ἀνθρώπου" reads more literally "He is Son of Man" – the only instance of this Christological title without articles before both "Son" and "Man" in the entire New Testament.[355] The author used this title for expressing "the transcendent character of Jesus' Messiahship and the all-embracing, present-and-future-encompassing mission of Jesus as the Son of God."[356]

Earlier in John 5:22 Jesus explained that God the Father judges no one, but grants such authority to the Son. Thus Jesus now claims to exercise it. During Jesus' early public life John records that Jesus promised to those who believed the sight of greater things of the revelation of the heavenly in the υἱὸς ἀνθρώπου (Jn. 1:50-51). In His dialogue with Nicodemus, He advances that promise, declaring that there was only one εἰς τὸν οὐρανὸν ("in the Heaven"), the υἱὸς ἀνθρώπου, and that this υἱὸς ἀνθρώπου must be lifted up so that all who believe in υἱὸς ἀνθρώπου might be saved (Jn. 3:13-15). God the Father no longer judges but is made known in and through the υἱὸς ἀνθρώπου.

---

[355] Andreas Köstenberger, *John*, 2004, 189.

[356] Herman Ridderbos, *The Gospel According to John*, 1997, 200.

Jesus proclaimed in John 5:25 ἔρχεται ὥρα καὶ νῦν ἐστιν ("an hour is coming and now is") in the context of God the Father has given the authority of giving life and bringing judgment. Now Jesus tells the Jewish religious leaders μὴ θαυμάζετε τοῦτο, because the handing over of Sabbath authority to Jesus does not remove their understanding of the eschatological time with its associated judgment.

Jesus repeats the phrase ἔρχεται ὥρα in John 5:28, but νῦν ἐστιν is omitted because the Jewish tradition of the eschatological expectations. In the future there will be a time when the physically dead will hear the voice of the Son and come out of the tombs into either the resurrection of life or judgment (Jn. 5:28-29; cf. Dan. 12:2). Those who τὰ ἀγαθὰ ποιήσαντες ("have done good") will rise to live forever, and those who τὰ φαῦλα πράξαντες ("have done evil") will rise to be condemned. For this Borchert argues that a person is to be judged on what he or she does, and not merely on what he or she says, because believing often proves superficial (eg. John 2:23-25).[357] Borchert does not mean the salvation by works, rather the life that one has manifests the test of the faith.[358]

Despite the ζωὴν αἰώνιον ("eternal life") believers claim to possess now, the reader or implied reader realizes the eschatology of John 5:24 might be the continued reality that everyone must come to face: the fact that everyone experiences life and death. The physical reality of death and life is within the dominion of God as He is in the role of life-giver, and judgement within the dominion of the Son. Thus, acceptance or refusal of the Son now must be the

---

[357] Gerald Borchert, *John 1-11*, 1996, 241.

[358] Most of the Reformed scholars agreed with Calvin, stating "He marks out believers by their good works, just as elsewhere He says that a tree is known by its fruit (Matt. 7:16). He praises their good works, which began when they were called." (John Calvin, *The Gospel According to St. John 1-10*, 1961, 133).

crucial factor of how one's life will be on the other side of the tomb (John 5:28-29).

The reader or implied reader notices that the conclusion of Jesus' first section of the polemic discourse in John 5:30 is much a repeat of opening remark in John 5:19. As mentioned earlier the difference is the change of the pronoun, third person to the first person. Jesus emphasizes the total dependence on the will of God the Father who sent Him. As God the Father is the judge, so also is the Son, Jesus. Jesus' judgment is thus righteous and just because it is based on the will of God the Father. Therefore, His healing of the lame man cannot be judged in terms of the man-made Jewish regulations on Sabbath observance. The characterization of the lame man makes apparent Jesus' identification.

A trial is in progress in which the Jewish religious leaders are the prosecutors and Jesus is the defendant. The charges were Jesus' claim to work on a Sabbath as the Father does and the blasphemy of His claim of the Son, equality with God the Father (Jn. 5:17-18). Jesus accuses them of not understanding the revelation of the Sabbath work of God in Jesus. Nor do they understand the Son has authority to give life and judge like His Father. Thus, the reader realizes that actually they are guilty of not honoring God the Father inasmuch as they are not honoring the Son, Jesus (Jn. 5:23).

6.7.2 Jesus' calls for witnesses (Jn. 5:31-47)

As the trial continues, the narrator tells us that Jesus calls witnesses for His defense against the Sabbath law breaking and blasphemy charges put forth by the Jewish religious leaders. For the reader or implied reader is a jury, and Jesus accepts the need for witnesses and thus He fulfills that need. Soon the reader or implied reader realizes the inability of the Jewish religious leaders to recognize God's revelation of the Son. Thus, Jesus tells them that Moses' writings accuse them.

At first, Jesus points out that ἐὰν ἐγὼ μαρτυρῶ περὶ ἐμαυτοῦ, ἡ μαρτυρία μου οὐκ ἔστιν ἀληθής·("If I bear witness about Myself, My testimony is not true") in John 5:31.[359] Under Jewish law it was not enough for the accused to prove ἀληθής: two or three witnesses are required (Deut. 19:15), and those testimonies have to be brought forward. Jesus acknowledges and accepts this situation. Thus, He points toward ἄλλος ἐστὶν (present tense) ὁ μαρτυρῶν περὶ ἐμοῦ ("there is another witness about Me"). Although the reader or implied reader might understand that the ἄλλος ἐστὶν ὁ μαρτυρῶν is God the Father, this is not the case for the Jewish religious leaders. So, Jesus turns to witnesses they have seen and heard, that is John the Baptist (Jn. 5:33-35) and Jesus' miracle works of signs and wonders (Jn. 5:36). In John 5:33 Jesus reminds that they sent ἱερεῖς καὶ Λευίτας to John the Baptist for his identification (Jn. 1:19). At that time John the Baptist witnessed to Jesus as ὁ υἱὸς τοῦ θεοῦ ("the Son of God") (Jn. 1:34) and ὁ ἀμνὸς τοῦ θεοῦ ("Lamb of God") (Jn. 1:36). Jesus calls John the Baptist a λύχνος ("lamp") that burned and shone (Jn. 5:35), and the reader knows that he is not τὸ φῶς ("light") (cf. Jn. 1:7-9). But the Jewish religious leaders are unable to see Jesus as the Jesus to whom John the Baptist bore witness. However, the author expresses more powerful witnesses for Jesus. He performed ἔργα ("work") that has its origins in God the Father (cf. 4:34). What the author may label "σημείων" is simply carried under His ἔργα. His ἔργα thus include the σημείων but are not limited to them. Everything He does is His entire ministry.[360] He continues to follow and respond to the Father's will (cf. 5:30).

---

[359] οὐκ ἔστιν ἀληθής renders "not valid or verified" rather than "not true," indicating a courtroom setting (See Donald Carson, *The Gospel According to John*, 1991, 259; Leon Morris, *The Gospel According to John*, 1995, 287.

[360] Donald Carson, *The Gospel According to John*, 1991, 261.

These acts are seen in many ἔργα that Jesus accomplishes perfectly (Jn. 5:36a). Thus, His perfect accomplishment of ἔργα witnesses to the truth of His saying, ὁ πατήρ με ἀπέσταλκεν ("the Father has sent Me") (Jn. 5:36b).

The witness of John the Baptist and the ἔργα of Jesus could be seen and heard, but there is also direct testimony from the Father who sent Him (Jn. 5:37a). The μεμαρτύρηκεν (perfect tense) points to the confirmed state and the significance of God the Father's witness. Because it is God's testimony it is greater than men's (cf. 1Jn. 5:9). The problem is that the Jewish religious leaders have never heard φωνὴν αὐτοῦ ("His voice") nor seen εἶδος αὐτοῦ ("His form") (Jn. 5:37b). The narrator explains what is meant by φωνὴν and εἶδος in John 5:38b, telling ὅτι ὃν ἀπέστειλεν ἐκεῖνος τούτῳ ὑμεῖς οὐ πιστεύετε ("that you do not believe the one whom He sent"). The Jewish religious leaders take it for granted that they have the word of God abiding in them (Jn. 5:38a). But their rejection of the Son whom God has sent makes such a belief self-deceit. Jesus is God the Father's φωνὴν and εἶδος, but they don't hear or see Him as such. The author emphasizes that Jesus is ὃν ἀπέστειλεν by God the Father (Jn. 5:38b), and that "No one has ever seen God, the only God, who is at the Father's side, He has made Him known" (Jn. 1:18). The φωνὴν of God the Father is ὁ λόγος of the Son, Jesus.

The author continues to point to the Jewish religious leaders' failures. The Jewish practice of ἐραυνᾶτε τὰς γραφάς ("search the Scripture") is regarded as ζωὴν αἰώνιον ἔχειν ("to have eternal life") (Jn. 5:39), but they refuse to come to Jesus who gives ζωὴν αἰώνιον (Jn. 5:40). They could not recognize the Scriptures which bears the witness to the Son, Jesus. They need to understand its true Christological point of view and purpose. Their accusations are based on their own study of the Scriptures and their interpretation of the Sabbath traditions (cf. Jn. 5:18). The author, however, asserts that the Scriptures are the witness of the unseen God the Father to the Son, Jesus (Jn. 5:37, cf. Jn. 1:45; 2:22; 3:10; 5:45-47; 12:41; 20:9). However, according to the author, the Scriptures are being abused by the Jewish religious leaders and they not only refuse to come to Him, but try to persecute and kill Him. Their refusal is deliberate.[361]

For His defense, Jesus finally makes the accusation that the Jewish religious leaders do not have the love for God (Jn. 5:42), while Jesus emphasizes that He has no interest in δόξαν παρὰ ἀνθρώπων ("glory from men"), human recognition (Jn. 5:41). From ἔγνωκα ὑμᾶς ("I have known you") Jesus rebukes them because they show no sign of loving God whatever their claims from the Scriptures might be. This leads them to the rejection of the Son sent ἐν τῷ ὀνόματι τοῦ πατρός and the easy acceptance of those who come ἐν τῷ ὀνόματι τῷ ἰδίῳ ("in the name of the own") (Jn. 5:43). Jesus' authority comes from God the Father who sent Him, but this truth is rejected as they accept all those who might come with nothing more than the authority of their own name. Jesus has rejected δόξαν παρὰ ἀνθρώπων, but they pursue it. Their inability to believe the Son, Jesus, comes from settling for the δόξαν παρὰ ἀλλήλων λαμβάνοντες ("receiving glory from one another") (Jn. 5:44a). Their delusions by misunderstanding and misinterpreta-tion of the Scriptures caused them not able to seek and find τὴν δόξαν τὴν παρὰ τοῦ μόνου θεοῦ ("the glory from only God") that all men should seek (Jn. 5:44b). Jesus appeals to a principle which applies to all men: No one is to seek his or her own glory, but only the glory of Him who sent Jesus.[362] Brown states that the failure to accept Jesus is really a preference of self, seeking δόξαν παρὰ

---

[361] Raymond E. Brown, *The Gospel According to John vol.1*, 1966, 225.

[362] Jesus said, "If anyone's will is to do God's[a] will, he will know whether the teaching is from God or whether I am speaking on my own authority. The one who speaks on his own authority seeks his own glory; but the one who seeks the glory of him who sent him is true, and in him there is no false-hood." (Jn. 7:17-18)

ἀνθρώπων.[363] Their self-love caused them to reject the Son, God-sent Messiah.[364]

Jesus brings up another witness for Him, Moses. Moses was regarded as the mediator between God and Israel. He intercedes before God the Father for people of Israel, the Jews (cf. Ex. 32:11-14, 30-33; Deut. 9:18-29). By God the Law had come to the Jews through Moses, but God also gives ἡ χάρις καὶ ἡ ἀλήθεια διὰ Ἰησοῦ Χριστοῦ ἐγένετο ("the grace and truth came from Jesus Christ") (cf. Jn. 1:17). Both have been given by God's will, but the Jewish religious leaders are rejecting the latter. Therefore, ἔστιν ὁ κατηγορῶν ὑμῶν Μωϊσῆς ("there is one who accuse you, Moses") (Jn. 5:45b). The reader or implied reader already knows that the Scriptures bear witness to the Son, Jesus (Jn. 5:39). If they believe in Moses, they would believe Him, περὶ γὰρ ἐμοῦ ἐκεῖνος ἔγραψεν ("for he wrote concerning Me") (Jn. 5:46). But they have not believed in Moses. The readers are familiar with the author's pattern in Johannine narrative of a statement in the affirmative followed by the converse. The author is saying that they are wrong to accuse Jesus on the basis of their misinterpretation of the Law. The reader or implied reader understands the continuity between τοῖς ἐκείνου γράμμασιν ("his writings") of Moses and τοῖς ἐμοῖς ῥήμασιν ("My words") of Jesus which are the same revelation of God. If they are unable to believe τοῖς ἐκείνου γράμμασιν of Moses, they cannot believe τοῖς ἐμοῖς ῥήμασιν of Jesus.

6.8   THE SIGNIFICANCE

In the lame man's healing narrative, the author establishes that the lame man and the story of his healing are intertwined with the

---

[363]   Ibid., 228.

[364]   Donald Carson, *The Gospel According to John*, 1991, 264.

characterization of Jesus as the Son whom God the Father sent to do God's work. Jesus has the divine authority and power to heal the lame man. The reader or implied reader clearly sees that the Jewish religious leaders' charges against Jesus are false because the healing was God's act and Jesus did the healing according to God's will. The author also shows through Jesus encounters with the Jewish religious leaders that the lame man healing miracle sign has eschatological implications. The lame man's healing belongs within the horizon of eschatology as it had been prophesied by Isaiah, "then the lame man shall leap like a deer" (Isa. 35:6).[365]

In His discourse of defense, Jesus as the Son of God the Father reveals God who has the authority to perform miracles and values the giving of life over the Jewish Sabbath tradition. Jesus demonstrated His divine authority to forgive sin and give eternal life to those who believe in Him. Another aspect of Jesus' healing the lame man on the Sabbath is judgment. While God the Father alone is called the judge, who will exercise the eschatological judgment, this authority has been delegated to the Son, Jesus, because of the relationship between the Father and the Son. At this eschatological judgment everyone will be raised. The Son, Jesus, will judge based on belief or unbelief concerning Him: a resurrection of life or a resurrection of condemnation. Because of their delusion or blindness and looking for glory from men, the Jewish religious leaders could not see their own spiritual depravity. So, they accused and tried to kill Jesus, the Son. The reader or implied reader can see that Jesus choosing to heal the lame man on the Sabbath has significant messianic implications. It presents Jesus as the promised Messiah. Therefore, like their forefathers failed to enter the promised land because of unbelief, the only way to live forever is through faith in the Son, Jesus. Culpepper points out, "The heart of the conflict, however, is less a difference in the

---

[365] Edwyn Hoskyns and F. N. Davey, *The Fourth Gospel*, 1947, 263.

concept of God than a difference in the locus of God's ultimate self-revelation. Jesus claims of preeminence over all prior revelation, claims which express the Christology of the church, are the point of the contention."[366] The author also expressed that unlike the Jewish religious leaders, Jesus is not looking for His own glory, but for the glory of God the Father. All human beings are made for His glory.

6.9   CONCLUSION

It was most likely John's intent as author to lead the readers to compare the response of the lame man in John 5 with that of man born blind in John 9. Both encountered Jesus and were healed; their responses, however, differ. In examining the similarities of the two men, Bennema compares the two episodes well:[367]

1. Both men had been disabled for a long time and excluded from the community.

2. Both were healed by Jesus on Sabbath.

3. In both episodes there is the mention of a pool: one a pool of Bethesda, the other a pool of Siloam.

4. The Jewish religious leaders investigated both healings.

5. In both episodes Jesus finds the healed person later to offer not physical but spiritual healing, the eternal life

However, the responses of the two men to Jesus and to the Jewish religious leaders are rather different, even opposite. The lame man betrays Jesus to the leaders while the man born blind

---

[366]   Alan Culpepper, *Anatomy of the Fourth Gospel*, 1983, 114.

[367]   Cornelis Bennema, *Encountering Jesus*, 2009, 195.

defends Jesus and is also persecuted. The lame man is unable to heed Jesus' warning and does not progress in his knowledge of Him and there is no indication that he comes to believe in Him, while in contrast, the man born blind progresses in his knowledge of Jesus in a way similar to the Samaritan woman in John 4 even as he stands up to the Jewish religious leaders. Also, when Jesus finds the man born blind later, he perceptively responds with belief, something we do not see with the now-healed lame man. Taking all of these differences in responses into account, the reader or implied reader should interpret the lame man narrative negatively. For the author, the miracles are signs that reveal Jesus' true identity for the purpose of his writing (cf. Jn. 20:30-31). But as we see in the characterization of the lame man, even miracle signs do not necessarily lead to authentic faith.[368]

For this narrative, the observation of the Sabbath is the essential literary and theological background. The reader or implied reader was asked to believe that Jesus was the Son of God who made God known (Jn. 1:18). What Jesus had done in the Jewish temple for the lame man on the Sabbath was not only a sign, but also a shadow of the gift of God in the Son who gives life and judges everyone at the eschatological time. Jesus is above the Sabbath and the works He does, which are always good, are allowable on the Sabbath as God Himself. It is impossible to honor and glorify God of the Sabbath without honoring and glorifying His Son. The author demonstrates that it is the Jewish religious leaders who are lost and are judged because they do not accept Jesus as the Son who gives life.

---

[368] See Alan Culpepper, *Anatomy of the Fourth Gospel*, 1983, 138 and also see James Howard, "Significance of Minor Characters," 2006, 72.

CHAPTER 7

The Man Born Blind (John 9:1-41)

THE NARRATIVE OF HEALING THE MAN BORN
blind in John 9 is a widely recognized and well known story
as one of the masterpieces of the Johannine narrative. It involves
multiple characters, multiple interactions, and multiple outcomes
reflective of character development as a result of the work of the
Messiah in healing the blind man. Central to the narrative, of
course, is the man born blind himself and the impact of his healing,
the focus of the story. As Reimer opines, "The character of the man
born blind in John 9 does represent a rare development of character and plot twists that are intriguing and worth noting."[369]

The author places this narrative the portion of his gospel known
as the "Festival Cycle" (Jn. 5-12), specifically placing it during the
time when the people of Israel celebrate the Feast of Tabernacles
(Jn. 7-10). It is in the "Festival Cycle" section of John's gospel that
the narrator develops the theme of increasing prosecution of the
Son who gives life by the Jewish religious leaders. This prosecution
and increasing hostility begins with Jesus' healing of the lame man
on the Sabbath in John 5. The Johannine narrative of "Cana Cycle"
(Jn. 2-4) and the "Festival Cycle" (Jn. 5-12) is woven together with
the profound theological view of the author. There are two related
motifs woven together in the "Festival Cycle": the repeated assertion by the author that Jesus is the Son of God who gives the life,

---

[369] Andy Reimer, "The Man Born Blind: True Disciple of Jesus," 2013, 429. He
refers to Brown's commentary on this text.

and the increasing hostility of the Jewish religious leaders toward Jesus.[370] The author is showing and telling that Jesus is the Son who, as the Messiah, fulfils the hopes and joys of the festivals that are taking place. In the meantime, the reader or implied reader clearly sees that Jesus' claims cause vigorous opposition by the Jewish religious leaders, thus fulfilling the author's words: εἰς τὰ ἴδια ἦλθεν, καὶ οἱ ἴδιοι αὐτὸν οὐ παρέλαβον ("He came to His own, and His people did not receive Him") (Jn. 1:11).

The author places the narrative of the healing of the man born blind after Jesus leaves the temple (Jn. 8:59). There is no indication of a change of time as the author closes one episode and opens the next. Most scholars agree that Jesus' presence in the temple is due to the Feast of Tabernacles (cf. Jn. 7:2, 37). During each morning of the feast, water is drawn from the pool of Siloam and taken in a procession to the temple, and each evening lamps are lit to illuminate Jerusalem.[371] The author implies that Jesus is the giver of living water (Jn. 7:37-39; cf. Jn. 4:10-14) and the light of the world (Jn. 8:12; 9:5). Jesus, the God-sent Son heals the man born blind as he restored sight. Culpepper argues that the man born blind is characterized as a representative figure, for all humanity are born blind and need to be restored to light.[372]

This narrative of healing the man born blind involves so many characters, perhaps the most characters (Jesus, disciples, man born blind, the neighbours, his parents, and the Pharisees) in a single Johannine narrative. In addition to the use of parallel or contrasting characters, the narrative contains ironic double entendre with terms that have multiple physical and spiritual implications.

---

[370] See Harold Songer, "John 5-12: Opposition to the Giving of True Life," *Review & Expositor 85*, 1988, 459-71.

[371] See J. C. Rylaarsdam, "Feast and Facts," *The Interpreter's Dictionary of the Bible*, 1962, 2:263.

[372] Alan Culpepper, "The Plot of John's Story of Jesus," 1997, 188.

Jesus is on the scene only in the opening and the closing. The man born blind, the main character, is heavily involved in the entire narrative. The reader can see his progress with Jesus' identification in the narrative like the Samaritan woman's. However, this narrative of healing the man born blind parallels the narrative of healing the lame man in John 5. Culpepper describes 11 parallelisms:[373]

1. The man's history is described (38 years, 5:5; from birth, 9:1)

2. Jesus takes the initiative to heal (5:6; 9:6)

3. The pool has healing powers for some (Bethesda; Siloam)

4. Jesus heals on the Sabbath (5:9; 9:14)

5. The Jews accuse Him of violating the Sabbath (5:10; 9:16)

6. The Jews ask who healed him (5:12; how he was healed, 9:15)

7. The man does not know where Jesus is or who He is (5:13; 9:12)

8. Jesus finds him and invites belief (5:14; 9:35)

9. Jesus implies a relationship between sin and suffering (5:14, Jesus rejects sin as the explanation for the man's suffering, 9:3)

10. The man goes to the Jews (5:15; The Jews cast the man out, 9:34-35)

11. Jesus must work as His Father is working (5:17; 9:4)

Both narratives are bound with a discourse on the Sabbath tradition as well as themes regarding sin, God's work and glory, and Jesus' identity. Thus, the two narratives signify the Christological and doxological points of view of the author.

---

[373] Alan Culpepper, *Anatomy of the Fourth Gospel*, 1983, 139. Schneiders explains well the comparison and the contrast between John chapter 5 and 9 (Sandra Schneiders, *Written that You May Believe*, 2003, 152-53).

As Martyn argues, there is an ancient maxim that no more than two active characters shall normally appear on stage at one time, and that scenes are often divided by adherence to this rule.[374] As an example, Martyn uses John 9 to read John's gospel as having two levels of drama, in which Johannine narratives are both the story of Jesus as well as the story of Johannine community. Although the majority of scholars agree his reading approach, the reader or implied reader could maintain that Johannine narratives are primarily the story of Jesus, and that the man born blind healing story is authentic and historically reliable.[375]

The man born blind healing narrative can be divided into eight acts as some scholars do.[376] The narrative structure can thus be viewed as follows:

Narrative structure (Jn. 9:1-41)

Act I: The Setting, Jesus and His disciples (Jn. 9:1-5)
Act II: Jesus and the man born blind I (Jn. 9:6-7)
Act III: The man born blind and his neighbors (Jn. 9:8-12)
Act IV: The man born blind and the Jewish religious leaders I (Jn. 9:13-17)
Act V: The Jewish religious leaders and the man born blind's parents (Jn. 9:18-23)
Act VI: The man born blind and the Jewish religious leaders II (Jn. 9:24-34)
Act VII: Jesus and the man born blind II (Jn. 9:35-38)
Act VIII: Jesus and the Jewish religious leaders (Jn. 9:39-41)

---

[374] James Martyn, *History and Theology in the Fourth Gospel*, 1979, 26.

[375] See Cornelis Bennema, *Encountering Jesus*, 2009, 245.

[376] Bultman, Beasley-Murray, Culpepper, Duke, Kim, O'Day and Resseguie divide the chapter into seven scenes. Painter and Lee do it into eight scenes. Moloney does it into eight but extends the narrative to chapter 10:12.

The man born blind in this narrative moves progressively toward full sight physically and spiritually as mentioned earlier. Contrastingly, the narrative shows the growing spiritual blindness of the Jewish religious leaders, the Pharisees. This anonymous man is blind from birth, and a beggar in the region of the temple in Jerusalem (Jn. 8:59-9:1; 9:8). It is also clear that he is a young adult, since the author tells ἡλικίαν ἔχει, αὐτὸς ("he is of age") (Jn. 9:21), indicating that he has passed his thirteenth birthday and therefore he had reached the age of legal responsibility.[377] Even so, he was probably rejected for going into the temple and participation in worship by Jewish customs, indicating the man was born blind and was a social and religious outcast.[378] At that time in Palestine, the blind or invalid would position themselves near the temple, hoping that worshippers would give money (Jn. 9:8; cf. Acts 3:2).

7.1 ACT I: THE SETTING – JESUS AND HIS DISCIPLES (Jn. 9:1-5)

The author opens by proclaiming that Jesus encountered an anonymous blind man who has not seen light from his birth. The man born blind is introduced, but he is not involved in the subsequent dialogue that takes place between Jesus and His disciples. He and his situation are the object of the dialogue, but he himself is not the central topic of the conversation. Brodie states that the blind man "lacks life" in a Johannine literature sense.[379] In the context of Johannine narrative, the author cast the healing in terms of light/darkness imagery. Just as Jesus claims that He is τὸ φῶς

---

[377] Raymond Brown, *The Gospel According to John*, 1966, 374; Beasley-Murray, *John*, 1991, 157.

[378] Cornelis Bennema, *Encountering Jesus*, 2009, 245-46.

[379] Thomas Brodie, *The Gospel According to John*, 1993, 345.

τοῦ κόσμου ("the light of the world") (Jn. 8:12), so He will show Himself to be τὸ φῶς τοῦ κόσμου (Jn. 9:5) by giving sight to him.[380] Lindars says that the man born blind healing narrative is presented not as an act of restoration, but as a creative act by Jesus who is τὸ φῶς τοῦ κόσμου.[381] That said, the reader or implied reader could see the man's healing both ways, either an act of restoration or as an act of creation.

The author uses the phrase of τυφλὸν ἐκ γενετῆς ("blind from birth") that emphasizes the heightening the miraculous work.[382] The reader or implied reader notices that there is no interaction between Jesus and the man born blind. Instead, in John 6:2, suddenly we see the disciples in conversation with Jesus after having not been a part of the narrative plot since John 6. The disciples suddenly show up here for the characterization of the man born blind. His disciples ask a logical question: τίς ἥμαρτεν, οὗτος ἢ οἱ γονεῖς αὐτοῦ, ἵνα τυφλὸς γεννηθῇ; ("who sinned, this man or his parents, that he was born blind?") (Jn. 9:2). Who is responsible for this man's suffering due to his being born blind? Is it sinful parents, or this man who committed a sin while still in the womb? Rabbis believed in a direct cause and effect relationship between sin and suffering. Underlying the disciples' question is the concern not to charge God with inflicting suffering on people for no cause, and to instead recall the teaching of the Mosaic law such as Exodus 20:5 and Numbers 14:18 and determine if the blindness of the man may be the result of parental sin. Going back to Jesus' instructions to the healed lame man in John 5:14 to "sin no more, that nothing

---

[380] Graig Keener, *The Gospel of John*, 2003, 779.

[381] Barnabas Lindars, The Gospel of John, 1972, 341.

[382] C. K. Barrett, *The Gospel According to St. John*, 1978, 356.

worse may happen to you," the disciples assumed suffering was a punishment for sin.[383]

The question of the disciples is answered shortly in John 9:3-5, but a full response of Jesus is not available until the end of this narrative. Jesus tells them that the man born blind situation exist ἵνα φανερωθῇ τὰ ἔργα τοῦ θεοῦ ἐν αὐτῷ ("that the works of God should be displayed in him") (Jn. 9:3). He rejects any connection between the man born blind's suffering and any sin. O'Day points that Jesus answers the question of the purpose of the man's blindness while the disciples asked about the cause of his suffering.[384]

The author's point of view that Jesus does not perform His works on His own authority but God's (Jn. 5:19-30) has earlier been established. Now, God is to reveal His works in the events of the life of the man born blind, with the author having pointed out that even suffering caused by evil ultimately contributes to the greater glory of God.

Jesus includes the disciples in His work, saying, ἡμᾶς δεῖ ἐργάζεσθαι τὰ ἔργα τοῦ πέμψαντός με ("We must work the works of the one who sent Me") (Jn. 9:4a).[385] Morris explains that δεῖ implies Jesus is not merely speaking convenient advice, but is

---

[383] Rudolf Schnackenburg, *The Gospel According to St. John vol. 2*, 1980, 240.

[384] Gail O'Day, *The Word Disclosed*, 2002, 67. He also argues that if the suffering of blindness is understood only as physical, then the presence of God in the healing will be missed or misunderstood. He has been blind since birth, but more is at stake in this healing than the gift of sight.

[385] Many scholars argue that "We" may include the disciples (see Donald Carson, *The Gospel According to John*, 1991, 362; Leon Morris, *The Gospel According to John*, 1995, 426; Herman Ridderbos 1997, *The Gospel According to John*, 334; Francis Moloney, *The Gospel of John*, 1998, 292). Martyn argues that it requires a reading on a higher level; it reflects the experience of Christian living at the time of the Gospel was written (James Martyn, *History and Theology in the Fourth Gospel*, 1979, 24-26).

articulating a compelling necessity.[386] The disciples are now associated with the work of Jesus, the Son who was sent by God the Father.[387] Of course, there are limitations that have been imposed on this work of revealing God. Since Jesus is τὸ φῶς τοῦ κόσμου ("the light of the world"), the darkness of νὺξ brings the day to an end, at which point He is gone from this world. No one can do the work of revealing God then (Jn. 9:4b). The reader can infer that the time of Jesus working in this world is short, creating an urgency to the task of doing God's work. For this period when Jesus is associating with them, God the Father continues to be revealed. His disciples can continue the works of Jesus because ὅταν ἐν τῷ κόσμῳ ὦ, φῶς εἰμι τοῦ κόσμου ("While I am in the world, I am the light of the world") (Jn. 9:5). The contrast between day and night reminds the reader of the conflict between τὸ φῶς and ἡ σκοτία in John 1:5. In the Johannine narrative τὸ φῶς or ἡ σκοτία symbolizes contrasting origin and qualities because τὸ φῶς is often used for righteousness and ἡ σκοτία is for perversity.[388] Barrett explains that it appears that τὸ φῶς is not a metaphysical definition of the person of Jesus but a description of his effect upon the cosmos: He is τὸ φῶς to judge or save.[389] In the author's point of view Jesus is the true and living φῶς (cf. Jn 1:1-13). In Him was life, and the life was the light of men (Jn. 1:4). As τὸ φῶς to shine ἡ σκοτία, ἡ σκοτία has not overcome it (Jn. 1:5). τὸ φῶς τὸ ἀληθινόν ("the true light") gives φῶς to everyone in the world (Jn. 1:9).

---

[386] Leon Morris, *The Gospel According to John*, 1995, 480.

[387] Kim suggests that the use of ἐργάζεσθαι recalls John 5:17, which justifies Jesus' healing of the lame man on a Sabbath by the continuous work of God. Jesus' healings are part of God's commissioned and redemptive activity (Moon Hyun Kim, *Healing Hurts*, 2005, 100).

[388] Kim refers to Charlesworth's Johannine narrative comparison with Qumran documents (Kim, Ibid., 101).

[389] C. K. Barrett, *The Gospel According to St. John*, 1978, 357.

The reader or implied reader will discover that Jesus' words in the setting of the man born blind story would prove significant in terms of his characterization. Brown summarizes well the opening setting of the scene of the healing narrative of the man born blind: "Before narrating the miracle, the evangelist is careful to have Jesus point out the meaning of the sign as an instance of light coming into darkness. This is a story of how a man who sat in darkness was brought to see the light, not only physically but spiritually. On the other hand, it is also a tale of how those who thought they saw that the Pharisees were blinding themselves to the light and plunging into darkness. The story starts in vs. 1 with a blind man who will gain his sight; it ends in vs. 41 with the Pharisees who have become spiritually blind."[390]

7.2 ACT II: JESUS AND THE MAN BORN BLIND I (Jn. 9:6-7)

Once again, the author lets the reader or implied reader know that Jesus initiates the miracle as He did to the lame man in John 5:6. The man born blind or his parents did not ask for healing. The author didn't mention any request from them or even prior conversations.[391] Sovereignly Jesus approaches him, forms mud from the dust with saliva, and puts the mud on the man's eyes (Jn. 9:6).[392] The use of saliva is also mentioned in the healing of the deaf and mute man in Mark 7:33 and of the blind man in Mark 8:23. The narrative shows the primitive character of the healing act as being curative, as it was regarded at the time. However, since the healing

---

[390] Raymond Brown, *The Gospel According to John*, 1966, 376-77.

[391] Herman Ridderbos, *The Gospel According to John*, 1997, 335.

[392] It is a traditional practice that the forming saliva with mud is believed to have medicinal value (C. K. Barrett, *The Gospel According to St. John*, 1978, 357-58).

takes place only after he washes in the pool of Siloam, there is also a natural dimension to the supernatural nature.

Forming mud with saliva is a violation of Sabbath regulations, one of the 39 forbidden forms of work on the Sabbath.[393] Both Jesus' healing miracles – the lame man (Jn. 5) and the man born blind (Jn. 9) – violated Sabbath regulations, leading to confrontation with the Jewish religious leaders. While the Jewish leaders see a Sabbath violation, the reader or implied reader sees Jesus' act of touching the blind man's eyes with mud as healing of a man expecting a miracle in his encounter with Jesus.

Jesus then tells the man born blind to go and νίψαι εἰς τὴν κολυμβήθραν τοῦ Σιλωάμ, ὃ ἑρμηνεύεται Ἀπεσταλμένος ("wash in the pool of Siloam, which means Sent") (Jn. 9:7). The author does not tell how the blind man makes the trip to the pool of Siloam, but the reader could imagine that it's not easy in total darkness. Interestingly, although clearly He could Jesus does not heal the man right away; instead, He directs him to go and wash. Ridderbos argues three reasons why the man born blind was sent to Siloam:[394]

1. To wash the mud out of his eyes

2. To evoke the blind man's faith

3. To carry out ritual purification (cf. Lk. 7:14)

The reader or implied reader can see in this story of healing the author's point of view that Jesus enhances or initiates faith with the intent of eliciting an adequate response of belief.

The man born blind responds immediately without question. In order to show his radical response to Jesus's word, the

---

[393] Rudolf Schnackenburg, *The Gospel According to St. John vol. 2*, 1980, 242.

[394] Ibid., 336. Interestingly Carson also adds another reason to correlate the Pharisees' unbelief with a prophecy of judgement in Isaiah 8:6 (Donald Carson, *The Gospel According to John*, 1991, 365).

author uses three active verbs: ἀπῆλθεν καὶ ἐνίψατο, καὶ ἦλθεν ("went and washed, and came") in John 9:7b. As earlier in the narratives in John 4:46-54 and in John 5:2-9, the author shows that the acceptance of Jesus' word leads to a miracle. But, for the author there is more important theological point of view than just physical healing of the restoration of sight. The author thus adds an explanation of the significance of Siloam, which means ὁ ᾽Απεσταλμένος. As the author adds an explanation to make it clear, Moloney argues the water of Siloam is crucial within the context of the Feast of Tabernacles, because the blind man is not healed because of the contact with the waters of Siloam, but rather instead because of the man's contact with the Sent One.[395] Malina and Rohrbaugh add to the meaning of Siloam the patron-client system of the Mediterranean world in the first century.[396] In fact, the author mentions 51 times that Jesus is sent by God the Father. God is the ultimate patron. Thus, the reader or implied reader may identify a messianic association with Siloam. Many scholars think that the author here establishes an allegorical connection between the water of the spring and Jesus as the Sent One of the Father.[397] The man born blind is healed in the water by the Son God has sent. Jesus as τὸ φῶς τοῦ κόσμου (Jn. 9:5) and ὁ ᾽Απεσταλμένος (Jn. 9:7) is able to restore sight to a man born blind. This miracle is described later as σημεῖα by the Jewish religious leaders in verse

---

[395] Francis Moloney, *The Gospel of John*, 1998, 292.

[396] Bruce Malina and Richard Rohrbaugh, *Social-Science Commentary on the Gospel of John*, 1998, 115-18. They say that patronage language is common in Johannine narrative, but such language ironically serves the author's anti-societal purposes.

[397] See Donald Carson, *The Gospel According to John*, 1991, 365; Leon Morris, *The Gospel According to John*, 1995, 428; Herman Ridderbos, *The Gospel According to John*, 1997, 336; Andreas Köstenberger, *John*, 2004, 284.

16. The plot of the narrative is composed of a promise in John 9:5 and its fulfillment in John 9:7.

7.3 ACT III: THE MAN BORN BLIND AND HIS NEIGHBORS (Jn. 9:8-12)

The author notes that Jesus' healing of the man born blind does not lead people to glorify God automatically. Rather, the people surrounding him are just surprised and confused at his healing. His neighbors and those who have seen him begging ask, Οὐχ οὗτός ἐστιν ὁ καθήμενος καὶ προσαιτῶν; (Is this not the man who was sitting and begging?") (Jn. 9:8).[398] Begging as a way of life of the invalid was a common feature in first-century Palestine.[399] It may be the only way the blind man could make a living at that time. Staley considers it significant that the man is identified as a beggar by his neighbors, and ἦν τυφλὸς καὶ ἀνέβλεψεν ("he had been blind and received the sight") by the narrator when identifying the man's parents in John 9:18.[400] In Judaism, the giving of alms was considered to be of greater significance that all the commandments as a way to gain merit with God.[401] The author uses his neighbors as witnesses to this man's healing in the narrative.

A debate ensures in verse 9: Some say that this man is he, but others say that Οὐχί, ἀλλὰ ὅμοιος αὐτῷ ἐστιν ("No, but he is like him") (Jn. 9:9a). But the healed man keeps saying, "ἐγώ εἰμι" (Jn. 9b). The author designates the healed man with ἐκεῖνος, the

---

[398] Ridderbos states that Οὐχ οὗτός ἐστιν assumes an affirmative answer (Herman Ridderbos, *The Gospel According to John*, 1997, 338; cf. Leon Morris, *The Gospel According to John*, 1995, 428-29).

[399] Joachim Jeremias, *Jerusalem in the Times of Jesus*, 1969, 116-19.

[400] Jeffrey Staley, "Stumbling in the Dark, Reaching for the Light," 1991, 66.

[401] Andreas Köstenberger, *John*, 2004, 284.

anonymous blind beggar associated with poverty and dependence. The reader or implied reader can be sure that the man in question is indeed the same man who had been born blind. The man does not know how or why the miracle has happened to him. When the people asked him how his eyes opened, he can only tell the physical facts of the mud with saliva, the command to go to Siloam washing, the obedience, and the sight (Jn. 9:10-11). The author thus mentions for the first time the question of how the man born blind receive his sight in this narrative, with several subsequent references to this question by the Jewish religious leaders (cf. Jn. 9:15, 16, 19, 21, 26). Schnackenburg argues that it is certainly the author's intention to point out the miracle's revelatory effect even on people who are not yet open to God's work.[402]

As to the question of who healed, the previously blind man can only answer ὁ ἄνθρωπος ὁ λεγόμενος Ἰησοῦς("the man who called Jesus")[403] and as to the question of how he was healed, he answered ὁ ἄνθρωπος ὁ λεγόμενος Ἰησοῦς πηλὸν ἐποίησεν καὶ ἐπέχρισέν μου τοὺς ὀφθαλμοὺς καὶ εἶπέν μοι ὅτι ὕπαγε εἰς τὸν Σιλωάμ ("The man who called Jesus made mud and anointed my eyes, and said to me that go to Siloam") (Jn. 9:11). The narrator uses two aorist verbs, ἐποίησεν and ἐπέχρισέν, which means that Jesus was not just putting physical mud but also spiritual anointing on his eyes. Kim argues the reason that the narrator omits the word 'pool' of Siloam as Jesus initially asked (cf. Jn. 9:7) is because he wants to emphasize the meaning of ὁ Ἀπεσταλμένος.[404]

When people ask the man ποῦ ἐστιν ἐκεῖνος (where is he?"), he responds οὐκ οἶδα ("I don't know") (Jn. 9:12). In contrast to

---

[402]   Rudolf Schnackenburg, *The Gospel According to St. John vol. 2*, 1980, 246.

[403]   The healed man gives an accurate testimony, apparently aware that the healer was Jesus although he has not seen Jesus yet until John 9:35 (Donald Carson, *The Gospel According to John*, 1991, 366).

[404]   Moon Hyun Kim, *Healing Hurts*, 2005, 109.

the healing lame man episode at Bethesda in John 5, Jesus makes no appearance at all, not even to answer the Pharisees later. The author probably composed the narrative in this way deliberately because Jesus has already withdrawn and broken off all discussion with the Jewish religious leaders. The healed man cannot yet identify Jesus who has given the light to restore his sight, so he admits his ignorance.[405] He does not know much else about Jesus, although he does knows the name of his healer, unlike the lame man in John 5. Morris states that the man's limited response concerning ὁ ἄνθρωπος ὁ λεγόμενος Ἰησοῦς ("the man called Jesus") may indicate that he knew little about Jesus.[406] He still has a long way to go to have faith in Jesus. Brown, however, points out that the healed man's repeated and humble confession of ignorance (Jn. 9:12, 25, 36) is designed to contrast with the Pharisees' bold statements (Jn. 9:16, 24, 29).[407] O'Day also notes the humility of the healed man quite willing to admit his ignorance in contrast to the arrogance of the Pharisees, asserting this is the author's intention to present to the reader or implied reader a healed blind man who is naïve, innocent, and guileless enough to say, οὐκ οἶδα.[408]

7.4   ACT IV: THE MAN BORN BLIND AND JEWISH RELIGIOUS LEADERS I (Jn. 9:13-17)

The previous scene in John 9:8-12 caused the man born blind to be brought to the Pharisees by the people (Jn. 9:13) who are

---

[405]   Francis Moloney, *The Gospel of John*, 1998, 293.

[406]   Leon Morris, *The Gospel According to John* , 1995, 429.

[407]   Raymond Brown, *The Gospel According to John*, 1966, 377.

[408]   Gail O'Day, *The Word Disclosed*, 2002, 70.

presumably this man's neighbors.[409] The author notes that the day on which Jesus made the mud for the blind man and restored his sight was a Sabbath (Jn. 9:14). Therefore, they ask πῶς ἀνέβλεψεν ("how he had received sight"), and the healed man replies πηλὸν ἐπέθηκέν μου ἐπὶ τοὺς ὀφθαλμούς, καὶ ἐνιψάμην, καὶ βλέπω ("He put mud on my eyes and I washed and I see") (Jn. 9:15). His answer to the Pharisees is not exactly the same as that given to his neighbors in John 9:11a, πηλὸν ἐποίησεν καὶ ἐπέχρισέν μου τοὺς ὀφθαλμοὺς ("He made mud and anointed my eyes"). To the Pharisees he says, "Put the mud on my eyes," not the more detailed description given to his neighbors that Jesus had "formed the mud and anointed my eyes." Likewise, by leaving out Jesus' command, ὕπαγε εἰς τὸν Σιλωὰμ καὶ νίψαι ("go to Siloam and wash") the man says, ἐνιψάμην, καὶ βλέπω("I washed and I see") in John 9:15b. Thus, the reader or implied reader may infer that the man is attempting to protect Jesus from the Pharisees' suspicion of His having broken a Sabbath regulation. Also, the man does not mention the name Jesus, although he gave the name to his neighbors (cf. Jn 9:11). Why not this time? O'Day and Staley argue that the blind man may be seen as protecting Jesus by not disclosing His

---

[409] Some scholars argue that the intentions of the man's neighbors were not necessarily hostile (see George Beasley-Murray, *John*, 1999, 156; Donald Carson, *The Gospel According to John*, 1991, 366-67; Leon Morris, *The Gospel According to John*, 1995, 430).

name.[410] The Pharisees now see Jesus as having broken one of the Sabbath regulations in His forming of the mud.[411] Unlike the case of lame man healed in John 5, the Pharisees are not interested in the man born blind being healed, nor in the person of Jesus reflected in a supernatural healing. In actuality, the Pharisees do not even believe that a healing has happened until the point that they clarify through the man's parents both that he had been born blind and now was healed (Jn. 9:18).[412] Their focus has been on the question of keeping the Sabbath regulations and any violation the mere forming of the mud represented.

Moreover, some of the Pharisees claim that οὐκ ἔστιν οὗτος παρὰ θεοῦ ὁ ἄνθρωπος ("this man is not from God") because Jesus does not keep the Sabbath, while others point to Jesus' τοιαῦτα σημεῖα ποιεῖν ("do such signs") as an indication that He could not

---

[410]   Jeffrey Staley, "Stumbling in the Dark, Reaching for the Light," 1991, 67. O'Day also says, "As much as Jesus is talked about in the interrogations of John 9:8-34, Jesus' name is never named [by a character] after [9:11] … There are many reasons for this reluctance to name Jesus' name. The Pharisees do not name the name of Jesus because to do so would give credence and standing to the one who bears the name. The man born blind does not name the name because the significance of the name will only dawn on him as the narrative advances. The man's parents do not name because they are afraid to do so [9:23]" (Gail O'Day, *The Word Disclosed*, 2002, 71).

[411]   Carson explores more reasons that Jesus may have broken the Sabbath according to the Pharisees: 1) since he was not dealing with life or death situation, Jesus should have waited until the next day to heal; 2) Jesus had formed the clay with his saliva to make mud, and forming was included among the 39 classes of work forbidden on the Sabbath; and 3) later Jewish tradition stipulated that it was not permitted to anoint eyes on the Sabbath, although opinion seems to have been divided (Donald Carson, *The Gospel According to John*, 1991, 367).

[412]   Ridderbos interprets ὅτι ἠνέῳξέν σου τοὺς ὀφθαλμούς as "since you say he opened your eyes" (Herman Ridderbos, *The Gospel According to John*, 1997, 339), and Barrett translates ὅτι as "with regard to the fact that" (C. K. Barrett, *The Gospel According to St. John*, 1978, 360).

be sinful (Jn. 9:16). As using the plural, τοιαῦτα σημεῖα, the author reveals that they are already aware of other miracle signs performed by Jesus. The reader or implied reader can think of the healing of the lame man in John 5, which involves the same conflict as that of the John 9 healing of the blind man because of the breaking of a Sabbath regulation. That said, there was no mention of a division among the Jewish religious leaders in John 5. In this case of the healing of the man born blind here in John 9, the Pharisees are divided as they debate His origins.[413] Some Pharisees deny His origins with God the Father, while others are open to such a possibility. However, the reader or implied reader knows that Jesus has already in John 5:19-30 explained His activity as being tied to the basis of His origins; however, it seems that the Pharisees have already forgotten Jesus' explanation. Schnackenburg states, "Jesus' work of revelation drives them into greater and greater despair and perplexity (cf. John 11:47). Revelation has a critical function."[414] From the author's point of view, it is clear that Christological concerns raised by Jesus' various healings prevail with the John 9 healing of the blind man.

Given all though, it is interesting that in John 9 the Pharisees did not question the fact of the miracle, nor the name of Jesus mentioned. Although the healed man is the one who is questioned, Jesus is the actual target of their investigation. They returned and merely ask the healed blind man, Τί σὺ λέγεις περὶ αὐτοῦ ("What do you say about Him")? Like the testimony of the Samaritan woman in John 4:19, the blind man confesses without hesitation προφήτης ἐστίν ("He is a prophet") (Jn. 9:17), having previously

---

[413] Carson points out that the division apparent in here roughly follows the differing ways of reasoning followed by the schools of Shammai and Hillel, referring Schlatter' remark (Donald Carson, *The Gospel According to John*, 1991, 367).

[414] Rudolf Schnackenburg, *The Gospel According to St. John vol.2*, 1980, 248.

described Jesus as "ὁ ἄνθρωπος" (Jn. 9:11). Morris states that προφήτης may well have been the highest position that he knew to ascribe to Jesus.[415] His understanding of Jesus' identity progresses from ὁ ἄνθρωπος ὁ λεγόμενος Ἰησοῦς to προφήτης. However, the term "προφήτης" has no messianic significance since the healed man is first brought to this kind of faith by Jesus Himself.[416] At this point the curiosity of the reader or implied reader is piqued as to how far this formerly blind man will grow having faith in Jesus.

7.5 ACT V: THE JEWISH RELIGIOUS LEADERS AND THE MAN BORN BLIND'S PARENTS (Jn. 9:18-23)

As the man healed from being born blind progresses, the Jewish religious leaders move in the direction of the prosecutorial mood toward Jesus because they do not believe in the healing of the man born blind (Jn. 9:18). Keener highlights the Pharisees' repeated ignoring of the testimony of the miracle itself, rather focusing on Jesus' alleged Sabbath violation.[417] From this scene on in the narrative, the author uses "οἱ Ἰουδαῖοι" for the Jewish religious leaders instead of "οἱ Φαρισαῖοι."[418] They did not believe that the man born blind has had sight restored. They must have all the facts first. Then they must try to prove that he did not come to sight by testimony of his parents who are qualified the best to testify (Jn. 9:18b). But the Pharisees attempts to establish that

---

[415] Leon Morris, *The Gospel According to John*, 1995, 432.

[416] Rudolf Schnackenburg, *The Gospel According to St. John vol.2*, 1980, 248.

[417] Craig Keener, *The Gospel of John*, 2003, 786.

[418] Carson attributes the shift from "Pharisees" to "Jews" to the author's penchant for stylistic variation (Donald Carson, *The Gospel According to John*, 1991, 368). Schnackenburg thinks that the change serves to indicate the "official character" of the inquiry (Rudolf Schnackenburg, *The Gospel According to St. John vol.2*, 1980, 249).

the man's parents have been lying about their son ultimately fail. The author uses two rhetorical questions that the Jewish religious leaders presuppose in attempting to establish that the healed man was not born blind and parents should not claim that he was (Jn. 9:19a). They are unwilling to go beyond the question of how the miracle happened, so continue to ask, πῶς οὖν βλέπει ἄρτι; ("how then does he see now?") (Jn. 9:19b). They challenge the absurdity of their claim.[419] The parents can only confirm the fact that οὗτός ἐστιν ὁ υἱὸς ἡμῶν καὶ ὅτι τυφλὸς ἐγεννήθη ("this is our son and that he was born blind") (Jn. 9:20b). The man born blind may have been staying at his parents' house as he spent his days begging in the temple. Their testimony gives further insight to the characterization of the formerly born blind man. The reader or implied reader learns more of the man through other characters, even if the man himself is not on the scene. The fact of the miracle has been told twice: one from the healed man himself and the other from his parents now. Belief, however, is still beyond the Pharisees. The author seems to point out that faith in Jesus does not depend on such facts, but on the identity of Jesus, τὸ φῶς τοῦ κόσμου (Jn. 9:5) and ὁ Ἀπεσταλμένος from God the Father (Jn. 9:7).

The parents of the man born blind wanted to withdraw from the discussion, so they send the Jewish religious leaders back to their son, αὐτὸν ἐρωτήσατε ("Ask him") (Jn. 9:21) – he is old enough, so he will speak for himself – because they were afraid of the Jewish religious leaders who had already decided that anyone who confessed that Jesus was Χριστός would be expelled from the

---

[419] Herman Ridderbos, *The Gospel According to John*, 1997, 340.

synagogue (Jn. 9:22).[420] The author wants the readers to know that the parents spoke not from ignorance but out of fear. Brown argues that the parents are "crypto-Christians" – those who know who Jesus is and what He does, or who even actually believe in Jesus, the Messiah, but are afraid to confess Him out of fear of being excommunicated from the synagogue.[421] The synagogue was not only the center of religious life but also communal life, and its excommunication and removal represented a severe form of social outcast. For this reason, the parents tried to avoid Christological discussion with the Jewish religious leaders by once again sending them back to their son (Jn. 9:23). Moloney points out that the parents "had forged their Christology within a context of hostility and conflict."[422] Lee, meanwhile, notes that the parents do not want to be involved in such discussion and place the responsibility to answer the Christological question back on their son, determined not to acknowledge who Jesus is.[423]

The reader or implied reader knows that the Jewish leaders rejected Jesus' claims of τὸ φῶς τοῦ κόσμου and ὁ Ἀπεσταλμένος from God the Father, and thus rejected all those who accepted them. The reader or implied reader can sense the powerless of the parents before the overwhelming powers that the Jewish religious leaders might have at that time.

---

[420]   Schnackenburg states, "If the term, ἀποσυνάγωγος does refer to the later period of the end of the first century, and since no measure of this sort can be shown to have been in use in Jesus' time, the only possible historical sanction is (ordinary) excommunication from the synagogue, which had a limited effect of up to thirty days. Whether the authorities took such a measure again Jesus' followers remain uncertain." (Rudolf Schnackenburg, *The Gospel According to St. John vol.2*, 1980, 250)

[421]   Raymond Brown, *The Community of the Beloved Disciple*, 1979, 71-73.

[422]   Francis Moloney, *The Gospel of John*, 1998, 294.

[423]   Dorothy Lee, *Flesh and Glory*, 2002, 179.

7.6 ACT VI: THE MAN BORN BLIND AND JEWISH RELIGIOUS LEADERS II (Jn. 9:24-34)

The now-healed man born blind is summoned by the Jewish religious leaders a second time. His characterization is more fully developed by this scene. During his first encounter with the leaders, the man said he did not know the whereabouts of Jesus (Jn. 9:12). In this second encounter, however, the leaders are direct, saying ἡμεῖς οἴδαμεν ὅτι οὗτος ὁ ἄνθρωπος ἁμαρτωλός ἐστιν ("We know that this man is a sinner") (Jn. 9:24b). They do not hesitate to claim that they know οὗτος ὁ ἄνθρωπος, proclaiming Jesus is a sinner. They subsequently ask the healed man, "δὸς δόξαν τῷ Θεῷ."[424] The Jewish used to employ an oath of giving glory to God before taking a confession of guilty (cf. Josh. 7:19; Jer. 13:16). Brodie states that δὸς δόξαν τῷ Θεῷ should have been extremely intimidating, though brief.[425] With this proclamation, the now-healed man born blind has no choice but to tell the truth before God.

Of course in this scene of the Jewish religious leaders encountering the now-healed man formerly born blind, their God is not the God of Jesus, τὸ φῶς τοῦ κόσμου and ὁ Ἀπεσταλμένος. The author wants to point out who can really δὸς δόξαν τῷ Θεῷ. Only those who know the God of Jesus, τὸ φῶς τοῦ κόσμου and ὁ Ἀπεσταλμένος can. Thus, in this context the man born blind indeed will δὸς δόξαν τῷ Θεῷ. The author's doxological point of view is closely related with his Christology. The reader or implied reader knows that the Jewish religious leaders' knowledge of God is not same as that of the healed man's. Thus, the healed man could

---

[424] Referring to Conway, Köstenberger suggests that the phrase δὸς δόξαν τῷ Θεῷ constitutes a solemn exhortation to tell the truth and to make a confession, with the implication that the person has done wrong (Andreas Köstenberger, *John*, 2004, 289).

[425] Thomas Brodie, *The Gospel According to John*, 1993, 350.

not accept their request because he does not οἶδα whether Jesus is a sinner, but he says that ἓν οἶδα, ὅτι τυφλὸς ὢν ἄρτι βλέπω ("one thing I know that I was blind, now I see" (Jn. 9:25).[426] Schneiders says correctly, "The man's replies indeed giving glory to God, testifying that he doesn't know whether Jesus is sinner or not (something only God can finally know about anyone) but he does know that He opened his eyes (something he experienced and will not be intimidated into denying)."[427] Brodie suggests, "Through this brief statement the man avoids becoming entangled in their confused condemnatory world. And he managed instead to bring the debate back to the central fact."[428]

The author reminds the reader of the question, πῶς δύναται ἄνθρωπος ἁμαρτωλὸς τοιαῦτα σημεῖα ποιεῖν; ("How can a man who is a sinner do such signs?") (Jn. 9:16b), a question asked by some of the Pharisees as important to answer before they decide to close their minds against Jesus. The Jewish religious leaders ask again how Jesus opened his eyes and τί ἐποίησέν σοι ("What did He do to you") (Jn. 9:26a)? Now at a loss, they ask the healed man to recount the details of the miracle.[429] They are still interested in the method of how he was healed, not who the Healer was that healed him. The healed man seems to be annoyed and wondered why they want to hear the testimony again, leading him to reply, εἶπον ὑμῖν ἤδη καὶ οὐκ ἠκούσατε ("I told you already and you did not listen") (Jn. 9:27a). He is saying that they don't need

---

[426]   Carson states that this may be an instance of the author instructing his readers that a person of committed faith ought to bear personal witness, having given the importance of witness in his narrative (Donald Carson, *The Gospel According to John*, 1991, 373).

[427]   Sandra Schneiders, *Written That You May Believe*, 2003, 155.

[428]   Thomas Brodie, *The Gospel According to John*, 1993, 350.

[429]   Herman Ridderbos, *The Gospel According to John*, 1997, 344-45. Perhaps they hope that he would contradict himself in recounting the story.

to hear his testimony again unless they are truly listening. The now-healed man somewhat rhetorically asks if their intention is to become Jesus' disciples by continuing to ask to hear the story of Jesus' miraculous work (Jn. 9: 27b). His question μὴ καὶ ὑμεῖς θέλετε αὐτοῦ μαθηταὶ γενέσθαι; ("Do you not also want to be His disciples?") implies that he already considered himself to be Jesus' disciple.[430]

The Jewish religious leaders in response disparaged and insulted the healed man and say, σὺ μαθητὴς εἶ ἐκείνου, ἡμεῖς δὲ τοῦ Μωϊσέως ἐσμὲν μαθηταί ("You are his disciple, but we are disciples of Moses") (Jn. 9:28). Since they consider Moses as their religious authority, they have no need for Jesus or His teaching. Perhaps because they realize that the healed man has seen through their attempts to trip him up, the Jewish religious leaders insult him.[431] They could not be moved by his testimony, in part because their thinking was based on the knowledge ὅτι Μωϊσεῖ λελάληκεν ὁ θεός ("that God has spoken to Moses") (Jn. 9:29a). The problem is that they don't know where Jesus comes from: τοῦτον δὲ οὐκ οἴδαμεν πόθεν ἐστίν ("however, we do not know where this man comes from") (Jn. 9:29b).[432] That's why they cannot accept Jesus. However, the reader or implied reader knows that Moses is not Jesus' opponent but a witness to him (Jn. 5:45-47). The leaders' mindset is locked into the Law that came through Moses, and

---

[430] Ramsey Michaels, *John*, 1989, 169; Charles Talbert, *Reading John*, 1992, 160; Leon Morris, *The Gospel According to John*, 1995, 437. Kim also says, "By doing so, he also demonstrates the courage that is required of genuine discipleship (Moon Hyun Kim, *Healing Hurts*, 2005, 117).

[431] Donald Carson, *The Gospel According to John*, 1991, 373.

[432] Barrett and Carson point out that on a formal level, the present statement stands in contradiction with the Pharisees' earlier comment in John 7:27, that is simultaneously and ironically true as in John 9:29 (C. K. Barrett, *The Gospel According to St. John*, 1978, 363; Donald Carson, *The Gospel According to John*, 1991, 373).

they reject ὁ Ἀπεσταλμένος from God the Father because they will not accept its truth. They insist upon the revelation of God as received through Moses, including both the Pentateuch and oral tradition, rather than choosing to attach to Jesus who claimed to be the source of new revelation from God.[433] For the author the origin of Jesus is one of the ultimate themes of his narrative.[434]

Then, the healed man becomes a bit agitated and tries to argue with them, saying ἐν τούτῳ γὰρ τὸ θαυμαστόν ἐστιν ὅτι ὑμεῖς οὐκ οἴδατε πόθεν ἐστίν, καὶ ἤνοιξέν μου τοὺς ὀφθαλμούς (for this is an amazing thing, that you do not know where He comes from, and yet He opened my eyes") (Jn. 9:30). Lindars states, "At this point the man himself becomes the teacher, echoing the kind of argument used by Jesus Himself in other discourse."[435] He thinks that there must be a connection between the fact that ἐκεῖνος opened the man born blind's eyes and πόθεν ἐστίν, his origins. He continues to press on, saying that we both know that God listens to people who will do His will, and not to sinners (Jn. 9:31). The author refers ἁμαρτωλός to reflect their assumed knowledge about Jesus in John 9: 24, 29. Now he earnestly defends Jesus, saying that nobody has ever heard of opening the eyes of a man born blind (Jn. 9:32). Never before in the history of God's people has a person who was born blind had his sight restored. If Jesus was not παρὰ Θεοῦ, He could not perform the miracle (Jn. 9:33). Brodie notes that his statement is not only an attack on their religious tradition and theology, but also is suggesting to them the unprecedented reality,

---

[433] Donald Carson, *The Gospel According to John*, 1991, 374; George Beasley-Murray, *John*, 1999, 158.

[434] Not only in this story of the man born blind, but also in many episodes. For instance, John 3:31, 34; 5:43; 6:38, 46; 7:28-29; 8:33, 42.

[435] Barnabas Lindars, *The Gospel of John*, 1972, 348.

the reality of God in Jesus.[436] Conway remarks that his courageous behavior before the Jewish religious leaders closely resembles that of Jesus Himself.[437] The author reveals that even the healed man knows that there must be a special relationship between the person who performs the miracle and God who makes it possible. How come the leaders don't acknowledge this fact even if the man did! Some of them had debated earlier whether Jesus could be from God (Jn. 9:16), but ultimately, they decided against this possibility (Jn. 9:24, 29). In depicting the now-healed man born blind's strong courage and confidence, the author's characterization of the man clearly differs from that of the cowardice demonstrated by his parents. Rensberger argues that this testimony explains why Jesus is not there from the central episode of the plot; His role is taken over by the man himself.[438]

Unable to win the debate with the healed man, the Jewish religious leaders employ a personal attack on the man.[439] They cannot accept the truth of which he testifies, so they expel him from the synagogue. It was a response in anger at the fact that they have been forced to listen to an uneducated man born blind telling them that they, the Jewish religious leaders, are incapable of assessing God's activity.[440]

In the meantime, the reader or implied reader can see the progress of the healed man since he now says, εἰ μὴ ἦν οὗτος παρὰ Θεοῦ, οὐκ ἠδύνατο ποιεῖν οὐδέν ("if this man is not from God, He could do nothing") (Jn. 9:33) while he described Him earlier to his neighbors as ὁ ἄνθρωπος ὁ λεγόμενος Ἰησοῦς ("the man

---

[436] Thomas Brodie, *The Gospel According to John*, 1993, 352.

[437] Colleen Conway, *Men and Women in the Fourth Gospel*, 1999, 133.

[438] David Renseberger, *Johannine Faith and Liberating Community*, 1988, 42.

[439] Colleen Conway, *Men and Women in the Fourth Gospel*, 1999, 132.

[440] Rudolf Schnackenburg, *The Gospel According to St. John vol.2*, 1980, 251.

called Jesus) (Jn. 9:11). He continues to grow in his understanding of Jesus based on the fact of the miracle that restored his sight. In contrast, the Jewish religious leaders accuse him of being born in utter sin and cast him out because he attempts to teach them a proper understanding of God (Jn. 9:34).[441] The reader or implied reader knew that Jesus had in John 9:3 already dismissed the disciples' question in John 9:2 about the sin origin of the man's blindness. It was the religious leaders' uninformed understanding of the reason for the man's being born blind that prevented them from seeing God's work in Jesus' healing of the man born blind.[442] They correctly characterize him as a teacher who takes over their privileged role to teach. Unlike his parents, the author shows that the formerly born blind man is not afraid of the threat of excommunication. That is a character of a true disciple of Jesus.

7.7   ACT VII: JESUS AND THE MAN BORN BLIND II (Jn. 9:35-38)

The author keeps noting that God watches and hears the faithful one who does His will (cf. Jn 9:31). Jesus shows up in the scene after hearing that the formerly born blind man had been excommunicated, finding him to ask: σὺ πιστεύεις εἰς τὸν υἱὸν τοῦ ἀνθρώπου ("you believe in the Son of Man") (Jn. 9:35b).[443] The author has indicated that Jesus uses the term ὁ υἱὸς ἀνθρώπου in

---

[441]   Carson states that the man's growth in faith and understanding was predicated upon his decisive break with the Jewish religious readers (Donald Carson, *The Gospel According to John*, 1991, 375).

[442]   Gail O'Day, *The Word Disclosed*, 2002, 82.

[443]   Köstenberger thinks that Jesus probably sought him out rather than finding him accidently, having heard of his excommunication from the synagogue and if so, this would be in keeping with the narrator's portrayal of Jesus as the "good shepherd" in the following discourse (Andreas Köstenberger, *John*, 2004, 294 referring Ridderbos).

order to refer to His role of making God known in the human history (cf. 1:51; 3:13-14; 5:27; 6:27, 53, 62). Jesus' presence in the world as ὁ υἱὸς ἀνθρώπου is very important as He reveals God and brings judgment, but the completion of His revealing role is yet to come.[444] Jesus' question to the healed man also contains a promise: if he believes in Jesus as ὁ υἱὸς ἀνθρώπου, Jesus will take him with Him in to his glory.[445] The reader or implied reader may recall Jesus' action towards the Samaritan woman in John 4:23-26 as Jesus reveals Himself at the following scene.

The healed man might be surprised by Jesus's question and answers with his own question: τίς ἐστιν, Κύριε, ἵνα πιστεύσω εἰς αὐτόν; ("who is he, Lord, that I may believe in Him?") (Jn. 9:36).[446] He is eager to believe in ὁ υἱὸς ἀνθρώπου ("the Son of Man"), but he does not yet know who Jesus is. His question brings to mind for the reader or implied reader the question posed by the Samaritan woman in John 4:19-26.[447] He calls Jesus "Κύριε," seeking more

---

[444] Bennema states that ὁ υἱὸς ἀνθρώπου is used exclusively by Jesus Himself, mostly referring to His death expressed as being "lifted up" (Jn. 3:14; 6:62; 8:28; 12:34), but it also denotes Jesus as a mediator, the point of contact between heaven and earth (Jn. 1:51; 3:13) (Cornelis Bennema, *Encountering Jesus*, 2009, 253).

[445] Rudolf Schnackenburg, *The Gospel According to St. John vol.2*, 1980, 253.

[446] Morris points out that the conjunction ἵνα here is based on an elliptical "tell me" and conveys purpose (Leon Morris, *The Gospel According to John*, 1995, 440).

[447] Duke calls his question in John 9:36 an irony of identity in Johannine narrative and relates it closely with the scene of the Samaritan woman in John 4:19-26. In both cases, a character who doesn't know Jesus calls Him Κύριε and make reference to Messiah or Son of man – thought to be absent. Jesus then quickly reveals His identity in the most appropriate way. To the Samaritan woman who is given to misunderstandings He speaks directly, "ἐγώ εἰμι, ὁ λαλῶν σοι" in John. 4:26. Now to the formerly born blind man Jesus beams, saying "ἑώρακας αὐτὸν καὶ ὁ λαλῶν μετὰ σοῦ ἐκεῖνός ἐστιν John. 9:37 (Paul Duke, *Irony in the Fourth Gospel*, 1985, 123).

information on ὁ υἱὸς ἀνθρώπου. While nothing more than a respectable address by the formerly born blind man is implied here, it evolves to become a theologically rich confession in John 9:38.[448] The reader or implied reader may conclude that Jesus is very impressed and satisfied with the man's response, saying "ἑώρακας αὐτὸν καὶ ὁ λαλῶν μετὰ σοῦ ἐκεῖνός ἐστιν ("you have seen Him, and he who is speaking to you") (Jn. 9:37). Jesus' deliberate use of "ἑώρακας" is all the more significant given that the healed man had not seen anything until very recently.[449] Moloney does well to note, "Terms central to the Gospel's Christology are combined. It is impossible for anyone to see God or come to the knowledge of God (cf. 1:18; 57), but Jesus reveals what He has seen (cf. 1:34; 3:11, 22; 8:38). He speaks what He has seen with the Father (cf. 6:46; 8:38)."[450] Thus, Jesus is inviting the healed man to recognize and believe that God is made known to him in ὁ υἱὸς ἀνθρώπου as he is willing to believe. Ridderbos says that by believing he truly δὸς δόξαν τῷ Θεῷ ("gives glory to God") (cf. Jn. 9:24), the now-healed man formerly born blind emerges as the one who sees in more than one sense.[451] The reader or implied reader knows that Jesus is the incarnation of ὁ λόγος ἦν πρὸς τὸν θεόν ("the Word was with God") (cf. Jn. 1:1, 14). Jesus speaks of what He knows from God the Father, and He speaks with God's authority. Jesus said to the Samaritan woman that the one who reveals God in a unique way, the ἐγώ εἰμι ("I AM"), speaks to her (Jn. 4:26). Beasley-Murray states, "The effect of this revelation is as overwhelming as that of

---

448   Andrew Lincoln, *The Gospel According to John*, 2005, 286-87.

449   Ibid.

450   Francis Moloney, *The Gospel of John*, 1998, 295-96.

451   Herman Ridderbos, *The Gospel According to John*, 1997, 349.

the Samaritan woman: the latter runs to her village to proclaim the advent of the Messiah, the former prostrates himself before Jesus."[452]

The healed man accepts Jesus invitation as he responds, πιστεύω, Κύριε ("I believe, Lord) (Jn. 9:38a). This confession leads him to a total surrender and bowing down to worship. He already responded to Jesus' earlier question, calling Him "Κύριε," (Jn. 9:36), but the reader or implied reader may sense the same Κύριε has its full Christological meaning as a disciple's ultimate confession. The healed man also accepts Jesus as the King of kings as he προσεκύνησεν αὐτῷ ("worshiped Him"). His twofold response of a verbal confession and a nonverbal act of worship is the climax of this healing narrative plot. Thus, the reader or implied reader sees his progress of faith in Jesus as reflected in his moving from calling Him "ὁ ἄνθρωπος" (Jn. 9:11) to "προφήτης" (Jn. 9:17) to "οὗτος παρὰ Θεοῦ" (Jn. 9:33). Now he finally confesses in faith before Jesus that He is "Κύριε," (Jn. 9:38) so that Jesus' earlier remarks to His disciples may have fulfilled (Jn. 9:3). The reason this man being born blind was ἵνα φανερωθῇ τὰ ἔργα τοῦ θεοῦ ἐν αὐτῷ ("that the works of God might be displayed") as the author characterizes his journey from blindness to sight. Like the Samaritan woman in John 4, but unlike the lame man in John 5, the man born blind reaches the saving faith which is a true disciple's mark.

Stibbe argues that in the Johannine narrative "one can introduce a character as 'a shadowy and indeterminate creature' who only becomes a living, definable personality after responding to various events – the emergence of the complete character from the action."[453] The character of the man born blind is a classic case of this.

---

452 George Beasley-Murray, *John*, 1987, 159.

453 Mark Stibbe, *John as Storyteller*, 1992, 25.

7.8 ACT VIII: JESUS AND THE JEWISH RELIGIOUS LEADERS (Jn. 9:39-41)

After his polemic confession and the act of worship, the healed man disappeared from the scene. However, the author relates the transformation of the man born blind against the Jewish religious leaders' stubborn unbelief.[454] His confession and act of the transformation function to explain the narrative of the final scene. The reader or implied reader sees the contrast between the Jewish religious leaders' entrenched and obdurate knowledge with the progressive knowledge of the man born blind. Although it is not quite the whole truth that the religious leaders are content and even complacent with the knowledge that God spoken to Moses, in their arrogant attitude of self-sufficiency, the Jewish religious leaders have become blind (Jn. 9:39).[455] Carson thinks that this final scene must have occurred in a public place so that the Pharisees were able to overhear what was said between Jesus and the man born blind, although the conversation was private.[456] Jesus tells them that they brought judgment upon themselves. Ridderbos comments that the judgment referred to here by Jesus

---

[454] O'Day states the author tells about Jesus' speaking of sight and blindness on another level, and about how physical sight can become spiritual blindness (Gail O'Day, *The Word Disclosed*, 2002, 85).

[455] Schnackenburg says that this paradoxical language reflects the author's sense of the strangeness of unbelief in the face of Jesus, the revealer (Rudolf Schnackenburg, *The Gospel According to St. John vol.*2, 1980, 255).

[456] Donald Carson, *The Gospel According to John*, 1991, 377.

is the division of humanity into believers and unbelievers brought about by His coming into this world.[457]

After hearing Jesus' remarks, some of them ask, ἡμεῖς τυφλοί ἐσμεν; ("Are we blind?") (Jn. 9:40). The author introduces them without much elaboration about the situation. The reader or implied reader knows that the questioners represent the Jewish religious leaders. Barrett explores that both giving sight to the blind and the blinding of those who see are common Old Testament themes (cf. Ps. 146:8; Isa. 29:18; 35:5; 42:7, 18).[458] They are familiar with the metaphorical use of blindness. Thus, the reader or implied reader knows well that Jesus means spiritual blindness.

The author closes this discussion with Jesus' claim of their sinfulness (Jn. 9:41). Because they claim βλέπομεν even though they actually are not, ἡ ἁμαρτία ὑμῶν μένει ("your sin remains"). The allegation of sin is transferred from the blind man and Jesus to the Jewish religious leaders.[459] There is no room with them for the new revelation from Jesus, leaving them guilty. If they had been prepared to admit humbly their need for light, they would have had no guilt. Because of this, the religious leaders are under judgment. Ridderbos points out that it is not the Pharisees' sin but rather their repudiation of grace that renders them lost, a point Jesus makes quite clear.[460] There is no salvation for people who reject the only way there is and no hope for those who are arrogant, saying βλέπομεν in their own eyes which are actually blind.

---

[457]   Herman Ridderbos, *The Gospel According to John*, 1997, 350. Also, Schnackenburg says, "His coming means a κρίμα, 'a sentence or judicial decision', here technically equivalent to κρίσις, Jesus in practice exercises the judicial activity, κρίνω, mentioned in John 5:22, 27, 30" (Rudolf Schnackenburg, *The Gospel According to St. John vol.2*, 1980, 255).

[458]   C. K. Barrett, *The Gospel According to St. John*, 1978, 365-56.

[459]   Dorothy Lee, *Symbolic Narratives of the Fourth Gospel*, 1994, 162.

[460]   Herman Ridderbos, *The Gospel According to John*, 1997, 351.

Schnackenburg comments well, "The search for one's own glory, which in the case of these Jews even uses God's glory as a pretext (cf. 9:24; 16:2), is the real source of this refusal and blindness (cf. 5:40-44; 8:49; 12:43). The 'sin' of the Pharisees is illustrated by their attitude towards the man born blind, boundless and impenetrable rejection of God's messenger and hatred of Him and His worshippers."[461] Brodie also comments, "It is a reminder that the full acceptance of the Son of humanity involves not only humble self-acceptance, but the acceptance of a self who faces death."[462] While the man born blind becomes progressively receptive and finally makes a full confession of faith and worship Jesus, the Jewish religious leaders become progressively blind to Jesus. They are ending up in total darkness and face the judgment of God. The author shows a double narrative movement where the man born blind progresses from blindness to sight not only physically but also spiritually, while the Jewish religious leaders move in the opposite direction although they have physical sight.[463]

7.9   THE SIGNIFICANCE

Through this narrative the reader or implied reader clearly sees the author's point of view in his revealing of not only the authentic faith of the man born blind becoming a true disciple, but also the significance of Jesus' miracle of restoring his sight and soul. In this narrative of healing the man born blind, Jesus is teaching the spiritual blindness of everyone, especially those who are arrogant not knowing their ignorance of the truth. Like the man born blind, anyone could be healed only by Jesus' divine authority and power.

---

[461]   Rudolf Schnackenburg, *The Gospel According to St. John vol.2*, 1980, 256.

[462]   Thomas Brodie, *The Gospel According to John*, 1993, 353.

[463]   Dorothy Lee, *The Symbolic Narratives of the Fourth Gospel*, 1994, 162.

Only Jesus Christ, the Messiah as τὸ φῶς τοῦ κόσμου (Jn. 9:5) and ὁ Ἀπεσταλμένος (Jn. 9:7) can give eternal life to those who believe in Him. Thus, if people acknowledge their blindness and want to receive the light, Jesus will show and enable them to see. Those who accept the light will receive the eternal life and become God's children. But those who reject the light will continue in darkness and face His judgment.

In order to emphasize the point of Christology and doxology in the narrative, the author also reveals Jesus' identity. The reader or implied reader knows that God is associated with the giving sight to the blind in the Old Testament as a sign of messianic activity. Thus, this healing narrative of the man born blind has deep messianic implications. This miracle of restoring sight provides a type of the messianic blessings to be realized through faith. As the author mentions τὰ ἔργα τοῦ Θεοῦ ἐν αὐτῷ ("the works of God in Him") (Jn. 9:3) before the miracle happens, the man born blind has tasted these blessings, and he acknowledged it (Jn. 9:33). And the healed man δὸς δόξαν τῷ Θεῷ ("gives glory to God") (Jn 9:24-25). Keener points out that this miracle of restoring sight is also significant in that it demonstrates Jesus' divine authority to judge those who reject Him, as Jesus declares in John 9:39 and as the author indicates in the healing narrative of the lame man (Jn. 5:22).[464] The Jewish religious leaders are a perfect example, as shown in the last scene of narrative. Barrett says, "The effect of the true light is to blind them [the Pharisees], since they willfully close their eyes to it. Their sin abides precisely because they are so confident of their righteousness."[465]

The reader or implied reader notices that the core of this narrative is a dualistic but nuanced movement between light and

---

[464]   Craig Keener, The Gospel of John, 2003, 794.

[465]   C. K. Barrett, *The Gospel According to St. John*, 1978, 354.

darkness.[466] Brown summarizes well this narrative of the healing man born blind: "This is a story of how a man who sat in darkness was brought to see the light, not only physically but spiritually. On the other hand, it is also a tale of how those who thought they saw (the Pharisees) were blind themselves to the light and plunging into darkness. The story starts in John 9:1 with a blind man who will gain his sight; it ends in John 9:41 with the Pharisees who have become spiritually blind."[467]

7.10 CONCLUSION

In this healing narrative, the author intends to show the contrast between the man born blind and the Jewish religious leaders. Bennema explains this contrast with three points;[468]

1. While the man starts out being born blind and gains both physical and spiritual sight, the Jewish religious leaders start to claim to have spiritual sight but turn out to be blind.

2. While the man testifies boldly before the Jewish religious leaders in the face of persecution and is even excommunicated, his parents withhold their testimony out of fear.

3. The man born blind progresses in his understanding of Jesus before the Jewish religious leaders and eventually reaches an authentic faith like a true disciple, while the Jewish religious leaders are proclaimed even guiltier for their blindness because they have rejected the Light they have been shown in Jesus.

---

[466] See James Resseguie, "John 9: A Literary-Critical Analysis," 1993, 296-98.

[467] Raymond Brown, *The Gospel According to John*, 1966, 377.

[468] Cornelis Bennema, *Encountering Jesus*, 2009, 255.

With this narrative, the reader or implied reader can clearly understand the characters of the man born blind. He is obedient, courageous, open-minded, willing to give testimony, taking risks, and remains faithful to Jesus until the end. He displays a remarkable progress in his understanding of Jesus. In this way, his characteristics are very similar to that of the Samaritan woman. However, the man born blind reaches his understanding of Jesus not in a reflective encounter with Him, but in a confrontation with the hostile Jewish religious leaders.[469] That shows his faith developed more stronger than the Samaritan woman.

The author develops Christological and doxological themes more in the narrative of the man born blind as the Jewish religious leaders' opposition is growing. In the context of the Feast of Tabernacle, he demonstrates Jesus the Messiah, τὸ φῶς τοῦ κόσμου ("the light of the world") and ὁ Ἀπεσταλμένος ("the One who sent") from God the Father, who fulfills the joys and hopes of the festival. Jesus offers eternal life to those who believe in Him and they δὸς δόξαν τῷ Θεῷ ("give glory to God"). But Jesus will judge those who reject the offer.

---

[469] David Renseberger, *Johannine Faith and Liberating Community*, 1988, 46.

CHAPTER 8

Summary And Concluding Remarks

T HE AIM OF THIS STUDY HAS BEEN TO CLOSELY
examine anonymous minor characters found in the Johannine
narrative, especially those in John 4, 5, and 9 in order to find out
the author's Christological and doxological point of view as reading
by means of a narrative-socio-cultural- historical approach. This
final chapter will summarize significant findings and conclusions
that have been offered at the end of each of the preceding chapters,
and also discuss the implications of the significance of the characterization and of theology in this study of the Johannine narrative.

8.1 SUMMARY

After introductory comments, Chapter 1 briefly surveyed the
current debate on characterization in Johannine narrative. It also
addressed the gospel's context in terms of its literary structure
and how this would be examined as part of the plan of this study.
Throughout, this study has taken a high view of the authority and
canonicity of the entire text of Johannine narrative.

Chapter 2 explored current research on characterization in the
Johannine narrative over the past decade or so, especially examining narrative theories and methods that have been developed.
In the process, this study identified a significant research gap:
although modern scholars have approached characterization based
largely on whether or not they see characters primarily as plot

functionaries, ignored has been the integral relationship between the characters of narrative and the narrative's plot. Johannine characters are best understood by their interactive relationship to other characters and to the structural systems of meaning that compose a narrative. In their encounters with Jesus and others, the author reveals Jesus' identity. It is very important in reading the Johannine minor characters that not only a narrative text-centered approach but also a socio-cultural-historical approach is used. It is in this way that an argument could be made for the doxological and Christological significances of the anonymous minor characters in the narratives of the Samaritan woman in John 4, the invalid at the pool in John 5, and the man born blind in John 9.

Chapter 3 presented the method used in this study. After examining and applying multiple approaches in looking at the minor characters in John's gospel, it became clear that narratives use plots and interrelationships among characters to project an ideological or theological point of view. The narrator reveals the true identity of Jesus through conversations that these characters have with either Jesus or with other characters. Subsequently, to fully understand the text and thus recognize the ideological or theological perspective of the narrator, the reader or implied reader needs to consider the characters' social, cultural and historical contexts.

The author's theological points of view as shown in the Prologue repeatedly appear in the anonymous minor characters in John 4, 5, and 9. The Prologue prepares the reader or implied reader by setting the stage so that the Johannine narrative can be approached with knowledgeable anticipation, while the main themes regarding the deity and glory of Jesus Christ are developed in John 4, 5, and 9 and, of course, throughout the narrative. As the Johannine plot unfolds, the revelation of God evidenced in the words and works of Jesus Christ generates a diversity of responses among the characters from rejection to belief. These characters' responses to the revelation of the Father through the Son in terms of their identity, character, mission, and relationship further serve the author's goal. The criterion for the author's characterization is the characters' response to Jesus and God's revelation as revealed in Christ, His teachings, and His works. The Johannine plot, meanwhile, revolves around John unfolding the revelation of the Father through the Son, Jesus Christ, in terms of the individuals' response as well as their identity, character, mission, and relationship. Having defined this methodology, the following chapters will employ this social-cultural-historical approach together with a narrative approach to identify the theological points of view of the author as John 4, 5, and 9 are analyzed and exegeted. The significance of this will be evidenced in the glory of Jesus Christ who came to this world to save through faith in Him.

Chapter 4 presented the first minor character to be examined: the Samaritan woman at the well in John 4. Her response to Christ's approach and the redemptive-historical importance of Jesus approaching the woman both entail significant theological truths. In response to Jesus, even though the Samaritan woman does not clearly confess Jesus as her Savior, it is evident that through the narrative the Samaritan woman progressively overcomes the barriers, eventually shows her faith in Christ, and acts as a true disciple as she shared her testimony. She moves from hesitation to engage with Jesus in this unusual and culturally unacceptable situation (Jn. 4:7-9), but ultimately to a willingness to talk, even if in a conversation met with misunderstanding (4:10) and even a challenge to what Jesus is asserting (Jn. 4:11-12). Jesus is still able to capture her attention and interest, and although she still does not understand (Jn. 4:13-15), she seems honest and open minded. As such there is a progressive nature in her faith portrayed through the conversation that takes place (Jn. 4:19-20, 25, 29), and in the end she proves seriously open to the idea that Jesus might be the Messiah. That's why she gives her testimony to the people and their confession shows that she has drunk of the living water. The characterization of the Samaritan woman in the narrative is thus most evident in her progressive transformation as her honesty, open-mindedness, perceptiveness, responsiveness, and boldness to witness is depicted through her progressive acceptance of and faith in Christ.

Of course, beyond the Samaritan woman's character as a model of faith, her very ethnicity as a Samaritan also is significant from a redemptive historical perspective. John seeks to use the narrative story of the woman at the well to show Jesus' affirmation that although His coming was first to the people of Israel (Jn. 4:22), the salvation historical pattern of the Old Testament remains intact, moving from the people of Israel to the Gentiles. Jesus' ministry moves beyond Israel through His encounter with the Samaritan woman, just as Isaiah prophesied to the people of Israel, "I will also make you a light for the Gentiles, that you may bring my salvation to the ends of the earth" (Isa. 49:6b). This leads to a theological tension, sending a message to the people of Israel that while the Messiah came first to them, others too would be the beneficiaries of his ministry. Of course, even while the encounter with the Samaritan woman demonstrates Christs' willingness to break through the sociocultural barrier separating Jews from gentiles, the focus of His ministry would remain primarily on Israel until the point of the crucifixion as the Jew's. In sum, through the plot and characterization of Jesus and the Samaritan woman the narrator reveals his theological messages to the reader or implied reader, points that include Jesus' mission given by the Father to reach out beyond Jews to the Samaritans, the meaning of living water and true worship, the ideal type of discipleship, and Jesus' identification as the Messiah and the Savior of the world.

The next chapter examined the healing of the son of the royal official found toward the end of John 4. The author portrays the royal official as the object or target of Jesus' word and action to give or restore life as the beneficiary of Jesus' second miracle sign. The development of faith seen in the official is a reflection of the significance of one's faith response in Jesus, the Messiah, Son of God. In coming to Jesus with faith that He would be able to heal his son, the official either knew about Jesus' power and authority to perform miracles because he had heard it from the Galileans who had been there in Jerusalem, or he may have been there for the Passover Feast in John 2:23. So it was with an initial faith that the ruling official approached Jesus to ask and beg to heal his dying son. In response, Jesus challenged the official to go beyond a belief that is merely based on miraculous signs, to which the official. responded to Jesus' challenge by believing in Jesus' word. Finally, his belief was confirmed and deepened to a true knowledge of Jesus. Therefore, the royal official represents those who initially believe in Jesus on the basis of His signs and wonders but are able to progress toward more on Jesus' words and knowledge of who He is for an authentic faith.

The healing narrative of the royal official's son is designed to demonstrate the journey of a faith from being superficially and externally based on signs and wonders to authentic faith, and to recognize that those miracle signs characterize Jesus as the life-giver. It is a climax to the series of encountering people with Jesus in the Cana Cycle of John 2-4. Both the Samaritan woman and the royal official reach an authentic and deepened faith in Jesus and testify to others so that they have become the authentic believers. It shows the power of the witness of the authentic faith in Jesus who is the life-giver for those who respond with faith in His words. Thus, the royal official is more than a type of positive faith-response to Jesus. The reader or implied reader can understand the official as a character who reveals some individuality, and in the process learn something of his authentic faith through this character. The author may have also have intended here for the reader or implied reader to make a connection between Jesus' life giving word and the Word of life (cf. Jn. 1:1).Through the first four chapters of John's gospel, the reader is instructed in some of the most important Johannine beliefs. What has been said in the Prologue (Jn. 1:1-18) is being proclaimed and acted out in the story of Jesus (Jn. 1:19-4:54). Above all, the reader now knows the nature of a right relationship with Jesus. The Prologue's teaching on the life-giving power that comes from believing and receiving the incarnated word (Jn. 1:12-13) happens in the story of Jesus as people accept or reject his word.

The next chapter addresses the narrative of the lame man's healing found in John 5. In this narrative, the author establishes that the lame man and the story of his healing are intertwined with the characterization of Jesus as the Son whom God the Father sent to do God's work. Jesus has the divine authority and power to heal the lame man. The reader or implied reader clearly sees that the Jewish religious leaders' charges against Jesus are false because the healing was God's act and Jesus did the healing according to God's will. The author also shows through Jesus encounters with the Jewish religious leaders that the lame man healing miracle sign has eschatological implications. The lame man's healing belongs within the horizon of eschatology.

In His discourse of defense, Jesus as the Son of God the Father reveals God who has the authority to perform miracle and values the giving of life over the Jewish Sabbath tradition. Jesus demonstrated His divine authority to forgive sin and give eternal life to those who believe in Him. Another aspect of Jesus' healing the lame man on the Sabbath is judgment. While God the Father alone is called the judge who will exercise the eschatological judgment, this authority has been delegated to the Son, Jesus, because of the relationship between the Father and the Son. At this eschatological judgment everyone will be raised. The Son, Jesus, will judge based on belief or unbelief concerning Him: a resurrection of life or a resurrection of condemnation. The Jewish religious leaders were blinded to their own spiritual depravity because of their religious delusion and search to receive for glory from men. So, the leaders accused and tried to kill Jesus. The reader or implied reader can see that Jesus choosing to heal the lame man on the Sabbath has significant messianic implications. It presents Jesus as the promised Messiah. The author also made clear that unlike the Jewish religious leaders, Jesus is not looking for His own glory, but for the glory of God the Father. All human beings are made for His glory.

The John 5 narrative of the lame man must also be viewed in the context of the subsequent John 9 story of the healing of the man born blind. It was most likely John's intent as author to lead the readers to compare the response of the lame man in John 5 with that of man born blind in John 9. Although others encountered Jesus and were healed, their responses differ. In examining the similarities of the two men, both men had been disabled for a long time and excluded from the community.

The responses of the two men to Jesus and to the Jewish religious leaders are, however, rather different, even opposite. The lame man betrays Jesus to the leaders while the man born blind defends Jesus and accepts persecution as a result. The lame man is unable to heed Jesus' warning and does not progress in his knowledge of Him, and there is no indication that he comes to believe in Him. In contrast, the man born blind progresses in his knowledge of Jesus in a way similar to the Samaritan woman in John 4, even as he stands up to the Jewish religious leaders. Moreover, when Jesus later encounters the man born blind, the man perceptively responds with belief, something we do not see with the now-healed lame man. Taking all of these differences in responses into account, the reader or implied reader should interpret the lame man narrative negatively.

Although providing examples of characterization both positively (Samaritan woman, man born blind) and negatively (healed lame man) in individuals, of course these passages also have theological significance, particularly Christologically and eschatologically. As John makes clear, the miracles are signs that reveal Jesus' true identity for the purpose of his writing (cf. Jn. 20:30-31). For the narrative of the lame man healed in John 5, the Sabbath observation is the essential literary and theological background. The reader or implied reader was asked to believe that Jesus was the Son of God who made God known (Jn. 1:18). What Jesus did in healing the lame man in the Jewish temple and on the Sabbath was not only a sign, but also a shadow of the gift of God in the Son who gives life and judges everyone at the eschatological time. Jesus is above the Sabbath and the works He does, which are always good, are allowable on the Sabbath as being done by God Himself. It is impossible to honor and glorify the Sabbath God without honoring and glorifying His Son. The author demonstrates that it is the Jewish religious leaders who are lost and are judged because they do not accept Jesus as the Son who gives life.

The next chapter explored the healing of the man born blind in John 9. Through this narrative the reader or implied reader clearly sees the author's point of view in his revealing of not only the authentic faith of the man born blind becoming a true disciple, but also the significance of Jesus' miracle of restoring his sight and soul. In this narrative of healing the man born blind, Jesus is teaching the spiritual blindness of everyone, especially those who are arrogant not knowing their ignorance of the truth. As in the case of the man born blind, anyone could be healed only by Jesus' divine authority and power. Only Jesus Christ, the Messiah as τὸ φῶς τοῦ κόσμου (Jn. 9:5) and ὁ Ἀπεσταλμένος (Jn. 9:7), can give eternal life to those who believe in Him. Thus, if people acknowledge their blindness and want to receive the light, Jesus will show and enable them to see. Those who accept the light will receive the eternal life and become God's children. But those who reject the light will continue in darkness and face His judgment.

In order to emphasize the point of Christology and doxology in the narrative, the author also reveals Jesus' identity. The reader or implied reader knows that God is associated with the giving sight to the blind in the Old Testament as a sign of messianic activity. Thus, this healing narrative of the man born blind has deep messianic implications. This miracle of restoring sight provides a type of the messianic blessings to be realized through faith.

The reader or implied reader notices that the core of this narrative is a dualistic but nuanced movement between light and darkness. This is a story of how a man who sat in darkness was brought to see the light, not only physically but spiritually. On the other hand, it is also a tale of how those who thought they saw (the Pharisees) were blind themselves to the light and plunging into darkness. The story starts in vs. 1 with a blind man who will gain his sight; it ends in vs. 41 with the Pharisees who have become spiritually blind.

In this healing narrative, the author intends to show the contrast between the man born blind and the Jewish religious leaders. The reader or implied reader can clearly understand the characters of the man born blind. He is obedient, courageous, open-minded, willing to give testimony, taking risks, and remains faithful to Jesus until the end. He displays a remarkable progress in his understanding of Jesus. In this way, his characteristics are very similar to that of the Samaritan woman. However, the man born blind reaches his understanding of Jesus not in a reflective encounter with Him, but in a confrontation with the hostile Jewish religious leaders. That shows his faith developed stronger than the Samaritan woman.

The author develops Christological and doxological themes even further in the narrative of the man born blind as the Jewish religious leaders' opposition to Christ, His teachings, and His work is growing. In the context of the Feast of Tabernacle, the author reveals Jesus the Messiah, τὸ φῶς τοῦ κόσμου and ὁ Ἀπεσταλμένος from God the Father, who fulfills the joys and hopes of the festival. Jesus offers eternal life to those who believe in Him and they δὸς δόξαν τῷ Θεῷ. But Jesus will judge those who reject the offer.

8.2   IMPLICATIONS

8.2.1 The significance of characterization in John 4, 5, and 9

Most of the Johannine characters demonstrate a representative type that portrays a particular characteristic in relation to the Messiah, Jesus Christ. The anonymity of the minor characters in John 4, 5, and 9 implements a representative characterization. The Samaritan woman, the royal officer, and the man born blind demonstrate for the reader or implied reader a scope of faith response to Jesus' words. In particular, the royal officer whose son is healed, and the man born blind show the progress of a genuine and authentic faith, directly contrasting with the Galileans. The Samaritan woman, the royal officer, and the man born blind give witness to the faith and discipleship of their community.

On the other hand, the lame man was not desperate to request healing from Jesus, unlike the royal official's strong entreaty that Jesus heal his son. Instead the lame man complains of his inability to benefit from the magical sign from the pool of Bethesda. Even in the absence of a clear request to heal, Jesus sovereignly initiates the healing of the lame man. While the Samaritan woman and the royal officer are influential characters in bringing the people of the Samaritan village and the household of the royal officer, the lame man is an instrumental character in bringing the confrontation with the Jewish religious leaders that result in persecution of Jesus. Thus, the lame man is representative of the unbelieving type, contrasting with other minor characters of the Samaritan woman, the royal officer, and the man born blind. Despite Jesus having healed him, the lame man remains lamed spiritually. The author's negative characterization of the lame man is clearly contrast to other minor characters, especially to the man born blind, whom the author depicts as claiming Jesus as the light of the world and demonstrating genuine and authentic faith and discipleship.

Throughout these narratives, the author depicted the controversy at the time centered on the identity of Jesus Christ. The lame man seems to align himself with Jewish religious leaders who deny Jesus' divine healing power. However, the man born blind confesses and describes Jesus as the Son of God who comes from God with divine power and authority. Therefore, the dynamics of encountering anonymous minor characters with Jesus ultimately present Jesus' true identity.

8.2.2 The narrative-socio-cultural-historical approach with other characters in Johannine narrative

This study, in looking at these minor character case studies in John 4, 5, and 9, demonstrated that the author assumed the reader or implied reader of his narrative has a good knowledge of the contemporary first century world of the incarnated λόγος, Jesus Christ. Also, the author also assumes the reader or implied reader is familiar with the Old Testament. For these reasons, , the narrative-socio-historical approach was applied here and used to analyze the anonymous minor characters in John 4, 5 and 9. Beyond these cases, however, the same approach could apply in the analysis of other characters in Johannine narrative in order to determine the author's theological point of view.

As evident from his soteriological point of view articulated in John 20:31, the author wants the reader or implied reader to evaluate the character's response to the incarnated λόγος, Jesus Christ. The author's characterization of those individuals fits into his dualistic world view. The characters represent the range of responses that people make in life, while these responses are eventually and starkly evaluated as, from a divine perspective, being either acceptance or rejection. Jesus Christ came to the world to reveal God and to bring people eternal life, an everlasting relationship with God from people's darkness and lack of true knowledge. People who encounter the incarnated λόγος Jesus Christ must either accept or reject Him. Of course, their responses are varied in terms of speed (instantly or progressively), clarity (ambiguous or obvious), and content (positive or negative). Progressing faith is not always linear, let alone constant: people's faith may often not be consistent or progressive depending on their circumstances. Culpepper explores the types of response to Jesus as follows;[470]

1. The first response is rejection, the rejection of the world hostile to Jesus

2. The second response is acceptance without open commitment.

3. The third response is acceptance of Jesus as a worker of signs and wonders.

4. The fourth response is belief in Jesus' words.

5. The fifth response is commitment in spite of misunderstanding.

---

[470] See Alan Culpepper, *Anatomy of the Fourth Gospel*, 1983, 146-48.

6. The sixth response is paradigmatic discipleship.

7. The seventh response is defection, and Judas is its infamous paradigm.

Again, however, John in his gospel demonstrates a dualistic world view, people ultimately either accept or reject the incarnated λόγος, Jesus Christ. Since characters depicted in the narrative are ultimately designed to represent real people, the author's characterization of their responses to the incarnated λόγος, Jesus Christ, demonstrates both how Jesus approaches real people and how those people respond with their choices in real life.

8.2.3 Theological significance of the Johannine characterization in John 4, 5, and 9

Broadly speaking, the Johannine narrative integrates both redemptive historical and individual theological truths. The narrator portrays Jesus affirmation that His coming was first to the people of Israel, showing how Jesus asserted Jewish salvation historical primacy, but then also keeps the salvation historical pattern of the Old Testament intact in showing that salvation is moving from being based primarily on the people of Israel to the Gentiles. Jesus' ministry opens up beyond Israel as He encounters the Samaritan woman. During this transition, we see either outright rejection of Christ or only superficial faith in Galilee, while authentic faith is represented in characters such as the woman at the well or the royal official. In addition to providing examples of individual faith, both good and bad, in response to Jesus, the author also makes clear to the reader and implied reader that Jesus as the Son of God has the power and authority to give or restore life, such as revealed in by the author in the healing narrative of the man born blind in John 9. It is precisely in the flesh of His earthly incarnation that ὁ λόγος reveals the underlying divinity of Christ. His powerful works become crucial witnesses to which belief cannot be refused and at the same time σημεῖα which manifest His δόξα.

The reader or implied reader may think the healing narrative of the royal official's son is very similar to the healing miracle of the lame man in John 5 in terms of healing at a distance demonstrating Jesus' power of the restoration of life. Jesus as a life-giver is developed by the author in the revelation discourse. Both narratives emphasize Jesus' life-giving word as well as hearing and believing in that word. The contrast between the two miracle signs in John 4 and 5 relates primarily to the response of those most immediately impacted by them. The author wants to show that the miracle signs do not always lead to an authentic faith. In the process, the author portrays Jesus as the Messiah, the Son of God who gives the eternal life and shows His glory.

In the lame man's healing narrative, the author establishes that the lame man and the story of his healing are intertwined with the characterization of Jesus as the Son whom God the Father sent to do God's work. Jesus has the divine authority and power to heal the lame man. The reader or implied reader clearly sees that the Jewish religious leaders' charges against Jesus are false because the healing was God's act and Jesus did the healing according to God's will. The author also shows through Jesus encounters with the Jewish religious leaders that the lame man healing miracle sign has eschatological implications.

In His discourse of defense, Jesus as the Son of God the Father reveals God who has the authority to perform miracle and values the giving of life over the Jewish Sabbath tradition. Jesus demonstrated His divine authority to forgive sin and give eternal life to those who believe in Him. Another aspect of Jesus' healing the lame man on the Sabbath is judgment. While God the Father alone is called the Judge, who will exercise the eschatological judgment, this authority has been delegated to the Son, Jesus, because of the relationship between the Father and the Son. At this eschatological judgment everyone will be raised. The Son, Jesus, will judge based on belief or unbelief concerning Him. Because of their delusion or blindness and looking for glory from men, the Jewish religious leaders could not see their own spiritual depravity. So, they accused and tried to kill Jesus, the Son. The reader or implied reader can see that Jesus choosing to heal the lame man on the Sabbath has significant messianic implications. It presents Jesus as the promised Messiah. Therefore, like their forefathers failed to enter the promised land because of unbelief, the only way to live forever is through faith in the Son, Jesus. The author also expressed that unlike the Jewish religious leaders, Jesus is not looking for His own glory, but for the glory of God the Father. All human beings are made for His glory.

Through this narrative the reader or implied reader clearly sees the author's point of view in his revealing of not only the authentic faith of the man born blind becoming a true disciple, but also the significance of Jesus' miracle of restoring his sight and soul. Jesus is teaching the spiritual blindness of everyone, especially those who are arrogant not knowing their ignorance of the truth. Like the man born blind, anyone could be healed only by Jesus' divine authority and power. Thus, if people acknowledge their blindness and want to receive the light, Jesus will show and enable them to see. Those who accept the light will receive the eternal life and become God's children. But those who reject the light will continue in darkness and face His judgment.

The author also depicts the identity of Jesus in a way that emphasizes key points of Christology and doxology in the narrative. The reader or implied reader knows that God is associated with the giving sight to the blind in the Old Testament as a sign of messianic activity. Thus, the characterization of the man born blind has deep messianic implications. This miracle of restoring sight provides a type of the messianic blessings to be realized through faith. The reader or implied reader further notices that the core of this narrative is a dualistic but nuanced movement between light and darkness.

8.3   CONCLUSION

In closing, these anonymous minor characters in John 4, 5, and 9 clearly show the author's Christological and doxological point of view. Each character is a model of belief or unbelief, accepting or rejecting the incarnated λόγος, Jesus Christ. Such is consistent with the author's purpose of leading the Johannine community to believe in the incarnated λόγος, Jesus Christ. These minor characters reflect some degree of change resulting from their encounter with Jesus Christ, either progress into an intimate relationship with Him or movement further away from Him. In either case, the author's characterizations demonstrate Christ's δόξα through the healings He conducts.

Works Cited

Ahn, Sanghee M. *The Christological Witness Function of the Old Testament Characters in the Gospel of John.* Eugene, OR: Wipf & Stock Publishers, 2014.

Aitken, Ellen B. "At the Well of Living Water: Jacob Traditions in John 4." In Craig A. Evans, ed. *The Interpretation of Scripture in Early Judaism and Christianity.* 2000.

Alter, Robert. "Biblical Type-Scenes and the Uses of Convention" in the *Art of Biblical Narrative.* New York: Basic Books, Inc., 1981.

Anderson, Paul N. *The Christology of the Fourth Gospel.* Valley Forge, Pennsylvania: Trinity Press International, 1996.

Aristotle, *Poetics* 6. Loeb Classical Library, Cambridge, Mass: Harvard University Press, 1092.

Ashton, John. *Studying John: Approaches to the Fourth Gospel.* Oxford: Clarendon Press, 1994.

Attridge, Harrold W. "The Samaritan Woman: A Woman Transformed." In *Character Studies in the Fourth Gospel. Wissenschaftliche Untersuchungen zum Neuen Testament 314,* 2013.

BAGD. *A Greek-English Lexicon of the New Testament and Other Early Christian Literature.* By W. Bauer, W. F. Arndt, F. W. Gingrich, and F. W. Danker. 2nd ed. Chicago: University of Chicago Press, 1979.

Bauckham, Richard. *Gospel of Glory: Major Themes in Johannine Theology.* Grand Rapids, MI: Baker Academic: 2015.

_____. *Jesus and the Eyewitnesses: The Gospels as Eyewitness Testimony.* Grand Rapids: Eerdmans, 2006.

_____. *God Crucified: Monotheism and Christology in the New Testament*. Grand Rapids: Eerdmans, 1998.

Barrett, C. Kingsley. *The Gospel According to St. John*. SPCK: London, 1978.

Beasley-Murray, George R. *John*. WBC vol. 36, Texas: Word Books: 1987.

BEB. Baker Encyclopedia of the Bible. Edited by W. A. Elwell. 2 vols. Grand Rapids, MI: Baker, 1988.

Beck, David R. *The Discipleship Paradigm: Readers and Anonymous Characters in the Fourth Gospel*. Biblical Interpretation Series 27, Leiden: Brill, 1997.

_____. "The Narrative Functions of Anonymity in the Fourth Gospel Characterization." *Semeia* 63, 1993.

Bennema, Cornelis. *Encountering Jesus: Character Studies in the Gospel of John*. 2nd ed.

Minneapolis: Fortress Press, 2009.

_____. "A Comprehensive Approach to Understanding Character in the Gospel of John" *Characters and Characterization in the Gospel of John*. Christopher W. Skinner, ed. London: Bloomsbury T & T Clark, 2013.

_____. "The Character of John in the Fourth Gospel." *Journal of the Evangelical Theological Society* 52, 2009.

Blaine, Bradford B. Jr. *Peter in the Gospel of John: The Making of an Authentic Disciple*. Academia Biblica, 27; Atlanta: Society of Biblical Literature, 2007.

Boer, Martinus C. de. "Narrative Criticism, Historical Criticism, and the Gospel of John." *Journal for the Study of the New Testament* 45, 1992.

Borchert, Gerald L. *John 1-11*. New American Commentary, Nashville: Broadman & Holman, 1996.

_____. *The Gospel and the Letters of John, Interpreting Biblical Texts.* Nashville: Abingdon, 1998.

_____. "The Passover and the Narrative Cycles in John." In *Perspectives on John: Method and Interpretation in the Fourth Gospel.* ed. Robert B. Sloan and Mikeal C. Parsons, Lewiston, NY: Edwin Mellen, 1993.

Brodie, Thomas L. *The Gospel according to John: A Literary and Theological Commentary.* New York: Oxford University Press, 1993.

Brown, Raymond E. The *Gospel according to John (I-XII).* Anchor Bible, Garden City, NY: Doubleday, 1966.

Bruce, F. F. *The Gospel & Epistles of John.* Grand Rapids, MI: William B. Eerdmans Publishing Co, 1983.

Bryan, Steven M. "Power in the Pool: The Healing of the Man at Bethesda and Jesus' Violation of the Sabbath (Jn. 5:1-18)." *Tyndale Bulletin* 54, 2003.

Burge, Gary M. *Interpreting the Gospel of John.* Grand Rapids, MI: Baker, 1992.

Bernard, J. H. *A Critical and Exegetical Commentary on the Gospel of John.* 2 vols. International Critical Commentary. Edinburgh: Clark, 1928.

Burnett, Fred W. "Characterization and Reader Construction of Characters in the Gospels." *Semia* 63, 1993.

Calvin, John. Trans. By T. H. L. Parker, *Calvin's New Testament Commentaries: The Gospel According to St. John 1-10.* William B. Eerdmans Publishing Co: Grand Rapids, MI, 1961.

Carson, D. A. *The Gospel According to John.* UK: Inter-Varsity Press: 1991.

Charlesworth, James H. "The Historical Jesus in the Fourth Gospel: A Paradigm Shift?" *Journal for the Study of Historical Jesus* 8, 2010.

Chatman, Seymour. *Story and Discourse: Narrative Structure in Fiction and Film*. Itaca: Cornell University Press, 1978.

Cho, Sukmin. *A New Perspective on John's Gospel*. Seoul, Korea: Solomon Publishing Co., 2008.

Collins, Raymond F. "From John to the Beloved Disciples: An Essay on Johannine Characters: An Essay on Johannine Character." In *Gospel Interpretation: Narrative Critical & Social Interpretation*, ed. Jack D. Kingsbury. Harrisburg, PA: Trinity Press, 1997.

_____. "The Representative Figures in the Fourth Gospel." *The Downside Review* 94, 1976.

Coloe, Mary L. "The Woman of Samaria: Her Characterization, Narrative, and Theological Significance." In *Characters and Characterization in the Gospel of John*, edited by Christopher W. Skinner. Library of New Testament Studies 461. New York: T & T Clark, 2013.

Conway, Colleen M. *Men and Women in the Fourth Gospel: Gender and Johannine Characterization*. Society of Biblical Literature Dissertation Series 167, Atlanta: Society of Biblical Literature, 1999.

_____. "Speaking through Ambiguity: Minor Characters in the Fourth Gospel." *Biblical Interpretation 10*, 2002.

Culpepper, R. Alan. *Anatomy of the Fourth Gospel: A Study in Literary Design*. Philadelphia: Fortress Press, 1983.

_____. *The Gospel and the Letters of John A Study in Literary Design*. Philadelphia: Fortress Press, 1998.

_____. "The Pivot of John's Prologue." *New Testament Studies 27*, 1980-81.

Darr, John. *On Character Building: The Reader and the Rhetoric of Characterization in Luke-Acts.* Louisville: Westminster/John Knox, 1992.

DJG. *Dictionary of Jesus and the Gospels.* Edited by J. B. Green, S. McKnight, and I. H. Marshall. Downers Grove, IL: Inter-Varsity, 192.

Dodd, C. H. *The Interpretation of the Fourth Gospel.* Cambridge: Cambridge University Press, 1953.

_____. *Historical Tradition in the Fourth Gospel,* Cambridge: Cambridge University Press, 1963.

EDNT. *Exegetical Dictionary of the New Testament.* Edited by H. Balz and G. Schneider. 3 vols. Grand Rapids, MI: Eerdmans Publishing Co., 1990-93.

Esler, Philip. and Piper, Ronald. *Lazarus, Mary and Martha: A Social-Scientific and Theological Reading of John.* London: SCM, 2006.

Fehribach, Adeline. *The Women in the Life of the Bridegroom: A Feminist Historical-Literary Analysis of the Female Characters in the Fourth Gospel.* Collegeville, MT: The Liturgical Press, 1998.

Forster, E. M. *Aspect of the Novel: The Timeless Classic Novel Writing.* Orlando, FL.: Harcourt, Inc., 1962.

Galef, David. *The Supporting Cast: A Study of Flat and Minor Characters.* University Park, PA: The Pennsylvania State University Press, 1993.

Genette, Gerard. *Narrative Discourse: An Essay in Method.* Translated by Jane E. Lewin, Ithaca, NY: Cornell University Press, 1980.

Giblin, Charles H. "What Was Everything He Told Her She Did?" *New Testament Studies 45,* 1999.

Guilding, Aileen. *The Fourth Gospel and Jewish Worship: A Study of the Relation of St. John's Gospel to the Ancient Jewish Lectionary System*. Oxford: Oxford Clarendon, 1960.

Haenchen, Ernst. *John*. 2 vols. Translated by Robert W. Funk. Philadelphia: Fortress Press, 1984.

Harris, W. Hall. "A Theology of John's Writings." *A Biblical Theology of the New Testament*, ed. Roy Zuck, 1994.

Hochman, Baruch. *Character in Literature*. Itaca, NY: Cornell University Press, 1985.

Hoehner, Harold W. *Herod Antipas. Society of New Testament Studies Monograph Series* 17. Cambridge: Cambridge University Press, 1972.

Hoskyns, Edwyn and Davey, F. N. *The Fourth Gospel*. 2 vols. London: Faber and Faber Limited, 1947.

Howard, James M. "The Significance of Minor Characters in the Gospel of John." *BibSac* 163, 2006.

Howard-Brook, Wes. *Becoming Children of God: John's Gospel and Radical Discipleship*. Maryknoll, NY: Orbis Books, 2001.

Hunt, Steve A. 'Nicodemos, Lazarus, and the Fear of the "the Jews" in the Fourth Gospel.' In

Gilbert van Belle, Michael Labahn and P. Maritz (eds), *Repetition and Variation in the Fourth Gospel: Style, Text, Interpretation*. Louvain: Peeters, 2009.

Hunt, Steven A., Tolmie, D. Francois, and Zimmermann, Ruben. eds. *Character Studies in the Fourth Gospel: Narrative Approaches to Seventy Figures in John. Wissenschaftliche Untersuchungen zum Neuen Testament* 314. Tubingen: Mohr Siebeck, 2013.

Hur, Ju "The Characterization of the Holy Spirit in Luke-Acts with Special Reference to Indirect Presentation." *Journal of the New Testament Society of Korea 22*, 2015.

Hylen, Susan. *Imperfect Believers: Ambiguous Characters in the Gospel of John*. Louisville:

Westminster John Knox, 2009.

_____. "Three Ambiguities: Historical Context, Implied Reader, and the Nature of Faith." *Characters and Characterization in the Gospel of John*. Christopher W. Skinner, ed., London: Bloomsbury T & T Clark, 2013

Iser, Wolfgang. "The Reading Process: A Phenomenological Approach." *New Literary History 3*, 1972.

_____. *The Act of Reading: A Theory of Aesthetic Response*. Baltimore: The Johns Hopkins University Press, 1978.

Keener, Craig S. *The Gospel of John: A Commentary* vol. 1. Peabody, MA: Hendrickson, 2003.

Kim, Dongsoo. *The Gospel of John in light of the Lens of Johannine Theology*. Seoul, Korea: Solomon Publishing Co., 2006.

Kim, Moon Hyun. *Healing Hurts: John's Portrayals of the Persons in Healing Episodes*. Seoul Korea: Korea Christian University, 2005.

_____. *People Who Encountered Jesus: Studies Johannine Characterization*. Seoul Korea: Spiritual Network Co, 2017.

_____. "The Samaritan Woman in John 4:3-42, Who is She?" Centering on the Literary 'Betrothal-Type' Scene & Characterization." *Hanshin Theological Studies 62*, 2013.

Kim, Moon Kyung. *Die "Johanneische" Theologie*. Seoul, Korea: Publishing House Korea Institute of Biblical Studies, 2004.

Kim, Stephen. "The Literary and Theological Significance of the Johannine Prologue." *BibSac* vol. 166, 2010.

Koester, Craig R. *Symbolism in the Fourth Gospel: Meaning, Mystery, Community*. 2nd ed. Minneapolis: Fortress Press, 2003.

Köstenberger, Andreas J. *A Theology of John's Gospel and Letters: Biblical Theology of the New Testament.* Grand Rapids, MI: Zondervan, 2009.

_____. *Encountering John: The Gospel in Historical, Literary, and Theological Perspective.* Grand Rapids, MI: Baker Academic, 1999.

_____. *John:* Baker *Exegetical Commentary on the New Testament.* Grand Rapids, MI: Baker Academic, 2004.

Kruse, Colin G. *The Gospel according to John.* Tyndale New Testament Commentary. Leicester: Inter-Varsity, 2003.

Kysar, Robert *John: The Maverick Gospel.* 3rd ed., Louisville: Westminster John Knox Press, 2007.

Laney, J. C. *John.* Moody Gospel Commentary. Chicago: Moody, 1992.

Lee, Dorothy A. *The Symbolic Narrative of the Fourth Gospel: The Interplay of Form and Meaning.* Journal for the Study of the New Testament: Supplement Series 95. Sheffield: JSOT Press, 1994.

Liddell and Scott. *An Intermediate Greek-English Lexicon,* 7th ed. Oxford: Clarendon Press, 1990.

Lincoln, Andrew T. "The Lazarus Story: A Literary Perspective." In Richard Bauckham and Carl Mosser (eds.), *The Gospel of John and Christian Theology.* Grand Rapids: Eerdmans, 2008.

Louw, J. P. "Narrator of the Father: ἐξηγεῖσθαι and the Related Terms in Johannine Christology." *Neotestamentica 2,* 1968.

MacLeod, David. "The Eternality and Deity of the Word: John 1:1-2." *BibSac.* vol. 160, 2003.

Malina, Bruce and Rohrbaugh, Richard. *Social-Science Commentary on the Gospel of John.* Philadelphia: Fortress Press, 1998.

Metzger. Bruce. *A Textual Commentary of the Greek New Testament,* 2nd ed. Stuttgart: Deutsche Bibelgesellschaft, 1994.

Metzger, Paul Louis. *The Gospel of John: When Love Comes to Town.* IVP Books: Downers Grove, IL, 2010.

Michaels, J. Ramsey. *John.* New International Bible Commentary. Peabody, Mass.: Hendrickson, 1989.

_____. "The Invalid at the Pool: The Man Who Merely Got Well." In Hunt, *Character Studies in the Fourth Gospel, Wissenschaftliche Untersuchungen zum Neuen Testament* 314. Tubingen: Mohr Siebeck, 2013.

Moloney, Francis J. "From Cana to Cana (John 2:1-4: 54) and the Fourth Evangelist's Concept of Correct Faith." In *Studia Biblica 1978*

_____. *Papers on the Gospels: Sixth International Congress on Biblical Studies, Oxford, 3-7 April 1978,* ed. Livingstone, Sheffield: *JSOT,* 1980.

_____. *Belief in the Word–Reading the Fourth Gospel: John 1-4.* Minneapolis: Fortress Press, 1993.

_____. *Signs and Shadows: Reading John 5-12.* Minneapolis: Fortress, 1996.

_____. *The Gospel of John, Sacra Pagina.* Collegeville, MN: Liturgical, 1998.

Morris, Leon. *The Gospel According to John.* Revised ed.: NICNT, Grand Rapids, MI William B. Eerdmans Publishing Co., 1995.

Mowvley, Harry. "John 1:14-18 in the Light of Exodus 33:7-34:35." *Expository Times,* 1984.

Newbigin, Lesslie. *The Light Has Come: An Exposition of the Fourth Gospel.* Grand Rapids, MI: Eerdmans Publishing Co., 1982.

Neyrey, Jerome H. *The Gospel of John in Cultural and Rhetorical Perspective.* Grand Rapids, MI: William B. Eerdmans Publishing Co., 2009.

_____. *An Ideology of Revolt: John's Christology in Social-Science Perspective.* Philadelphia: Fortress Press, 1988.

O'Day, Gail R. *The Gospel of John.* In The New Interpreter's Bible. Nashville: Abingdon Press, 1995.

Okure, Teresa. *The Johannine Approach to Mission: A Contextual Study of John 4:1-2. Wissenschaftliche Untersuchungen zum Neuen Testament.* Tubingen: Mohr Siebeck, 1988.

Porter, Stanley E. *John, His Gospel, and Jesus: In Pursuit of the Johannine Voice.* Grand Rapids, MI; Eerdmans Publishing Co., 2015.

Powell, Mark Allen *What is Narrative Criticism?* Minneapolis: Fortress Press, 1983.

Resseguie, James L. *A Narrative-Critical Approach to the Fourth Gospel in Characters and Characterization in the Gospel of John.* London and New York: Bloomsbury T & T Clark, 2012.

_____. *The Strange Gospel: Narrative Design and Point of View in John.* Biblical Interpretation Series 56, Leiden: Brill, 2001.

Rhoads, David. "Narrative Criticism: Practices and Prospects" In *Characterization in the Gospel: Reconceiving Narrative Criticism*, eds. David Rhoads and Kari Syredeni, England: Sheffield Academic Press, 1999.

Ridderbos, Herman N. *The Gospel According to John: A Theological Commentary.* Translated by J. Vriend. Grand Rapids, MI: Eerdmans, 1997.

Rimmon-Kenan, Shlomith *Narrative Fiction.* London and New York: Routledge, 1989.

Skinner, Christopher. *Characters and Characterization in the Gospel of John*, ed.; Library of New Testament Studies 461; London: T & T Clark, 2013.

_____. *John and Thomas: Gospels in Conflict? Johannine Characterization*

and the Thomas Question. PTMS, 115; Eugene, OR: Wipf & Stock, 2009.

Schnackenburg, Rudolf. *The Gospel According to St. John.* Crossroad, New York, 1990

Schneiders, Sandra. "Inclusive Discipleship (John 4:1-42)." In Schneiders, *Written That You May Believe: Encountering Jesus in the Fourth Gospel.* New York: Herder & Herder, 1999.

_____. *Written That You May Believe: Encountering Jesus in the Fourth Gospel.* Revised and expanded ed. NY: Crossroad Publishing Co., 2003.

Sloyan, Gerard S. *What are they saying about John?* Mahwah, NJ: Paulist Press, 1991.

Smalley, Stephen S. *John: Evangelist and Interpreter.* Nashville: Thomas Nelson Publishers, 1984.

Smith, D. Moody. *New Testament Theology: The Theology of the Gospel of John.* Cambridge, UK: Cambridge University Press, 1995.

_____. *John.* Abingdon New Testament Commentaries. Nashville: Abingdon, 1999.

Springer, Mary Doyle. *A Rhetoric of Literary Character: Some women of Henry James.* Chicago & London: University of Chicago, 1978.

Staley, Jeffrey L. "Stumbling in the Dark, Reaching for the Light: Reading Character in John 5 and 9." *Semeia* 53, 1991.

Stibbe, Mark W. G. *John as Storyteller: Narrative Criticism and the Fourth Gospel.* Cambridge; Cambridge University Press, 1992.

_____. *John.* Reading: A New Biblical Commentary. Sheffield: JSOT Press, 1993.

_____. *John's Gospel*. London and New York; Routedge, 1994

Thomas, John C. "'Stop Sinning Lest Something Worse Come Upon You': The Man at the Pool in John 5." *Journal for the Study of the New Testament* 59, 1995.

Thompson, Marianne M. "The Rising of Lazarus in John 11: A Theological Reading." In Richard Bauckham and Carl Mosser (eds), *The Gospel of John and Christian Theology*. Grand Rapids, MI: Eerdmans, 2008.

Van Aarde, Andries G. *Focusing on the Message: New Testament Hermeneutics, Exegesis and Methods*. Pretoria, Pretoria Book House, 2009.

Van Eck, Ernest. *Galilee and Jerusalem In Mark's Story of Jesus: A Narratological and Social Scientific Reading*. Hervormde Teologiese Studies Supplementum 7, 1995.

Van Tilborg, Sjef. *Imaginative Love in John*. Biblical Interpretation Series 2. Leiden: Brill, 1993.

Von Wahlde, Urban C. *The Gospel and Letters of John, vol. 2*. The Eerdmans Critical Commentary on the Gospel of John. Grand Rapids, MI: Eerdmans Publishing Co., 2010.

Waweru, Humphrey Mwangi. "Jesus and Ordinary Women in the Gospel of John: An African Perspective." *Swedish Missiological Themes* 96, 2008.

Zimmerman, Ruben. "The Narrative Hermeneutics of John 11: Learning with Lazarus How to Understand Death, Life, and Resurrection." In Craig Koester and Reimund Bieringer (eds), *The Resurrection of Jesus in the Gospel of John. Wissenschaftliche Untersuchungen zum Neuen Testament* 222; Tubingen: Mohr Siebeck, 2008.

CPSIA information can be obtained
at www.ICGtesting.com
Printed in the USA
LVHW022118290921
699079LV00001B/2